UNITY IN FLIGHT

SHORT FICTION
BY

Maropodi Hlabirwa Mapalakanye

Peter Rule

Zachariah Rapola

Michael Vines

Phaswane Mpe

Allan Kolski Horwitz

First Published in 2001 by BOTSOTSO PUBLISHING
PO Box 23910, Joubert Park, 2044, Johannesburg
ISBN 0-620-27234-1
Text:
Maropodi Hlabirwa Mapalakanye, Peter Rule, Zachariah Rapola, Michael Vines,
Phaswane Mpe, Allan Kolski Horwitz

Graphics:
Patrick Rorke, Anna Varney-Horwitz, Peter Rule, Ike Mboneni Muila, Michael Vines

Layout & Design:
ART STUDIO

Printed by:
Millionaire Printers

Funded by:

NATIONAL ARTS COUNCIL
OF SOUTH AFRICA

CONTENTS

Maropodi Hlabirwa Mapalakanye

Graphics by Patrick Rorke

SEARCH FOR HIM IN THE WILDERNESS

How many schoolgirls S'pekere fondles is none of your business. He fought hard for the cabinet post you people say has now put him on heat, as if it was easy risking his life fighting the Boers. And you watched, pretending you were unaware of the war for your own freedom. Now you open your big mouths so loud about children and rights and all that crap, as if you knew anything, and call S'pekere all sorts of names. In fact, it's not him running after the girls. It's them chasing after his status, seducing him even when he's with his wife and children, because you encourage them by pretending you don't know how nasty these sweet sixteens are. What do you know about rights that Spekere doesn't know, anyway? Who taught you about those rights if not S'pekere himself?

The little twits wear their sisters' perfumes and stockings and flash their thighs when he drives past, and when he stops, just to greet them, they rub their titties against his face, so he can smell the perfume and get mad. And when he's crazy, they jump into his car and turn the radio full blast on the freeway, as he drives from city to city, attending serious government business. They abuse his generosity, you see? Even messing with his executive cell phones and entertainment allowance. And I'm not going to tell you the things their little fingers do under his pants on the highways. Who's on heat then?

S'pekere fought hard for you people. Remember how he suffered that Easter weekend, the Good Friday of the last state of emergency, when I told that Boer colonel I was going to grill him for shooting my dog?

It was S'pekere, Zitha, Guvuto, Rocks and Slash, the Alex Big Five, at Rocks's place, right here in Alexandra. Their motto was no co-operation with the enemy. Smash him day and night, 'till he spews blood. Guvuto and Rocks must have coined it. Those two! Guvuto with his stubbornness, Rocks with those big eyes of his. I think Guvuto is the one who started the whole rigmarole. I don't know why they called him The General. Always looking for trouble.

You should've seen him giving police the slip from a car flying at two hundred kilometres per hour. He wore that brown overcoat of his. The wind tore away its buttons and it flew in the air like a balloon, and a police boy tried to give chase but ended up with broken legs and fingers. He cried like a baby, Guvuto gone and forgotten. That was Guvuto, the guy who was to land S'pekere in hot water on that Good

Friday.

You see they had gathered in the sitting room Rocks used to convert into a bedroom at night. They rose to pledge their commitment to the Cause. Rocks led them through their fighting prayer to the God of Avalanche. When Guvuto gave a cue, they stretched their arms in front and clasped each other's hands tightly. Rocks led them through the ultimate pledge:

War unto the enemy, total war and war, nothing else but war. Let blood flow.
Let it flood rivers. Let it flood the land. And the rivers and mountains must choke
in the flood.
The simple message to the enemy: No co-operation, no running away.
Arrogant cheek towards the Boer all the time. Harass him, haunt him day an
night.
Crush him 'till he spews blood. Our pledge: no running away,
No fear, no flight. Never co-operate with the enemy. Mislead him,
Haunt him. Crush him. Never run away. Don't fear a Boer.
Our pledge: Arrogant cheek towards the enemy!

They sat, Rocks on his sofa next to that window with opaque black glass which never opened. He wouldn't allow anyone on the sofa, including his father who always moaned about being bullied away from his own furniture by a won't-work. His elder brothers beat a speedy retreat to avoid torture by the hot balls in his face when Rocks entered the house those days. Remember how a charging police dog once made a quick turn after eye contact with him, and chased an innocent madman into the mucky waters of the Jukskei River? I don't want to talk about how those big eyes once caused the police to mistake Rocks for a petty thief, and chase him down Paul Kruger Street in Pretoria.

S'pekere nearly died that Good Friday, people. Yet, today he's still in trouble with you messing up his name, his official duty hardly giving him a chance to breath, and your teenage girls worsening his case, psyching the brains out of him, to pay for their nose rings and golden teeth from his executive medical aid. Everyone seems to have forgotten he's a very important government official, dealing with important issues. Everything you say about him is hot air. How can you say he's on heat?

I tell you, it's not fair, these sayings doing the rounds in the township about him, as if he had no shame. Mind you, he's still serving the Cause. He always donates generously from his own pocket towards the upkeep of the children he makes with the little twits. You don't know because you're jealous. Anyway, who has the right to say getting involved in steamy things in luxury cars with the girls you love is taboo? It's unfair.

S'pekere sustained the flames of revolution when police smashed your toes with sledge hammers in Lebowa. He defied assassins they hired to butcher you, right here in Alexandra. Even Vlakplaas was nothing to him. He fought them throughout when they blew up your corpses a million times with bombs, until they were sand. You people have no shame at all. It baffles me how readily the whole township forgets its heroes, I wish I was a white man.

You see, personally, the only thing I find dangerous about S'pekere is his habit of playing around with married women as if they are public property. Because, you see, no gluttony can equal that of a man when it comes to the prospect of sharing a woman. Not even casual lovers are shared with joy. Your own blood brother would kill you for messing around with those organs of his wife which her father would not touch. You don't just go about fiddling with another man's wife the way S'pekere does. As for the unmarried ones and the adventurous schoolgirls, for all I care, he can have them until he drops.

The man made his ultimate sacrifice on the Good Friday I told the Boer colonel I was going to sue him. I was about to instruct the Supreme Court to conduct a commission of enquiry into the matter when the neighbours begged, "Please Bra Crime, have mercy on the poor soul, drop the case!" But my dog. Tiger! I miss that dog.

Now, having reaffirmed their commitment and taken seats, the Big Five sat down for real business. Those ones! I'm telling you, they knew everything about the Struggle. I don't care who says what. They fought very hard for this township. But that Guvuto! I must confess. One day, I mean ... Well, forget it. But, he must watch out.

Anyway, an argument developed between Guvuto and S'pekere. I'm not quite sure whether it was Guvuto or S'pekere who insisted somewhere they should write 'squeeze the enemy's throat till he's cold'. I think it was Guvuto, because people agree S'pekere was insisting on 'muffle the throat' instead. What Zitha later confirmed to me personally was that Guvuto was screaming, "Squeeze the rotten throat; man, you bloody coward!"

That's when trouble started. All of a sudden Rocks jumped out of the window like an impala. His feet shut the opaque thing behind him with such unbelievable quietness on his way down. He had seen angels of terror enter the kitchen like ghosts in the daylight.

Guvuto and S'pekere stood there transfixed like a pair of rabbits blinded by car lights. Zitha can tell you how he grabbed the empty teapot on the table and pretended to perpetually pour tea into a used cup. S'pekere shuffled his hat a million times in an effort to hide his face. But, it was late, very late. Except for Rocks, of course.

After clearing the window, he landed in the kitchen of the house opposite. Being experienced in daring escapes and knowing his territory so well, he used another window to land in the bedroom of the third one. But you know Alexandra, no need to trace his way through more windows and passages like that until he reached Seventh Avenue and was gone and forgotten.

"*Nou ja, kêrels, wat*[1] ... the ghost, with lots of hair all over his body, began.

"*Nee, jong* Andries[2]," his companion corrected, "It's, 'hello gentlemen'."

"Okay, hello Kaffir gentlemen," Andries said whipping a hunting knife from his waist.

"No, Komrade Andries," his colleague disapproved and turned to the guys, "Gentlemen, we are your komrades. Other komrades are waiting outside. Can we invite them for tea?"

Silence.

"See?" Andries was angry, "Now, no more games. Who is Rocks?"

"Never co-operate with the enemy," they say Guvuto thought to himself.

"You see now komrades," the second ghost warned, "We come in good spirit but you start your trouble. Is that how you treat visitors?"

"Hey!" his friend shouted, slashing the air around Zitha with the hunting knife, "Who is Rocks?"

"This one," Guvuto said, pointing at S'pekere.

S'pekere was shocked with terror but took it like a comrade. He looked at the other comrades and saw them slightly nodding their heads as if to say, agree, mislead the bastards. He agreed he was Rocks and was taken off. At the kitchen door, holding him by the scruff of his neck, the Boers told Rocks's mother not to worry, her son would soon be back. S'pekere tried a magic trick. He clutched his chest and whimpered.

"*Wat makeer*[3], *kerel jong*?" Andries asked him.

"Tablets. My heart."

"Your heart on the right? No wonder you always see illusions of freedom," they laughed.

You see this Guvuto of yours now? People say I hate him for nothing. Just last week he called S'pekere names in a tavern, as if it was not him who sold S'pekere to those Boers like that. That's the problem with failures. They get obsessed with calling successful comrades names. Do you know what the miscarriage calls me? Do you know? He calls me 'Crime on Crime'. And why? All because I'm unemployed, I don't have a wife and a child and I have this drinking problem. He says these things do crime on me and, my actual name being Crime, I should be called 'Crime on Crime'.

Tell me, is this how comrades should talk to each other? And you laughing at the sick joke? Do you know what it means? You see, drink I do, but is that the way to talk? 'Crime on Crime'? Knowing that it's the Struggle that drove me to it? Look, *ek is ou Crime, ek*,[4] I'll get the bastard. The day I meet S'pekere's car stopping at a red robot in town I'm going to tell him this rubbish calls him a chicken murderer. Yes, that's what he calls him, and I'm going to tell S'pekere. I'll do it. I'll tell him man to man. I've had enough of this Guvuto thing. Wish S'pekere uses the secret police ... Look, nobody stopped him from getting a cabinet post. It was he who said even the municipal elections were rubbish. Now, why this jealousy towards S'pekere? S'pekere must activate the secret police. I mean, is it fair to call our people's leaders chicken murderers?

And those Boers didn't play games with S'pekere. They punched him and made him squirm and hit his head against the steel walls of their ugly truck. I mean, hitting his head like that, kicking him like he was a dog. That Guvuto thing! It's him who started all these insults that the township uses against S'pekere, calling him a child abuser and a chicken murderer.

And in that truck there were three other comrades bending and holding their knees for balance, as the police stood on their backs pointing their guns out. One of the comrades is now a premier. He was wearing that military jacket of his with decorations. That's why they tried killing him with S'pekere. I'm telling you, hell had just started for S'pekere.

They made him bend next to the premier and stood with their big boots on him as well. You think they took them to the police station right away? No! They drove around the streets of Alexandra the whole afternoon, kicking and poking them with rifle butts. Especially towards sunset, when the rotten police began to sing freedom songs, doing toyi-toyi[5] on their backs in the streets. I'm telling you ... Yet today you people have the nerve to say S'pekere is corrupt.

You should have seen the dogs walking the comrades through pools of blood in the police station. There were corpses all over, some with their entrails hanging out. It was the first time S'pekere was ever there.

"But, Sir ..." S'pekere began to protest.

"Wat?" It was the bloody Andries.

"I'm not Rocks. My name is S'pekere."

He shouldn't have said it. They whisked him to a car outside, stuffed him into the boot and drove him home to check on his identity documents. They did not care a damn about the steel things that hurt him, especially when they swerved round the bumpy corners at great speed. By the time they reached his home he was bruised all over.

"Do you know this terrorist?" they asked his mother who could hardly see through her tears of fear.

"Asseblief, my baas, hy is my kind[6]."

"Where are his papers?"

They scrutinised the papers and bid his mother farewell.

"Okay, sleep well mosadi[7]."

"What about my son?"

"This one? Search for him in the wilderness."

"Where, my baas[8]?"

"Maybe you lucky. Also try hospitals and mortuaries."

What woman could sleep well if S'pekere was her child? It was only after a week that a cleaner identified him at Thembisa Hospital. We had all given up hope, thinking his corpse was rotting somewhere in the mine dumps of Cleveland. S'pekere could hardly eat, drink or breathe properly. What with the plaster all over his body and a broken neck. We couldn't tell how many bones were broken, or the number of electric shocks he had gone through. And didn't you all say the dogs had killed him for nothing?

Now you hear this nonsensical gibberish about his fornication and lack of morals and say he is wrong. You're victims of the lies from this enemy of democracy called Guvuto. The swine has even turned against his closest friends. You know what he calls Rocks now? He calls him 'scavenger', all because Rocks works for the Intelligence. That one! He thinks he can make this country ungovernable with bitterness. I pray they cook a criminal case against him. Then he'll see 'Crime on Crime' and 'Scavenger' and 'Chicken Murderer' in the maximum prison.

Look, I don't care. I survive on piece jobs. S'pekere sacrificed more than all of us in this country, except the President and his cabinet, of course. Let the man enjoy the girls as much as he wants. That's his democratic right. I'm happy he successfully campaigned for the legalisation of prostitution and abortion with the other comrades in government. We fought for these rights. S'pekere can have them all. People! Stop troubling our leaders, this is a democracy. We're in a free country?

COW FOR SLAUGHTER

Mma Mahlatji sat silently by the open grave in Thembisa as priests took turns flaunting their hurt at the sudden death of her teenage son. The avowed servants of Him above, fuelled by earthly slogans and declarations, screamed to the skies, smacking their chests, denouncing the vile deeds of a deranged township where the innocent soul had been murdered and was now being buried. They despised the devil in tongues of angels and demons before the multitudes around the grave, for their fury knew no discrimination.

Fellow teenage Strugglers were in attendance, too. They kicked dust high, chanting, brandishing stones, knives, axes and toy guns made of cardboard, wood and wire. But their attire was genuine military uniform, complete with rank insignia, taken from the South African soldiers who were dying in the Angolan and Namibian wars. It was bought second-hand from shops in and around Johannesburg, in keeping with the craze of the Comrades who used to address each other in military terms those days. And the uniforms were so intimidating that soldiers besieged the burial ceremony as if they were in a war of attrition with the cemetery.

"Freedom now, education later!"

They tore their throats with chants of patriotism and words of abuse. They stomped the ground, shook their weapons to the police and stuck out their tongues, taunting and celebrating all at once. And the priests got more spirited in their sweat. They jumped high in a festival of colour, their cassocks ballooning in the air as the dogs of war salivated, implements of death at the ready.

Mma Mahlatji remained motionless.

Somewhere in Mohlalaotwane, right in the heart of Ga-Sekhukhune, the people of a peasant village with parched feet were dispersing from Mahlatji's home, after having buried the man of the house early in the morning. Among them were knots of gossips with caustic tongues. They had sought to know how on earth Phogole (being Mahlatji) could die on the same day as his only son. Then they strummed out their disgust with the woman who had had the nerve to divorce Phogole after his death. Their torn clothes flew about as they demonstrated their intent to uncover the root-cause of this despicable act.

"Mothers of Mohlalaotwane, hang your heads in shame," a whisper had incited vitriol from one tight knot to another.

"What a shameless bitch! A swine gobbling up its young and roasting its husband for supper."

"Has the witch really eaten up such an industrious man, Mologadi?"

"Oh no, mothers of Mohlalaotwane, what does this make of us? The men will have a field day scolding us."

"They've started already, Ngwan'a Masemola. We're called the bonfire clan."

"To think of the nerve to shun the burial of the man who paid for your dowry with twenty walking cattle and ten bleating sheep!"

"To destroy him, just like that? The man who put you into an immaculate four-roomed house in Thembisa and single-handedly polished you into a real white missus of Mohlalaotwane?"

"Oh, no, women of my village, it's a screaming shame! What are we now in the eyes of our men?"

"We are nothing anymore, my sister."

"What vulgarity?"

"Cursed be my daughters if I emulate such a serpent!"

"Indeed, cursed be all the girls of Mohlalaotwane if we join the sorceress, Hunadi. May their wombs shrivel with barrenness and their breasts run dry till eternity!"

They had spat into their left palms and beaten the saliva with two fingers of the right hand and pointed their index fingers to the skies in a vow that concluded by calling on a curse to descend upon the villain.

The village priest and elders had stood around the grave watching Mahlatji's coffin draped in a black ox-hide approach its final destination. They had bowed their heads with the shame of sharing blankets every night with witches they thought were loving wives. It had been beyond their comprehension how the sorceress called Mma Mahlatji could have subjected her husband and son to such undignified deaths. But then it had happened. Nothing could be said or done any more. Mahlatji was gone. Butchered just a week before.

It had happened at the beginning of a month-long consumer action in Thembisa. A call had been made for the residents to boycott business in town but Mma Mahlatji had only vaguely heard about it. Phogole referred her to their son, Lefata, when she sought to be assured on the eve of the boycott.

"I don't know, Mama. Mama, please, you're disturbing me. I want to sleep. Anyway, who said there was a boycott?"

Indeed, Lefata had heard little about the boycott and had never really taken it to heart. To him boycotts had just come and gone. Some worked. Others were only cheap scares made up by drunkards and chance-takers. This one could just be another of those scares. Otherwise, why were there no posters around? He found it strange that parents built mountains out of every grain of sand.

Now Mma Mahlatji recalled how she had stood there a while, her confusion momentarily giving way to a penetrating motherly warmth for the little bundle curled up on the tin bed against the wall. She had prayed that He in the dizzy heights above should please see to it that Lefata became a doctor one day. Then she had checked herself, planted a soft kiss on his brow, and left to join her husband in the other room.

Her concern arose from the fact that the following morning she had to pay the final installment on the steel plates for their coal stove. The Indian trader from whom she was buying them had threatened to cancel the deal if she failed to pay in full on the day.

"If only I knew. But why did I do it?" she thought, tasting salty tears in her mouth as the final stage of the burial ceremony was reaching a climax before the grave.

She had heard about people who would tie a person's hands at the back with wire, put a car tyre round his neck, dose him with petrol, force him to drink some of it and then set him alight. She had shuddered at the thought of it on her way to Johannesburg and continued to do so when she returned carrying the plates and a few household things that only motherly instinct would purchase. How she had wished to find Lefata waiting for her at the taxi rank, ready to assist her evade any possible trouble!

"Oh, God of Nazareth, please save your sinner. Deliver us from the necklace treatment, my Lord, just this moment, God of Abraham and Israel!"

"Target, target, target!" tiny voices suddenly accosted her.

She had dropped everything in fright, and gone down on her knees pleading for mercy. It was too late. The smell of dagga and cheap beer engulfed her. Someone among the teenagers surrounding her called out the name of her own son in an admonishing tone.

No, it can't be! She was dreaming. Yes, she was. But it was. No. It can't. Oh no! It's him. Could it be? No. He wouldn't. But it's him. Really? Oh, God! This drunk? It can't. Lefata? This drunk? What are our children up to during school holidays! No. Not Lefata!

"Please, my son, explain to your friends."

"Explain what?" he sneered, his head falling onto one side, eyes half-closed. "You think just because you are my mother you are free? No. It's a long walk to freedom."

Hands were pulling her this way and that, fists pounded and boots rained down. Her own son was leading the attack, bent on making history. For too long his peers had been accusing him of cowardice. Girls had called him insulting names. He would

now show them he was the bravest comrade. It had suddenly dawned on him how easy it was to become a Kathrada or a Mandela. There was no going back. At this moment, for him, the Struggle had begun.

It took them fifteen minutes of beatings and torture before Mma Mahlatji was left vomiting soap and cooking oil. Her stomach wrenched with pain, the boys left full of fun and victory. Neighbours found her writhing helplessly but she begged them not to say a word to Mahlatji about the involvement of their son. She had once seen him hurl a ticket examiner out of a moving train for calling her a kaffir meid and a bitch. It chilled her blood to imagine what he would do to the little drunken rat. But the two-legged township press had reached his fruit-stall at the Leralla Station before she could rest on the bed. They had dramatised the story for Mahlatji and expressed their profound shock at the boy who had had the nerve to abuse his own mother for the amusement of riffraff.

She heard his fruit cart squeaking its way to the storeroom. Phogole entered, the co-ordination in his limp knocked out by anxiety and agitation. His arms reached to her out of helplessness and the need to hold tightly onto someone to ease himself of the violent tensions mounting in his systems. For the first time Mma Mahlatji saw her husband gushing tears. She, too, burst out crying, more in sympathy due to her physical pain. How could she save her family?

He choked with the effort to utter a word. Then, after a while, he found his voice in a quiver, and said in front of everyone, "Gods forgive me if I kill my own son tonight!"

He looked up at the ceiling, shaking his head with much emotion. " I'll do it. Even though I could not kill that Boer who drove the Saracen over my leg in Sharpeville in 1960, I'll kill my son! I'll kill him. Tonight."

They heard him say, "I'll kill my son!" and attributed it to the usual effervescence of parental pain which was bound to soon bubble itself out. It was impossible that such a loving man could kill his only son. He was too rational for such an extremity. Many would do it, maybe, but not Mahlatji.

Someone said, "Please don't take it too much to heart, Phogole. It's the kind of mischief we have to put up with from our children these days," and they left him attending his wife's bruises, trying orange juice and milk to counter the effects of soap and cooking oil. What they didn't know was that they would be called again to his house that very night. They did not know that the whole of Mpho Section and parts of Difateng, Motheong and Lekaneng Sections, raging mad, were to besiege Mahlatji's house that very night.

When it all started, people were taken aback by shrill voices crying out, "Everyone out! A man has murdered his son! Mahlatji has killed Lefata!"

Neighbours who had earlier assisted his wife, confirmed that, indeed, Mahlatji had done it. They confirmed this when everyone came out to deal with him, and testified loud and clear for everyone to hear. Then they supported the youth who stormed the house of the beast and dragged Phogole into the streets for the necklace treatment.

The few adults who tried to plead for the man were chased down the streets by mad hordes of girls and boys until they would have nothing to do with his rescue anymore. Mma Mahlatji's protestations were drowned by wild excitement and hysteria. She stood with disbelief as they torched her husband, flames shooting high, consuming Phogole as it would any victim of the Ku Klux Klan. The sight induced paralysis in all her faculties. She fell, and came to only the next day. That's when the street committee ordered that Mahlatji be buried outside the township.

Her pleas to bury husband and son together fell on deaf ears. Phogole had been declared an enemy of the people. They denied her even the chance to accompany his remains to the village. His relatives came to fetch him. They were the least prepared to hear a word from Mma Mahlatji.

Poor woman!

Perhaps they should have been a little generous and attempted a semblance of sympathy, a pretext, to grant her last minute plea that the burials be delayed until the murderer of her son was found. They should have at least been less noisy, perhaps then she could have struggled through the paralysis that had befallen her and explained. Perhaps those who had separated the burials should have shown restraint and not sought to punish Phogole in his death. They should have had pity for her sake, allowed themselves to have second thoughts before passing the verdict on her husband. That could have lessened her grief at her son's open grave.

Ah, African mama! But it's done now.

The elders with the village priest around Phogole's grave had constructed frightening words of condemnation in their skinny bosoms. They called upon the ancestors to bring down their wrath upon the beastly calves that refused a father to be buried with his son.

"Cursed be the debased brats who feed upon their own fathers," they pronounced.

"May they bear pigs as pale as the white man!" the village priest demanded, inciting skilful women to prolong the customary wails that suddenly filled the cemetery.

Some women fell to the ground and were attended to, more fainted than was usually the case at such rituals. And the priest continued calling for the eternal destruction of a shameless breed whose mothers and fathers had strayed because they had never been to the mountain.

"These murderers," the elders added, "Get their witchcraft from their very uncir-cumcised mothers and fathers! Dung of the lowest township scum!" They spat hard on to the ground.

At that moment, a minibus had sauntered into the graveyard and stopped a few paces from the mourners. Four men and two women in colourfully embroidered African robes had stepped from it. Everyone around the grave had gone quiet, the mourners scrutinising the alighting strangers, wondering who they were. One of the strangers was obviously a convict by the way they had ruffled him up.

"Greetings, compatriots of Mohlaotwane," one of the strangers addressed the mourners, while the others pushed and pulled their victim forward.

"We drove all the way from Thembisa to make sure you know the truth before Comrade Phogole is buried. For the whole week we tirelessly hunted this man. Now we have him. It's a pleasure to find you still gathered like this, comrades," he paused with discomfort due to the blankness he read in the faces of the mourners.

"Is this how you treat functions such as this in your Thembisa?" the priest had began, "From which clan is your father?" he asked with mounting anger.

The villagers shook their heads and made 'tsk-tsk-tsk' sounds of disapproval with their mouths, a few craning their necks with curiosity.

"Please show respect, we are burying a man, not a dog," a village elder had ordered. "If you have anything to say to us, wait until we are done."

"There is not much to say, comrades," one of the women from the vehicle took over. "This is the man who has caused all the confusion. Do what you want with him."

Another man added, "He's all yours, comrades. We have done our bit. But if you are afraid, just give us a word, his necklace and petrol are in the car."

It shocked and infuriated the villagers all at once. Women clutched their wombs and whimpered. Others got bilious and wanted to vomit. Their stomachs were burn-ing with acid, their wombs went ice cold. Young men and women bayed for the strangers' blood.

"Destroy these harbingers of death!"

"Kill them!"

So went the battle cries, and the villagers scoured the ground for stones, eyes menacingly fixed on the intruders.

Then an elder intervened. Those who already had stones dropped them with reluctance. The strangers sighed with relief. The elder quietly signalled to the mourners to again converge in an orderly way around the grave. When all had returned to their places, he slowly turned to the terrified strangers and repeated what had already been said.

"Let us remind you once again, people from the slaughterhouse. We are burying a man, not a dog. If you don't know, this one, Phogole, was a hard-working man. He had many cattle, one of which has already been slaughtered to bury him. For us that's enough. We don't feed on humans, we are not cannibals."

"But ..."

"No more word from you again, woman. Your head is hardly covered. It's creatures like you who forced us into the curse of burying a man away from his son. Haven't you soiled us enough already? You've gone even further to desecrate not only the burial, but also the village. If you know what's good for you here in Mohlalaotwane, shut your mouth."

"For the last time, if it is in accordance with your ways in towns to bathe your dead in your fellow man's blood," the priest reiterated, "take your sacrificial cow to the abattoir you call home. Slaughter it there in Thembisa and offer its blood as libation to your gods of horrors, not here in Mohlalaotwane. You've defiled our village enough already. Please go away before I open my eyes."

Befuddled, the strangers mechanically propelled their 'cow for slaughter' to the minibus and drove off without delay. It took them the distance from Mohlalaotwane to Groblersdal to utter a word.

"Bloody village reactionaries!" the bearded one at last hissed between clenched teeth. Then he turned round, "No chance for you, sell-out. The comrades are waiting for you in Thembisa. Bloody murderer!"

The groups' embarrassment had given way to a sense of revenge, heating up to a horrifying urge. Again and again they called their 'cow' a murderer because under the cover of darkness he had killed Lefata with a blunt object inside his father's yard. He had done this to settle old scores with Phogole because Phogole had exposed the 'cow's' connivance with the police Special Branch in tracking down political activists in the township. The 'cow' also did it because he had wanted Phogole to be destroyed by the very people for whom he, Phogole, had been risking his life. Indeed, for many years the man had been smuggling trained guerrillas into the country to fight the 'cow's' masters. Now the 'cow' was in serious trouble.

And while the minibus accelerated so as to catch up with the other funeral in Thembisa, Mma Mahlatji sat almost transfixed, watching the gaping grave, only wishing her son's burial would pass quickly. Around her, the priests were joined by other speakers in their praise for the deceased. Each explored their oratory skills in applauding the child's political maturity and moral uprightness.

"He was a knight in the shining armour of valour, the neon light in the hearts of his peers and others who are patriotic to the land!" they endorsed, igniting slogans and raising red dust high in the air.

There was a moment of absolute silence though. This was after some men and women in bright trade union T-shirts shuttled forwards with purposeful urgency and whispered something to the leading priest. The clergy, with apparent deep scars of solemnity in their hearts, called upon the mourners to give the Comrades a chance to carry out the final patriotic deed.

The silence was now intense, allowing politicians to swing into action. With a dignified and heavy mood of pride and duty, they started pointing here and there, vigorously nodding their heads and making beckoning signs with their fingers, advising the Comrades on the next course of action and positions to hold. Then, at a given signal by the most important politician, the Comrades in military fatigue went into formation; toy guns pointed to the skies, and with the help of their mouths and mime, they carried out a 21 gun salute in honour of the departed compatriot. Yet, Mma Mahlatji heard none of these. She heard no speech nor slogan nor 21 gun salute. She was deeply engrossed, overwhelmed.

Nothing physical remained vivid any more, concrete structures had lost colour and form. She found it an insurmountable task to reconcile with the chilling deaths of her loved ones. Behind her a few people whispered among themselves with restrained appreciation. They said she was indeed a strong one, the fitting wife of Phogole, the cadre of the people.

"How does a useless woman face life when things go this way?" she kept asking herself, "What is there to still live for?"

But above all, there rose a sense of guilt. It had kept gnawing at her since her house was attacked and was again becoming strong amidst holy curses and political noises that were choking the air with dust.

"I should not have done it," regret repeated itself.

The youths sang with mad passion around the open grave. Cassocks flew in a myriad shades of colour and design as if to bring the departed soul back to life. The dogs of law licked their lips in anticipation. The minibus was flying at supersonic speed somewhere between Pretoria and Thembisa and, Mma Mahlatji was minutely recounting the series of events that had led to the tragic loss of her husband and son.

Then, something told her never to rest until the name Phogole was cleared. It had to be done. Soon. Now. The feeling built up strongly within her. Yes, Phogole was her man. He had rescued her from the line of fire on that terrible day in Sharpeville when people were slaughtered on account of the passbook. He had it done before they even knew each other. And, as a result of hs bravery, he had lost a leg. No, she was not going to cry any more. The man had loved her to the end. She must clear his

name. But first she must see his grave before going to bed. She was not going to waste a night without saying a word to him in that grave. Yes. She must go now. They can remain burying their hero. It's enough that she saw his grave, she must leave. There was no more time. She must leave for Mohlalaotwane. If anyone was going to try and stop her, they would have to turn her into a corpse. She must go, come what may.

Mma Mahlatji calmly rose to her feet and looked at the faces around her and at her son's coffin. Then, with deliberate slowness, she began walking away from the grave. No one could attempt a hiss or a touch of restraint. The calm in her eyes and demeanour were too authoritative to challenge. The priests and 'military youths' went abruptly quiet as she walked off as if in a trance.

Suddenly one of the youngsters in the uniform of the dead soldiers shouted, "Reactionary! Stop her ..."

He didn't finish what he intended to say. A tall, well-built woman dressed in black from head to toe smacked him with the back of her open hand. She caught him full in the face. He spun on his heels, yelping, clutching his cheek, then fell and rolled on the red soil, spitting out some of his teeth.

The woman gave him a sharp look, turned and hurried behind Mma Mahlatji. The crowd and the Boer soldiers made way for the two figures dressed in black. Not even the government licenced killers felt equal to that which moved the woman, and both the mourners and soldiers stood stupefied, watching as they vanished into the distance.

Perhaps in Mohlalaotwane sobriety might gather together the elders in Mahlaltji's home and his wife's family to discuss the whole matter, and maybe seek ways to cleanse her of the filth misfortune had heaped upon her. It might be agreed that the circumstances cried out for the slaughter of a beast which, Mahlatji's family, having been the aggressor in the matter, might be persuaded to provide, as well as granting her additional compensation for having treated her as if she was a witch.

The tall woman calmly reversed a Toyota sedan from her garage with motherly care. In the passenger seat was Mma Mahlatji, looking ahead to the long trip to Mohlalaotwane. She had to see Phogole's grave before going to bed that night. While she sat back in her seat, the minibus was negotiating a corner at the northern entrance to the township, the 'cow' still sweating inside.

UNITY IN FLIGHT

"Viva[9] Azania!"
"Viva the Land!"
"Power to the People!"
"Power to the Land!"
A church hall thundered with these chants one evening in Hamanskraal. It was the launch of the Azanian People's Party, exactly two months after the banning of the Azanian People's Union and the arrest of its entire leadership. As the ceremony began, Tau, a stocky man in his mid-forties, his clothes still smelling new, from white running shoes down to his underwear, was cutting corners at a trot between thorn bushes and open spaces.

He had left his home at Kwa-Thema just a few hours before, people still celebrating his return the previous day from Robben Island where he had served a twenty year term on suspicion of harbouring and then spreading barbaric thoughts in a Christian country.

Now, breathing the clean air of freedom, rhythms dictated by the moody terrain under his feet on the outskirts of Pretoria, he was fuelled by a mission in his heart — the zeal to avenge. And, there was no better place to settle old scores than at the launch of the Azanian People's Party.

"Viva Azania!"
"Viva the Land!"
"Long Live the Spirit of Maqoma, Sekhukhune, Moshoeshoe!"
"Buya[10] Bambatha! Mbuya Nehanda! Buya Modjadji!"
"Aluta Continua!!!"
Speech after speech, song after song, continued in the church, pulses agitated by war chants and dances. The youth, like well-fed calves prancing along the river bank at sunset, were showing off their health. They were flying all over the place, putting up posters on the walls, distributing pamphlets, showing new arrivals to benches and exchanging positions from time to time so as to guard doors and windows. They flaunted new energy in their commitment to the cause. They ducked imaginary blows and missiles, returned them with speed and accuracy, elbowed phantom soldiers, rattled mimed machine-guns seized in bayonet charges and viciously kicked around so many envisioned police dogs that you felt pity for their victims.

Their fists shooting in the air above the multitude of heads and war cries and dances, the mood seemed as if the hall would spill out and charge at the enemy in a conventional insurrection. It was as if it was just a matter of seconds before their hands mauled those who had invaded the Azanian soil, ravaged our pastures and made poverty our natural lot.

"The Dutch settler who rules us by coercion shall die!" a brave speaker pronounced.

"Same with their European brothers whose bellies are swollen with our fields and toil, for which they daily gang up to perpetually subjugate us," a woman added more fuel.

The speeches made ceaseless calls for the immediate execution of Ronald Reagan and Margaret Thatcher.

"The two are just like their imperial forebears who engineered our earlier defeats and slavery. Ronald Reagan and Margaret Thatcher are the worst exporters of modern rape, plunder and murder ... " a unionist rumbled on.

Ululations pierced the thick air inside the church. They competed with sharp whistles and slogans in urging on the fiery speeches. Orators, too, played their role to the full. They sang praises to the days when the African warrior knew how to emerge victorious from battle. The days of Shaka, Hintsa and Moshoeshoe, when the invading white pest would bombard the breeze with cannons petrified by its own nightmares about the enraged African lion whose lair had been invaded and whose cubs had been violated.

"Land scorching rapists!" they raged.

The cramped church hall was a volcano rearing to explode at the slightest provocation. Outside, the summer evening was clear, the moon shining bright, bright enough for one to pick out a figure a good few feet away, and peacefully cool, except for the police and soldiers who were heavily armed and had taken up strategic positions around the hall. But the volcano rumbled on.

"*Vuka*[1] *Hintsa! Vuka Lembede! Vuka Mantatise!*"

"*Vuka Lumumba!*"

"*Vuka Nzinga!*"

"*Me Katilili, Mantatise,*
Cuddle us, your children, let us feed from your breasts.
Nandi, Mother of Shaka, Mother of Us All,
May your sacred womb continue to bear
Brave sons and daughters of the soil!"

"*Viva Azania! Viva the Land!*"

"*Long Live the People's Party!*"

Those in the church and the agents of law outside stood like two bull buffalo

rearing to gore into each other's belly, ready to scatter offal all over the battlefield, to fill the air with the smell of dung. Already blood was lingering in the air.

Tau arrived sweating at the gate. Blinding lights fitted on armoured trucks flooded him. Video cameras started rolling his image into their files. He did not care a hoot. He knew the circus was a strategy to scare him from what was going on inside. He proceeded as if nothing was happening.

On either side of the footpath to the hall were heavily armed vampires. He could see others lurking in the small bushes within and outside the yard. This was sheer provocation but he was not prepared to be intimidated. Not even by their ghostly quietness. He had fought countless times in his life and knew how to render them useless. His mission needed to be accomplished. Someone had to pay!

"Viva Azania!"

"Viva the Land!"

"Izwe Lethu[12]!"

The multitude chanted continuously as the evening matured into night. Tau entered the hall, moving gingerly like a stalking leopard. The young marshals inside realised this was not a man to be guided nor disturbed. His soul and demeanour were fixed on something that would soon be seen. As for the rest of the hall, people paid little attention to the man, they were too engrossed with the work at hand. Those in front of him made way when he put his hands between them in a gesture that requested they separate long enough for him to pass.

A smartly dressed man called Mavaka stood up to address the throng. His confidence and the supporting cheers from the floor showed he was qualified for a top position on the executive body of the People's Party. He had the style, radiance and charisma of a natural leader. When he took the microphone and started talking about the aims and objectives of the organisation it was clear that he was no man to mess with. He knew his job. Especially when he spoke about the things that needed to be done to the oppressors.

"We will dig the snake out of its hole," he declared. "We will chase it down the tarred road on the hottest summer day. By God, we will pulverise it!"

"Viva the People's Party!"

"Viva!"

Mavaka continued in a strident voice, "And when we move on towards victory ..."

Suddenly his eye caught that of another man rooted in the centre of the hall. The fierce look in the man's eyes did nothing to conceal its hostility. Mavaka recognised him at once. He was the bull terrier who had never known how to let go in fist fights during their youth. The confrontational intent in him could not be mistaken. The pulse of slow death was radiating from him towards the stage. It crippled Mavaka for a while. His heart pounded and he remained transfixed behind the microphone, saying nothing.

The silence in the hall was unnerving. People nudged each other. Many of the grown ups knew the stranger. Most youths had heard about the man but could not link the name to the owner.

"Who is he?" they whispered.

"Who?"

"The stranger."

"Stranger? Tau? You don't know what you're talking about!"

"Tau? This short?"

"Who said he was tall?"

"I can't believe it. Can't be him."

"It is. Fresh from the Island."

"No, it can't."

"Are you sure?"

"It's him."

"But aren't they comrades?"

"They are."

"Now what is this?"

"Sh ..."

Everyone was becoming anxious. What was going on between the two men? One on the stage, the other in the centre of the crowd. Youths belted out chants to make up for the growing confusion.

"Viva Azania! Afrika Viva!"

"Sizobabamba nezingane zabo[13]!"

"Sizobabamba[14]!

"Sizobadubula ngombayembaye[15]!"

"Nang' uSobukwe[16]!"

"Viva the People's Party!"

"Izwe Lethu!!!"

History gripped Tau's mind as he stood keeping Mavaka captive with flaming eyes. He saw images of life on the Island. There were naked men freezing in winter. Rocks crushed their backs as they slaved in a quarry, goaded by the whip. Some were infected with lethal diseases, gripped by slow, painful deaths. All this flashed vividly before his eyes as if the horrors were happening right there in the hall.

Then came the worst of all. Tau himself was flung into a pit. He could feel coarse sea sand being thrown over his body, leaving only his cleanly shaven head to the mercy of the scorching sun. Hours on end, sand squeezed and compressed him so that he all but gave up life. That was when he visualised the usually doomed Red Indians in Wild West films, who would be pulled round and round on gravel by outlaws mounted on horses – they would die with no limb or hair left on their bodies. Then he saw his people threatened with extinction by bandits in their own motherland.

"Ah, life under foreign domination!"

He remembered how thirsty he had become in that position in the pit. He remembered how, when he begged for water, a pink-red drunken warder leisurely came to piss into his ears, nostrils and all of him that remained above surface. At first he was seized by a mad rage. Instinct had said, "Jump out and rip the Boer's wind pipe out!" but the earth had tightened its grip even more ruthlessly.

The acidic feel of urine, its stench of Klipdrift brandy and the helplessness of his situation collaborated to humiliate him. He boiled with such rage that he could hardly open his mouth with a simple curse. It was then, for the first time since he had been in prison, that he visualised Mavaka giving evidence at his bogus trial.

He had heard Mavaka tell the judges, "Tau incited us to kill whites with double edged pangas made from car springs." He saw it all as it took place in the small home garage which had been turned into a makeshift court. Yes, the judges themselves were imposters. They were nothing but disguised police officers full of hate. And not only did they make it a hush-hush thing, to hide the role of Mavaka and his like, they also propelled the farce at lightning speed to deny their victims a chance to obtain legal representation.

This was the trial that wasted twenty years of Tau's life. The same trial that flashed before his eyes now, showing Mavaka with a wild grin before a fake judge. Now watching all this replayed before him, shaking his head in the tense hall that not long before was full of life and verve, Tau did not realise his hands were folding into fists that Mavaka saw as solid rocks.

"*Viva Azania! Viva the Land!*"
"*Power to the People's Party!*"
"*Viva Peasants and Workers!*"
"*Down with traitors!*"
"*Ha bashwe bana ba baloi*[17]*!*"
"*Kill the traitor! Kill the dog!*"
"*Izwe Lethu!*"

Mavaka's hands searched for something unknown to him. His mouth went dry with bitterness. He swallowed with effort but nothing went down. He longed for the holy flesh and blood of the son of Judah to wet his throat although it was not sabbath day, nor was the occasion a sacrament ceremony. Shivers rocked his body. His eyes started to see juggled objects. For a moment he lost such control over his faculties that he could hardly feel the sweat running down his back. He felt mud in his shoes. His suit shrank and felt tight. It was as if Tau's stare had pulled his tie so tightly round his beefy neck that he felt strangled.

"*Viva Azania!*"

"*Viva the Land!*"

"*Power to the People!*"

"*Power to the Land!*"

The crowd repeated chants and slogans, yearning to devour the exploiters of the land, to pulverise imperialists, settlers and their running dogs, then paused.

Tau made good use of the break. He approached Mavaka, "Tell them about your noble contribution at the trial. All about pangas and Europeans being driven into the sea."

Mavaka's suit expanded ten times its size but he felt naked. "Please, comrade ..." his words pattered away for want of breath. Again he opened his mouth. Nothing came out. He made empty gesticulations, his mind working very fast. He thought of a few tricks but dismissed them as they came. Time was running out. If he could only get something to delay, something to shock. Something to give him enough chance to construct a safe escape from the quagmire.

Yes! Here it is. He sent his body into spasms, as if inflicted by the demons of spiritual revivalists. He tensed his eyes and buttocks and yelled, "Holy tight mission!"

Every muscle in his body was now taut. A noise of car tyres forced to a sudden halt while rotating at high velocity on a tarred road escaped the combination of his lungs and throat. He let loose a confusion of growls, snarls and groans. His body whirled in the air and hit the stage with a loud thud. The crowd held its breath with shock. But that was not all.

After a second or so, he sprang up, a totally changed creature. A complete image of the holy possessed by demons at the height of exorcism. He was experiencing raptures, seeing visions in the air. He spiced queer sounds with the kind of wailing you would hear during the confession of vice. His transformation was so hypnotising that people took it for a kind of magic.

Then, like a prophet at a Zion healing session, the transformed creature was spitting foam, mingled with barely audible groans. These subsided after a short while. At least a word or two could now be picked out from his utterances. He was flinging insults at himself. The young sought to bring him down from the stage for messing up the function, but they were soon hushed by the crowd and began to relax watching the free show. By this time the performer had shifted to another gear. He scattered energy in all directions. He coiled, twisted, jerked, twitched, squirmed, jumped and stomped the ground as if to say 'Hallelujah'! His eyes were bloodshot and the curses were becoming clearer.

"Holy tight mission!" he repeated. "*My gat, mos man*[18]! Let me die!"

He paused, red eyes challenging every face below the stage with the slowness only a madman could manage under the circumstances. The hall was held spell-bound. Fired by his own performance and still fixing his dilated eyeballs on the crowd, Mavaka took to front stage. A controlled long growl followed, shorter ones took over.

" What am I? Who am I? Why? Why? My gat, mos man!"

There were murmurs. People were now becoming restless, feeling he had gone too far. Mavaka stood for a while staring down at the auditorium without blinking. Then, still maintaining a controlled rhythm, he began tearing off his suit. Underneath the jacket a sound transmitting device was exposed.

"Look at me," he said. "I'm a traitor! I've sold my brother here," pointing at Tau. "Kill me! Now!"

The throng could not wait any longer. It surged forward. But the leadership raised their palms and shouted, "Order, order! Please, comrades!"

The wave calmed down uneasily, finally coming to a standstill though excitement still reared, ready to explode. It was then that an elderly man took the platform persuading everyone to take their seats. When all were seated he began talking with convincing authority.

"Comrades," he began in a deep voice, "it is our task to achieve radical change so as to ensure true human fulfilment. Our violence, carried out with informed purpose, should be ruthless and properly directed."

"*Viva!*"

"*Power to the People!*"

"It should seek to immobilise the settler government by striking decisive blows against the enemy's war machinery and the farmers who rape our land and drain the life of our peasants."

"*Power to the People!*"

"*Power to the Land!*"

"It should cripple the cannibalistic multinationals that exploit our workers in the mines and factories."

"*Viva the People's Power!*"

"*Peasants and workers, viva!*"

"Utilised this way, it is bound to destabilise the settler army and send a message to the imperial cowboys. This is the type of violence we need. To destroy powerful forces that connive to oil the Dutch oppressor. Not idiots like Mavaka."

"That one must die!" someone from the floor demanded, pointing at Mavaka.

"Now!" the whole house roared in unison.

"Kill the traitor, save the nation!"

"Kill him now, kill the settler later!"

"He must die!"

"Yes, he must die!"

"Kill, kill, kill!!!"

The old man stood with his head slightly bowed. The crowd repeated the cry, "Kill, kill!" till some leaders came to the rescue by waving to the house, urging everyone to settle down. The screams began to subside. The elder patiently waited for the last of the murmurs to wear themselves out. They did and he continued speaking in a calm but forceful voice.

"Whatever we do, sons and daughters of the soil, let us not be controlled by emotions. This man here," he pointed to Tau, "has just arrived this morning from Robben Island. He has made one of the greatest sacrifices in our struggle."

"Viva!"

"Long live Comrade Tau!"

"Now, before we even acknowledge his selflessness, we already want to kill in his name. Is it so thoughtful of us to do that and get the police on his back before he has even rested? Do we want such a brave warrior to be hanged for a dog like Mavaka?"

"Viva comrade Tau!"

"Viva!"

"Uyi bhubhezi Tau!"

"Uyibhubhezi[19]!"

"Viva the spirit of Mangaliso Sobukwe!"

"Viva!"

"Viva comrade Tau! Viva!"

"Izwe Lethu!"

"Besides, it is our duty to ensure that this launch of our People's Part is a success. At least to ensure our broader victory. We are not boys and girls in the streets seeking adventure. We are launching a revolutionary party in preparation for a very bitter struggle ahead."

Someone tried to throw in a word but was hushed down.

"Sons and daughters of the soil," the old one proceeded with great firmness, "Mavaka can no longer sell anybody. We now know him. His job is finished. Who can he fool after this exposure? Nobody. No longer will he be able to walk the streets with his head high. Children will jeer and spit at him for the rest of his life. Mind you, he still has to justify his salary, because no colonial pig is ever prepared to pay a monkey that cannot deliver. From now on his life is on fire. It is far worse than yours and mine. So why soil the noble task of this day with a dog's blood? We don't need it. Unless, mark me, unless we wish to reduce our noble war to a mere act of revenge. For that matter, we are not prepared to assist the dogs out there to disrupt this sacred occasion. Let their lackey join them. Go Mavaka. Do your job from the armoured trucks outside. Go. We will meet in the battlefield. Go now. Go, sell-out."

Mavaka could not imagine living with the consequences of ejection and isolation. Maybe he could do with an ace or two. He went totally berserk. With the speed of a striking cobra he smashed the sound-transmitting device on the stage. He clasped the back of his head with both hands and screamed.

"My *moer*[20], mos man!" he started insulting himself again. "I'm sick and tired! Fuck the Boer! Fuck the whole system! Who am I? A killer! What am I? No! Kill me! Destroy me! I want necklace treatment! Now! Burn me out! Now!"

Then, he paused for a moment and went on slowly with much intensity, "Oh yes, now. Now I point them out ... "

"What?"

"I point them."

"Who?"

"The others."

"Who?"

"Those I work with."

"Point them!"

"Point them!

"Point! Point! Point!"

"Out sell out, out!"

"Let them come out!"

"Let them!"

"Kill the sell-out!"

Mavaka's eyes started searching.

Towards the back of the hall a petrified man hesitated, then shot towards the door. He could not go far. In no time his legs were kicking in the air. Two muscular men had him by the scruff of his neck and were now carrying him towards the stage, their fists doing things to his ribs. Two more traitors were pointed out. Their sound-transmitters were repossessed for future use by the People's Party and all the traitors were lined up on the stage for everyone to see.

A shot rang out. It shattered the brains of the man standing next to Mavaka. Some of the brain matter covered Mavaka's face like cream. He dived for cover under the front benches. More shots followed. The other two sell-outs shrank in the face of

instant death while Mavaka watched. People panicked and screamed. The church hall was now being pumped with unrelenting fire. Most people jumped out of windows not knowing where the next bullet would come from. A few used the door to escape into the glare of the moon. Some of them got shot in the chest or between the eyes. There was now chaos both in the church hall and outside.

Comfortably set up in the police vehicles, a commanding officer had given the order. Realising the futility of keeping a spy who would expose more about the security machinery than he would benefit it, the commander had decided, in his commitment to the Volk[21], that a monkey's miscarried mission was a heavy liability: an empty-handed hunter, just like an empty stomach, was nothing but a heavy burden.

"Isn't it better then to get rid of the Kaffir monkeys?" the faceless man asked those of his tribe.

"Of course, there's nothing sweeter than seeing the savages scurry around terrified," they reasoned.

"Kill the Kaffir savages!" they chorused.

Outside the church hall the youth returned fire with stones, flammable liquids and a few small guns. Some men and women joined in with guns as well. Running battles ensued.

Tau scaled a high fence. He was part of a large group that only wanted to get away because they were neither armed nor organised. Once outside, in a desperate attempt to vanish from the firing line, they took to all directions, running away into the small bushes clumped around the hall. But their's was a blind escape. Some of them ran directly into the fire of the police and soldiers who were hiding in those bushes under the bright full moon. Tau, however, managed to flee.

After what seemed centuries of ducking bullets whistling past his head, he found himself among a group of about thirty people running on a gravel road. Behind was the unabated, sputtering gunfire which could still be heard as the group ascended what seemed an endless hill. Here many of the runners radiated to the flanks of the road, hoping to be swallowed by the darkness of long grass and scattered bushes. Tau continued straight on, another figure running in front of him. Nobody followed them.

When they descended the incline on the other side of the hill, he caught up with the other man. They ran side by side for some time, their footsteps harmonising, eyes on the road, ears primed, their breathing alternating in an uncomfortable rhythmic sound. Then they recognised each other. The other figure was Mavaka. But no more talking now. Only the stolen, regular darting of sideways glances at each other. No more settling ancient grudges. No. No more confessions. None of these. The fire in their chests was too hot, the fire behind deadly. The escape, a refuge.

They did not know where their route led. All that mattered was to get away. Neither uttered even the simplest of exclamations. Not even a curse. Every little grain of the remaining energy in their systems had to be saved for the task at hand. Quietly they ran under the glare of the full moon.

Suddenly something whizzed past their heads. Oh no! They must gather up whatever last strength was left in their bodies and accelerate. Tau was convinced some policeman had singled him out as the key target for the night. Mavaka similarly thought his end had dawned. They had to run.

"This way," Mavaka invited Tau.

The men took the direction Mavaka suggested. After some time they came to a *donga*[22] and jumped inside. The place was so dark! But then because of the darkness, their pursuers would find it difficult to spot them. They fell and groped. They ran, tripped and fell, picked each other up, ontinued running. How they ran and ran!

By morning, out of breath, they came to a highway. Carrying scars from the night of trampling on stones and tearing through bushes, their bodies were all bruised and cut, their clothes muddy and tattered. But at least they could still walk or, for that matter, crawl. Their hearts said, "Keep going!"

When they reached the highway, a huge truck emerged from the horizon. On its side in bold red letters. was written, ABNORMAL LOAD.

The men looked at each other. They looked at the road and took in its stretch. They looked at the truck and took in the stretch of road again. Then they nodded and understood each other without saying a word. Finally, they fixed their eyes on the oncoming vehicle, waving it down.

The big machine and its huge load came to a roaring halt.

"Where are you going?"

The driver squinted at them from the heat and the hubbub of the machine's entrails. The two men were exhausted. All they could do was point down the road and gesticulate their need for help. The driver signalled for them to jump in. Mavaka and Tau did so and sat very close next to each other, fearing to smear him with their mud. The truck took off, everyone's eyes fixed on the road ahead.

No one spoke.

They did not know where the machine was heading. So long as it took them far away from the guns and the cannons. It rumbled on to a destination they did not care to know.

At length, a soothing warmth began to seep in. Forgetfulness began to swallow their consciousness as the humming of the big machine became a lullaby for them. They found solace in deep sleep. The truck continued on its journey, pushing on and on with its load, the two exhausted bodies next to the driver, united in flight.

Peter Rule

Graphics by Anna Varney-Horwitz

Graphic on page 47 by Peter Rule

FIFTEEN YEARS AGO TODAY

Arriving in my car at Johannesburg Airport, we were assailed by the building alterations, road diversions, scaffolding and traffic congestion; dust and exhaust fumes. We sat in a queue to the drop-off zone with you checking your watch and perspiring in your suit, a forty year-old executive uncomfortably moving up in the world. Giant yellow cranes swung overhead and the sound of pneumatic drills seemed to rattle the windows.

"I hardly recognise the place anymore," you said. I could hear you breathing. You pulled at your tie. "It's like my life. With what you and Kevin have told me in the last few days, I don't know where I stand. I was the husband, the father and the brother; the three of you as the most important people in my life. Now Miriam has gone, and I discover that the two of you, the ones I have left, are really strangers to me. Where does that leave me?"

You climbed out of the car and heaved the suitcase off the back seat. Someone hooted behind us and I couldn't hear the words as your mouth moved. Were you cursing, or perhaps praying, as you smoothed your hair over your balding pate and the corrosion showed on your face? "Write it down for me, Elaine," you said, leaning at the window. "Words are your medium. Help me to understand it all."

You hurried off, on your way to negotiate a franchising partnership with a black empowerment consortium in Cape Town, like a man in flight.

And so I write it down for you, for myself, perhaps for Kevin, when he is ready. It begins with him. What I thought was dead and buried, thrown down the well of the past and filled in with sand, comes back to me with Kevin and what happened to him. It was he who called her back.

I was waiting for him in the Boys High car park after rugby practice as I have on Thursdays since Miriam died. As a freelance writer whose hours are flexible, this is one of the ways that I can support the two of you, the men in my life. His usual Under-16 troop came clattering up the concrete steps from the fields. They generally made a lot of noise, the chummy wisecracks and raucous jostle and shove of the rugby age regiment showing off its precocious masculinity, but this time they were quiet and Kevin was not among them. Something happened to their faces when they saw me. It was odd because they were used to saying hello with self-conscious courtesy: *Kevin's aunt with the nice legs,* I once heard the fullback remark. It passed over their faces like a change in the light. Some of them averted their eyes while others, those behind, looked at me with a hard secretive intentness. None of them said anything and they dispersed quickly as they passed.

I climbed out of the car and went to look for him. I thought he might have been taking a shower – although he always waited until he got to the flat – or was perhaps talking to the coach. It was unlike him not to arrive with the others, punching shoulders, handing out high fives, crashing into the seat next to me, bright-eyed and flushed with exertion; this boy growing into a man.

He was nowhere to be seen on the grandstand steps or the upper fields. The groundsman and his staff were marking the field on the far side, a distinct white line on the wintry turf. Otherwise the field was deserted. I walked across the yellow-grey grass thinking about how lovely a windswept day it was, one of those rare Johannesburg winter days when the wind blows the smog away and everything is pellucid. I was a small groundling crossing lines on a field beneath the intense blue of the sky, and then I saw him on the lower field.

He was sitting hunched over, his head down, a slight cramped figure under the posts. I called him but he didn't move. When he didn't respond the second time I began to run, my sandals flying off. There was something uncharacteristic in his posture, as if he were in prayer.

He looked up when I neared. His face was smashed in, his left eye closed and his lip split. His rugby jersey was torn down the front and there was a raw welt under his ear.

"What happened, Kevin? God, what happened to you? Who did this?"

Then I remembered the change in the boys' faces.

"Was there a fight? What were you fighting about?"

"You've come," he said in an unsteady, slurred voice, someone speaking out of a strange mouth. Without any sound he began to cry – this gangly teenager whose seven year-old tears I remember as he lay under a buckled bicycle in the driveway. I began to panic, talking about doctors and ambulances and assault charges and the principal, trying to help him to his feet and to make him lie down at the same time. He caught hold of my arm and pulled me down next to him. His face worked and eventually he got the words out.

"You want to know why they did it?" he said. "I'm gay."

"What do you mean, you're gay? What are you saying?"

"I told my class today."

"You did what?"

He swallowed and his face contorted. I thought he was too distracted to have heard my question. But suddenly he spoke.

" I told them in our English oral on identity. That I'm gay and it's part of my identity and I'm sick and tired of living a lie, hiding it from everyone when it's part of who

I am and it always has been. I saw Judge Cameron talking about it on T.V. and decided I'm not going to hide it all my life. Why should I? But those guys, my buddies," he stopped again, his breath jerking, his fingers digging into my arm, "my buddies said I was a *fucking moffie* who had betrayed them. They said they don't want a queer for a scrumhalf checking out their bums as he waited for the ball. Each of them hit me, even my friends. Some of them didn't want to, I could see, but the captain said that only moffies would refuse to do it. They took turns."

He looked at me, my godson, my nephew.

"What's the matter with me? Won't you just tell me — what's wrong with me? Why can't I be normal?"

"There's nothing the matter with you, Kevin," I told him. "It's not you. Listen to me! It's not your fault. It's not your fault."

I held him and we cried under the rugby posts, and I realised that I was crying more than him, and not only for him but also for myself. I realised, as I helped him to the car and took him to the clinic — "Bloody rugby again," said the doctor, "pastime of savages!" — that in holding him I was somehow, unexpectedly, holding and comforting myself. The years collapsed around me and I saw in his brokenness that girl who was raped as a fourteen year-old. It was he who called her back, through his broken lips.

"I'm sorry," I said. "I'm so sorry." I suppose I said it in shock and sorrow over Kevin, but I was also saying it to that destitute self who rose out of the years and rested her cheek suddenly between my shoulders. I suppose I was at last asking for her forgiveness.

It was not my fault, either.

Two men raped me at a party when I was fourteen years old.

Your head jerks up. The revelation arrests you and your throat moves in a strange way, the breath writhing there like a trapped animal. And that is the sound you make. Not a human sound but the sound of a large animal when the bullet enters its flesh.

Tell me what happened. I know it's probably difficult for you but I need to know exactly what happened.

What was it that I told you?

It was a long time ago, ages ago. I don't remember it very clearly. I was at a twenty-first birthday party. They followed me into the kitchen where I went to get a drink. They bolted the door and raped me. One of them held me down while the other one did it. Then they swopped.

Why the hell didn't you tell me, Elaine?

Why didn't I tell you, especially you, my big brother? The truth is, I could not tell you or anyone else in the house. It was unspeakable. If I opened my mouth, I might have lost myself completely, the self that all of you — especially Mom — carried through the troubled years afterwards. There was no doubt in my mind that I, the victim, was to blame. I did not know how I was to blame. I could not have explained my guilt to anyone. I felt it, and it destroyed the fourteen year old and her sense of her own value and her trust in her own body, the girl I left behind on the kitchen floor as they walked away, sated.

Of course, the incident had a social context. I thought about this a lot when I was older. They were from the southern suburbs, dressed in black leather jackets, the kind who shaved infrequently and walked around with motorbike helmets under their arms, who used to roar around the rich suburbs looking for chicks, loud music, a jol. It was a time before all the high walls and intercoms and electric fences. You could see and hear a party, the people and the music spilling out onto the pavement. I saw them a few times at parties in the north before it happened. Perhaps they thought it didn't count if you did it on that side of town, away from your family and acquaintances. Perhaps they thought it served the stuck up bitches right, their own depraved form of upward mobility. Perhaps they were beaten up by drunk fathers or sexually abused as children. I remember the click of the door and the snap of the bolt and a big hand over my face, the smell of Texan unfiltered and stale deodorant, my legs taken out from under me.

They had no right.

I am pleased that Kevin is staying with me while you are away. His face has nearly healed now, but there is something that is hidden away from me there, a hooded look. I think he is embarrassed that he cried when I found him under the rugby posts. It doesn't correspond to his image of himself as a teenager. He hasn't spoken to me again about being gay.

On the other hand, I don't think he resents me for knowing his secrets. We have long intellectual discussions about religion. "If Jesus came again," he announces, "he would be black and gay and female. Because those are the people who really suffer these days. He would be thrown out of the church. He would be arrested and beaten up in some stinking prison cell. He would probably have AIDS."

I wonder how you would respond to this, the staid church warden of your parish congregation. Is this little boy growing into a prophet, about to overturn the tables of respectability? All I know is that you would listen. This is something that you have learnt since your certainties were shattered by Miriam's death. As for me, I lost my faith with my virginity, although I still identify with the suffering of Christ the man, and his forsaken cry on the cross. Suffering seems to be the only constant.

I cannot explain how close I feel to him. He laughs at my laconic, off-hand jokes about politicians as we watch the eight o'clock news, the kind of remarks that make you uncomfortable. He is more like a younger brother than a nephew to me. And as I see him struggling with himself and who he is, at times in long interludes of silence, at times in sudden outbursts of anger that shake through his whole body — last night he dropped a bottle of milk in the kitchen and was stricken with rage, almost apoplectic — I feel some lost part of myself approaching, that fourteen year-old whom I shunned for so long. When I am with him, she comes into the room, returning into my proximity but, accustomed to being shunned, she remains just beyond reach.

There are two different people. The person who walks towards the moment through her first fourteen years and seven months, and the person who walks away from it through the next fifteen years. I am the second person, and the first is in many ways a stranger to me, an intimate stranger, like a daughter whose life I shared but now recall only remotely, a daughter who left, was banished, or perhaps died, on that evening fifteen years ago, whom I buried inside me. (Can one experience one's own ghost before dying, or do we all live with the ghosts of our several deaths?) But none of you knew of the passing. There was no mourning, no homily, no flowers for the family, no donations to a favoured cause, just the dead memory of the girl hidden away inside me, whom I could no longer feel. Only now, fifteen years later, do I begin to speak to her again in my silence. I find the words coming, my head turning to her in her corner, the one I could not bear to look at, whom I loathed and left behind, who remained.

Does it frustrate you that I move backwards and forwards, that the story does not progress in neat chronological steps? I know you prefer linear sequences. *Why can't you get your life in order?* I remember you once saying to me after I dropped out of the interior design course at Tech and was struggling over whether to travel to the Middle East or take up journalism. Even at Miriam's funeral you insisted that the tributes from family and friends should follow the stages of her life. Perhaps that orderliness helped you hold onto yourself in the sudden desolation of her absence. Strange that you, of all people, should have resorted to poetry in your own short tribute. "She was the flaming warmth of my life, and now I am cold. *She was the rain on my soils, and now I am dry. She was the quick stream in my desert, and now I am barren.*"

At the flat, I wash the back of Kevin's head, matted with blood, over the basin. The doctor has cleaned and stitched his face but his blonde hair is still clumped and discoloured. I cup his chin with one hand and pour the warm water from a jug with the other. The water rushes through his hair and swirls crimson down the plughole. Suddenly it comes back to me. *Uterine haemorrhage.* Words that are strangely distant to the girl and that seem to have little to do with her, like a label on an aerial photograph marking a bomb site, like Kevin's face when he lifts his eyes as I get near. That other doctor says them as if to himself, leaning over the carnage. He seems to need to talk to himself as he works down there where the girl can feel but not see, precise monotone syllables, his own language: *rupture, perineum, anaesthetic, incision.* She asks him not to hurt her. She asks him please not to hurt her. *Please. Please don't hurt me. Please don't. Please.*

"*Who did this to you?*" he says suddenly, his head flying up, small welts of tension under his eyes. "*You must report this to the police!*"

But she does not. He cannot make her, his face fading away. She knows about privileged information, about the doctor-patient relationship, about her right to his silence. What else is there to take away from her?

I have never told this to anyone but I told it to Kevin the day after his assault and I tell it now to you. She lay in the bath. afterwards. The hot water soaked into her. With her eyes closed, she could almost believe that it had never happened. It could not really have happened, not to her. When she opened her eyes it surrounded her, almost solid, coating her skin. For a moment she lay quite still, floating in her blood, bewildered. Then she screamed. It was all the more terrible because it was silent, her jaw snapping shut so that no one would hear and come running. I see her lying in the bath, opening her eyes and seeing the crimson clots coming out of her. She lay there as the scream expanded inside her and filled her head. It filled her body, a quiet destructive freezing of her insides. Her silent body screaming in its own blood. She did not die. No, she did not. She pulled herself up and climbed out of the bath. Holding a fist of cotton wool underneath her, she scrubbed the bath. She phoned her friend and sneaked out of the house to her place, the thick wad of pads hidden between her legs. "Shit, look at your face, Elaine. You're white as a ghost." They went to the doctor's room, a Saturday morning with ordinary people doing their shopping. I do not remember her walking there very clearly, except that she had to stop and lean over, suddenly cut in two, hoping that no one would notice.

The word got around. Not her word, that silenced girl who could not speak of it. *Their* word. She was an *easy lay.* She was *asking for it* and we gave it to her, *the little bitch,* the *slut.*

The crowd who invited me to the party avoided me.
Certain friendships evaporated.
I looked into the mirror and saw what they saw and I hated her.

She hit Marcus Woodley, the secretary of the school photographic club, when he tried to touch her breasts at the club's monthly movie three months later. It must have been her, that hidden girl, because I took a conscious decision to put the thing behind me and get on with my life. She hit him right off his chair and he lay there on the classroom floor immobile with shock, the click-clicking of the old school projector and the flickering colours going on around them. The others thought he had fallen off his chair and laughed. She felt a strange loathsome pleasure in seeing him like that. She left and ran six blocks home in the dark, keeping close to the walls of the houses, crouching behind bushes when headlights approached. The streetlights hurled her shadow against the walls as she ran, now in front of her, now behind, huge and distorted and silent, full of kinetic menace. The irony of it was that I fancied Marcus Woodley and thought his photographs displayed in the foyer of the school hall, the way he used light and shadow in his portraits of residents of an old age home, were works of budding genius. But when he began to touch me, his arm moving surreptitiously around my shoulders, his fingers sliding down my upper arm, an ugly heat rose in me. I hit him with the back of my hand just below the left cheekbone. He came to school with a red weal under his eye. He never looked at me or spoke to me again.

How long have I been running from her, her breath at my nape, her blood in my trail, running from her as I could not run from them? And when did I stop running and begin to walk resolutely on, refusing to look back, sure that I would outlast her, that she would wither and fade away? Of course it was too late to run. The time to run was then – and I re-enact it again and again in some recurring phase of my sleep that is the travail of labour without its release – biting through the hand of one, scratching out the eyes of the other; but then I cannot unbolt the door, I rebound against the walls with the shatter of glass and crockery, caged by their breaths that coat my skin, until their hands close around my ankles and down, down they drag me down. Years later I am sitting in an editorial meeting where journalists and sub-editors smoke and swear and suddenly I cannot bear to be in the room and I rush out with chairs falling and copy flying around me and hide my face in a corner of the bathroom, I who am a mistress of masks exposed by my own fright. No, no, I did not leave her behind me, she is inside me, but still I run, I run through the shadows but never fast enough. I lean over Kevin and see her in his eyes as he looks over my shoulder, and I feel the frailty of her against my backbone, her breaths against my skin.

Of course there are other ways of telling it. These are the words that run beneath the words that I chose for you. They come to me later as I lie rigid in bed after Kevin has finally gone to sleep and I can hear his breathing from the room next door, sonorous because of the swelling of his nose and lips. They held her down. They overpowered her, two young men with a girl. She did not understand what they were doing until it was too late. One of them put his hand over her mouth. He jerked her head back, his fist in her hair, his nails tearing across her scalp and her tight face pulled back. (It's funny, I remember the feeling of tightness around the corners of my eyes. I feel it sometimes when I turn away from the sun or a sudden blinding reflection on water. In that moment as I turn my head in the red ringing darkness. In this moment as I lie with my eyes squeezed shut. The other one climbed on her and ripped her skirt off. She could not move and then the first one sat on her face and pinned her arms down under his knees. She wanted it to end but it did not end. She wanted them to get off her but they did not get off her. She wanted to scream but she could hardly breathe. She wanted the pain to end but the pain got worse and the second one was worse than the first.

They were so big and she was small, just a girl. When I reach back for that girl, just past puberty, interested in shampoo and pop and nail polish, she turns her face and is a stranger, lying there, myself.

She wanted it to end but it did not end. Of course it had a beginning, middle and end like any other incident. But I am the event.

On the morning of the Monday after, I remember dressing for school, putting familiar clothes, my clothes, onto the body of a stranger. It was not just the yellow and purple marks on my thighs and the rawness between my legs and the searing pain in my neck and the scratch marks on my scalp and my breasts. All these physical things healed. It was the feeling of strangeness inside me, a bereavement without the ritual of mourning. And looking at myself in the mirror, I felt as though I had lost myself and that I was to blame. I knew this with the same certainty that I knew my own loss. And because it was my fault I could not tell you. It was my secret. The first person had gone away and would not be heard from again.

"She's a teenage rebel," said Dad. "It's just a phase. It happens to all kids and they grow out of it."

She slammed doors, spat insults at her mother when she dared to wait up for her, reviled her brothers. She locked her door and smoked cigarettes. She hated her figure and lost weight. Her hips were too wide. She wore long loose shirts to hide her bum. She had a tattoo done on her upper arm where they could see it at the dinner table. She deliberately dropped dishes when it was her turn to wash up.

Perhaps you remember this part. Once her brother jumped onto her bed while she was sleeping, harking back to the rough and tumble of childhood, the boyish pleasure in giving fright. She screamed and leapt away from him. She crouched in a corner of the room and cried and cried. She would not take her hands away from her face when he said sorry, tried to comfort her. Stupidly, he stood and looked at her from the doorway.

The bastards. If only I had known. If only I could have got my hands on them. Why didn't I know? Why wasn't I there? Why didn't I notice?

I was once struck by a television documentary about earthquakes, the narrow opening of the fault line that reached deep down into the earth. I covered up the fault lines. I used make-up to hide the scratches and bruises. I became more extrovert, I went to more parties. I was determined to have a good time. No one would ever touch me like that again. My skin thickened. I became stronger as I grew up physically, more stubborn. I learnt how to send out messages. I only let men approach me if I knew I could control them. I had a series of weak, troubled, dissolute boyfriends whom I was drawn to mother, to control, to redeem. Although I didn't recognise it, even then I was looking for myself in them, the first person, the lost daughter.

You did not notice because I did not allow you to notice. I did not need you to notice. I could handle it without you. I did.

But you have something of mine that I need more and more, Christopher, just as you have something of Kevin's that he will need from you in the coming months. You have some sense of that girl, the feeling of her. Of course you lost her too, but it was not out of loathing. Somewhere inside you, you hold her as you held her then, walking home from school with your arm around her, telling her about the charms and talents of your best friend who, you said, had fallen for her. She just listened to you and smiled. *What must I tell him?* you asked in exasperation.

Nothing, she said, flushing, her heart all awry. *Just tell him nothing.*

Also, I could not find the words. There were times when I thought of telling you, when I came close to it. But what are words? *Rape. Assault. Damage.* Just sounds and shapes in the mouth, nothing but air. Words had nothing to do with what happened to me, what happened inside me. Only much later, now that I have crossed the passage of years and found the shore of distance, only now can I begin to find the words to throw back across the water — I think I have learnt from Kevin the value of speaking these things, of sharing the burden — but I cannot throw very far and they are soon lost. A small disturbance, a ripple, and they are gone, and I am left once again alone. How many pebbles does it take to fill a sea?

Nevertheless I find myself scratching for words, choosing them, polishing them, flinging them out together. As the sea is to a puny handful of pebbles, so silence is to words. But as I get older I find that words are one of the things that I have left.

Be quiet. There's no need to rush around.

I talk to Kevin in the evenings when he gets home. He doesn't say much, but he seems to want to listen to me. I talk about her, myself, the fourteen year old. As he gets to know her, I find myself wanting to know her better too, to become reacquainted. How are you going to understand this when you read it? You who want the world to add up. You who want to walk in a straight line, through reliable terrain, from the past through the present to the future. Before Miriam died you used to talk about *plotting the trajectory of your life*, about five-year career plans But now you have been waylaid by a gay son and a sister who is a closet rape victim. No, a survivor. We have our own journeys to make, unknown paths, doubtful destinations, and we need your company.

I talk to her sometimes, after he has gone to bed, as I do the household chores, ironing, making his sandwiches. Is this a sign of insanity? Not just the common madness of verbalizing your own company, but sharing words with a self that is fifteen years younger? Of course, she does not speak to me and that is part of her loneliness, and of mine, but I hear her. I wish to be there, to accompany her, to be a bed beneath her back, a soft pillow under her head when she finds rest at last. Of course it is a vain and useless wish. Nevertheless, *Calm down, my love,* I say. *Take it easy on yourself. You are infinitely more lovely and more precious, my dear, than you think.*

Listen, Christopher, I'm nearly through. Your year of mourning is nearly over and when you return you will need to start again, like us, and we will be here. I want you to know that your son is tenacious. I drop him off at school and he walks through the gates with long strides, upright, alone. I see something of Miriam's fierceness, something of your obstinacy, and some grace all of his own as he chooses to make his way. Neither you nor I can go with him into the classroom, among the boys who beat him up and reviled him. But when he comes out again we are here, at least. As for me, I continue to breathe, but now I do not feel that every breath is one that I deprive of some other self inside me. She and I breathe together, but I do not say that breathing is easy. You see, Christopher, she survived, not without trauma, not without the mark of deaths, no thanks to me. Kevin brought her back to me and helped me to begin to receive myself. In this way only, one breath at a time, we choose to continue to live.

CHARCOAL

He has a soft place on the back of his head from where they dropped him on the concrete floor. He walks with a limp, his left foot turning sharply outwards, then inwards. People turn to watch him as he walks down the street, his hips swivelling awkwardly. He reminds them of that time. Some call out a greeting and he raises his hand, the one that isn't carrying the pad. He doesn't say much anymore, but seems to listen, his eyes immobile. They focus just to the side of his niece who speaks to him with her bird-face at the gate.

He sits under the apple tree on the chair, the one with a half-broken back, in his grandmother's small yard, sketching in his pad. He draws thick harsh lines that run down and diagonally across the page. Inside the lines there are thin elongated faces that have eyes but no mouths. These eyes are sudden openings in the prison of lines, serrated like the broken mouth of a bottle, the pupils black slits. Sometimes the faces seem to float without their bodies behind the mesh. At other times there are bodies that trail beneath them but they are incomplete, emaciated. He sketches one of these each day, his right shoulder tilted above the left, his head bent and rigid as he works, the muscles standing out in his neck. The piece of charcoal jerks, jerks, and then rests in his hand, poised above the paper, for hours.

At other times he watches the children playing in the yard, his nephews and nieces, cousins, neighbours. They are used to him and sometimes ask him to hold one end of the skipping rope or to watch over their clothes as they dance under the spray of grandmother's garden hose — she shouts out of the window to them not to stamp on her vegetables — but he does not call them or speak to them. His head is slightly bent, his eyes guarded. When his grandmother asks why he likes to sit there and watch them, he says it is for his pictures, which he also calls his photographs.

The children look at his pictures but do not see themselves. I am not so old, says his niece, wrinkling her nose as she looks. He draws the *amadlozi*, the old ones looking up at us from their graves, says his grandmother. The children ask where the sun is, and the flowers, marigolds and impatience, that grandmother cultivates in a neat bed beneath the kitchen window opposite the vegetable patch. He shakes his head, his lips working soundlessly, and they return to their game. He tears the page out carefully and inserts it at the back of his pad with the others and then leans over the new blank page, his arms rigid on his knees, neither watching the children nor drawing.

You see the ones who come to close your mouth, stop your legs from moving, take your breaths. Those who come to twist and turn your truths so that you no longer recognise yourself. You see the ones looking at you through the lines.
What did Mbuyazi see when he swallowed the razor blade after they had beaten him for those two days, forcing him to stand against the wall? The comrades that they arrested, that he swore never to inform on? Where did he get the razor blade from? Or was that just a story? Sometimes sounds come out of the mouth but you do not see it open, behind the walls. Sometimes sounds cut through the lines.

Can you see a bullet fly? This is what they argue about in the cell, after they have told and retold their stories, before they begin over again. The lines of the bars slide across the cell floor; it begins to get darker. No, a bullet moves too fast for the eyes. You hear the shot, you see where it has hit, but the bullet itself is invisible. It is not like a teargas canister which anyway sounds different when they shoot it, *boof-wshshshshsh*. Those things — you can dodge them and even fetch and throw them back so that they eat their own medicine. But what about those shining bullets that you can see, thin streaks of lightning? He does not believe it. He saw Kini diving through the fence of corrugated iron sheets and cardboard with the crack-crack behind them as they ran. And then he lay there. Come on, get up! We've got to keep moving! Wake up! Can't you hear the Casspirs closing in? But he did not move, the sudden quietness of lying there in the grass and cardboard and empty cartons and the smell of urine after all the running and the feeling that this could be the end as he ducks his head down beside his brother Kini and smells the roots of the grass and the dirt and they rush past in the street. And then he shakes Kini's arm but he does not move, he does not hear. He sees the hole under Kini's shoulder, but the blood comes out the front. Once those bullets get inside your body they become enraged, like a killer inside a hut. The straight line and then the broken lines, his face in your hands, his eyes. He did not say anything as he bled. What was there to say?

He sits at the front of the hall and watches them speak. The Truth Commission has come to town. Some people speak and others listen. Their mouths open and the crowd behind him murmurs. We did this, they say, but not that. That was someone else of whom we have no knowledge. Their mouths open but he sees their eyes through the lines. We received orders. It was a state of war, Your Honour, if I could put it like that. We had to restrain him in the cell because he resisted. I would not use the word torture, Your Honour, but the utilisation of interrogation methods. We were doing our job. It was the way things were at that time with the onslaught on our way of life.

He sketches more quickly. There are still the lines, the eyes, the faces, but now you see them over the shoulders, under the elbows, between the legs of those huge ones who move forward. You see the blank spaces of the backs of those ones as they press forward. Now they explain to the commissioners what happened, what they did, how they did it, why they did it. Now they give the commissioners their words. Their mouths move. *Detained. Restrained. Administered force. Subdued.* But the commissioners were not there to see them as they came forward. He sketches. What you do not see are their faces, which only the eyes can see, the eyes that now watch you as you look.

As for me, I am not one who can stand up there and speak about it. What is there to say? They did this, they did that. They blindfolded me, they lifted me up, they dropped me on the floor. They told me to wipe up my own mess. They wanted information but I did not know. Did Mbuyazi? They turned my truths around and made me eat them like shit. They made me stink in my own nostrils. Words get caught in the lines. I write my A's and B's but they slip down over the lines and the teacher pulls my ears. I draw under the desk, the tree in the schoolyard outside, the soldiers in the streets, the smoke rising over the houses. When the commissioners come, I try to think of words to carry what my eyes saw but by the time the words are ready no one is listening. They think I did not hear the question. I see the backs of their heads as they walk away. There are plenty of others that they have to interview. Anyway, what can words say? Mouths open and shut, but behind the words are those who breathe and under the words, lying silent in the ground, are those who do not.

Mbuyazi and Kini, my brothers, who lie here inside my pictures and watch me.

Me and Mbuyazi and Kini, the three that we called 'we', growing up close to each other like trees in the backyard of a matchbox house, sharing the sun, making space for each other's roots. The three of us who started the SRC and helped to form the street committee, who listened to Radio Freedom together late at night, who shared courage like bread. They cut down my brothers and left me standing, but I feel them under the ground.

He draws a flower for the children, but it seems to be struggling to straighten from the earth, which is a heavy mesh of lines. The petals are bold, pointed, but some curl downward at the tips. The sky is a coil of thin lines that seethes and glints just above the petals. He makes it shine with a high voltage. Would any flower dare to touch it? At the centre of the flower there are many eyes crowded together, too many for the drooping flower to bear. He thickens its stalk, strokes across the earth until it is black.

Doesn't every flower deserve to grow?

The children stand around him, looking at the picture in his lap. But a flower needs rain to live, says his niece. He draws a shower of spikes into the back of the earth, his hand jerking, his head still. The children look at the picture, and then at him – he feels their eyes – and then they slowly walk away.

We apologise, say the mouths. It was unfortunate. We would like to request forgiveness from those who suffered. He watches their eyes as they speak. He has his pad and draws their eyes surrounded by faces, all those who can no longer speak, who look on. He remembers the shape of Kini's head as he lifted his eyebrows and spoke at meetings. He had a smooth head that used to shine in the sun. As he draws, the heat of Kini's head that he held that night comes back into hands and his fingers, into the charcoal that he holds. Between them all there are lines with small, twisted barbs.

He walks to the station.

On the train there are mothers singing hymns.

Sitting under the tree, he looks carefully at the picture for hours.

Then he dreams that he is walking across the thorny veld, through long grass. His feet knock against spears and bones and empty cartridges. It is a countryside that he has seen once before, from the window of a train, when he was small. The vultures break out of the grass suddenly in front of him. The burnt huts and kraals smoulder. He finds charcoal inside the ruins of a hut and draws on a broken mud wall. Tall dark figures whose feet get caught in the lines as they run. There is no one at home. He walks on. He does not limp; his stride is long. He hears singing but sees no singers, a deep hum of men's voices. He stands still and listens, and then realises that it is coming from below. He can feel the vibrations through the soles of his feet and it grows within his bones and makes him taller. They are singing deep underground. Also, there is the rhythm of shudder and pause, of the earth at labour. He sees them in his hearing, their faces sweating, their eyes in the hot night of the earth, the glint of their picks as they swing and cleave into sand and rock and heave back. Bending over, he draws their song with charcoal on the palm of his hand, up the insides of his arms lest he forget it on his journey. But when he looks around him, there are only huge yellow mounds to be seen and great wheels on towers marking the places of the dead. He begins to run. His stride opens and the grass beneath his feet crackles and then changes to dirt and further on to tar. His soles burn but he runs faster as his shadow grows behind him. He is in the graveyard and there are funeral processions and speeches and the dust rising from the feet of those who dance and chant, and men in vans and trucks who watch from the gates with bristling weapons. He knows he has to get home before dark. Then he hears voices behind him. Can you run faster than bullets? they ask.

Isn't this the worst thing, my brothers, to be so afraid that you cannot control your fear? You cannot keep it in place. It comes back long afterwards. The time does not stay behind you. You sit down and suddenly it is there. What's the matter with him? He is crazy, they say. Isn't this the worst thing, my brothers?
   No, the worst thing is to be alone.

On the last day of the hearing he walks down the side aisle of the hall, his hips swivelling awkwardly, his pad beneath his arm, but he does not stop at the front where he usually sits. He continues past the row of tables and microphones where people are leaning over to whisper, shuffling notes, pouring out glasses of water. He sticks his pictures up on the wall behind where the speakers come to sit and to say their words. We did this, we did that. The orderly says that it is not permitted. He must take them down. But then the priest comes and stops the orderly. He has seen this priest sitting among those at the front, touching his forehead with his palm as he listens to them speak. Leave them up, he says. The orderly walks away and the priest puts his hand on his shoulder and looks at the pictures.
   These are photographs of Kini and Mbuyazi, my friends. And of me. If you take a photo, it is of you also.
   He has not spoken so many words for seven years. The priest looks and turns to him. Suddenly the priest reaches out to him and touches his head from the side, the soft place at the back. His lips move in a prayer. He hears the small noise in the priest's throat, like something hiding that stirs, and he faces the priest, looking just to one side.
   My child, I see, says the priest, taking out his handkerchief and unfolding it and wiping his face, his eyes. He has seen this priest wiping his small bright eyes with his handkerchief as they say their words. We did this, we did that.
   But why are you the one to cry? he asks.

FATHER'S NIGHT

She lost her libido beneath a pile of soggy nappies around an overfull bucket. A pile of disrupted nights unravelled like coathangers. A pile of things to do, people to arrange, chores to complete. Would she ever recover it? he wondered. A pile so intransigent that the small boy's dungarees at the bottom once changed colour. Sex was on her list, but at the bottom so that it slipped right off beneath the weight of items. She would look at him, like a housewife back from her monthly shop: Darn it (brushing the pale wisps from her eyes), I knew there was something I should have remembered. Sorry, love. But there'll be another time.

There wasn't.

He understood that all she wanted was to pull up her knees, curl into a quiet and barely recognizable familiarity within herself. Not that she had much chance to become reacquainted – once there she would sleep almost instantly. In another life (it seemed that remote) she might have painted willow patterns on china or written letters to her distant twin sister. Now she calmed her mauled nipples against a pillow and slipped quickly beneath the surface of breaths into the temporary relief of sleep.

Sleep.

The word had taken on an aura of nostalgia, the distant home of a migrant, the youth of seasoned traveller. Once part of the unconscious rhythm of life, as undeclared as breathing or, dare he think it, making love. Now a predator pinching at the corners of her eyes and mouth, stealing the gloss from her skin, dulling her hair, infiltrating the whites of her eyes. Sleep as a poverty of hours. Sleep as a poor woman's dream. Sleep as the ache of muscles and stiffness of limbs and apperception of age – sleep as any damn thing but itself.

"How do we get out of this cycle?" he asked as she stirred her morning tea and then watched the contained movement with languid eyes.

"I don't know."

"You have to help me with this, Julia. I'm struggling to cope."

"You're struggling to cope." A flicker in her voice, like a strip of colour in a monochrome sequence, but the retort landed flatly, her eyes still lapping the light of the liquid.

"If the kid would only take a bottle, then I could get up. We could share the nights."

"If only," she said. Her fingertips whitened for a moment against the mug. He stood up with a jerk, almost knocking his chair over. He strode around the table and

put his hands on her shoulders, caressing her through the cotton. But her flesh had taken on a defensive tone. He sensed the pores closing, the layers of skin hardening against him. Her body winked at him through its armour.

"I'll be late," he said.

"Be careful," she said. "Lock your doors."

You think you know a person, he thought, teeth bared against the traffic, his own knuckles white. Then she does not sleep through a night for seventeen months. You no longer know her. She no longer knows herself. There are strangers walking around the house, gesturing listlessly towards remembered lives, but without conviction. She no longer knows you, or even has the inclination. Her elbows at the ironing board say, I want to sleep. Also: the scrape of her slippers in the passage, the tendons of her throat as she speaks on the phone, the rise and fall of her collar bones. Please allow me to sleep. (Where the hell's your flicker? – opening the window to vent his fist. Do you think coloured lights are only for Christmas trees?) But she does not utter the words. Somewhere along the boundaries of sleep the small boy murmurs; together they tense up, expectant, listening – he might calm down on his own; it happens, sometimes. Then he squawks, and the sound comes jumping through the dark like a panicking frog, landing between their bodies; then again, louder: it's the nipple alarm. She hauls herself out of bed. (Do you think you're at Kyalami? – as his father would say. Do you think the traffic lights are there for decoration? Maniac! And where the hell did you buy your licence? Up yours too! All my expletives are cliches, he thought.) 11.47pm, 1.15am, 1.23am, 3.50am, 5.11am. "Darling, please get up and make the tea." She is still able to be civil, despite the sun rattling at the window. "It's time to get going."

For her there were countless antidotes, anecdotes, assurances, fail-safe strategies, three-night regimes. He saw the mother mafia surrounding her with condolences and advice at birthday parties, family occasions, creche meetings. Honey under his tongue just before he closes his eyes, dear. Late night car rides. A big supper will help him to settle. Let him cry; it's good for the lungs. "I can't let him cry," she said evenly. Is it a matter of principle? "It's a matter of what I can and cannot do. These are my limitations." (And aren't they your husband's limitations? A voice whispers among his glands.) Mother-in-law wrings her hands. Janine at the launderette pouts. Hazel rolls her eyes over scones.

Nothing helped.

For him there was the tight-skirted Ms Jamieson brushing past in the lift, leaving an understated but lingering scent on his lapel like some word she had said with lips close to his ear: How are things at home, Jeremy? The clip of her heels in the typing pool, the perfect contours of her calves, and the way she quite casually stroked her eyes over him when he was not looking. Or she thought he thought she thought he was not looking. Or perhaps that he was. Then the sense of the pulse in his own temples, a crooked narrow grey-blue vein growing more prominent with age. Ms Jamieson's eyes on him, stroking. The darkness, tactile and fecund, of exchanged breaths and conjured heats. Desire happened. Quite suddenly. Desire. Striking from within, the leap and twist of muscles below the gut. A loud rushing in his ears so that he thought people might hear and looked around furtively. Followed by a long slow wrenching tautness. Did it all eventually end? – a creeping numbness, the accommodation of loss. He wore Julia's absence on his body, under his skin, wherever he went. He remembered the moment when she had stepped down from the bus after a month away at her sister's, how his flesh had stood up and crept like a cat over his bones. She was every woman and none of them; hollow-eyed, bedraggled by the night, holding her mug with interlaced fingers. Oblivious of him and his clamouring tenderness. His love for her was a matter of the intestines, the vital organs. He could not live without her and so lived alongside her.

Then one morning she could not get out of bed. There was panic in her eyes. The doctor ordered bed rest: chronic exhaustion. She could barely move. Her bones seemed to lock in stubborn protest, her muscles to desist, as if she had climbed a mountain without training. She wept.

He brought her the small boy through the first two nights, and then decided.

"Wanna nipple, wanna nipple," the small boy wailed on seeing him appear.

"Nipples all asleep," he explained, proffering the alternative.

There was a moment of stunned deliberation.

Then the battle of the bottle commenced in earnest.

He pushed it towards a hand. The boy swatted it away with a rising yowl. He offered it again. The boy punched it clear across the room with a roundhouse right. He retrieved it and offered it again. The noise level was high. The boy swung both arms at it furiously, taking his eyes off it in his rage. He dodged under the outer defences and tried to plug it straight into the socket. The boy almost spat his entire tongue out, gargling apoplectically, rolling his head. When the counterfeit nipple persisted, he inhaled deeply, opened his eyes wide, and let rip. The scream shocked up through the top of his head and stapled him to the ceiling.

Truce. Truce. Or, to be frank, retreat.

"Okay, okay, okay. No bottle, no bottle. At least, not right now."

The boy eyed him suspiciously at oxygen refuelling stops.

"Wanna Mommy! Wanna Mommy!" His head reverberated with the sound, an ill-fitting key in a rusty lock.

So it went.

He made sure her bedroom door was tightly shut.

The days and nights began to fold in and out of each other like a book read without a proper sequence. He would wake with a shock from his dawdling at a meeting. Had he remembered to change out of his pyjamas? Was he wearing underpants? He would harangue with the deputy director long after he had gone to bed. "What's the matter?" Ms Jamieson asked at his desk. She looked alarmed. He had dismantled his ballpoint pen and was trying to squeeze the ink out of the wrong end. Why? She looked at him enigmatically and offered him a tissue for his stained shirt.

It was on the third successive night. He could no longer focus his eyes properly. The floors and the walls of the small boy's bedroom had begun to shift and sway. His entire body felt elongated so that he had to duck on entering and was conscious of the ceiling (or was it sinking slowly?). The small boy's voice had somehow come loose from his body, sounding in the opposite corner of the room (a junior ventriloquist?). He would turn in his anxious lassitude only to find that the boy was behind him; he was getting used to listening for the first birdsong in the dark before dawn.

Some time between four and five there was a long argumentative howling session punctuated by pitiful sobs and shudders in the cot. Then the small boy stopped, looked at him for a moment, lent over the cot rail and prised the bottle out of his unintelligent hand. Given its frequent flights across the room, he had grown accustomed to clutching it stubbornly. The boy lay back, scrutinized the nipple for a few seconds, shook it with a wry expression, inserted it into his mouth and — was it all just the hallucination of his sleep-starved brain? — began to suck. He shook his head, blinked, tried to arouse himself from his waking slumber. Was it possible? He doubted it. But there was the sound of bubbles stringing up from the nipple to the growing reservoir of air behind the milk. It was an ethereal sound, the secrets of small angels flitting between night and day. For the first time, he felt the boy's eyes close peacefully on him. He lay down on the carpet and slept.

Lying completely still, he eased down the passage, touching open the door, finding her form in the sheets, compassing the sleep of her body in the quiet movement of his mind, breathing in her nearness without need of word or touch. He sensed the curve of her spine in the dark. From the rise and fall of her nape, and then the lift and dip and lift along the stepping stones of the vertebrae, he moved carefully, filled with wonder at the smoothness of her. He paused in the shadow of the shoulder blades, before him her quiet flesh opening out to a plateau. And then the hillocks of muscle running alongside the track and the narrowing of the gauge between finely downed tightening slopes and beneath the whole warm world of the body humming and chiming with its hidden rhythms of bone and pulse and breath and then the bump of the coccyx at the terminus. As a child, he had once stood beside a railway .

track with a train rushing past, the blurred faces at the windows, the air in his face and then gone. He found himself beside their bed. She stirred in herself. He could hear the evenness of her breathing in slumber; her back to him.

When he awoke the sun was a bright patchwork on the wall behind the cot. It lit up Humpty Dumpty's eyes as he teetered and shone on the side of Jack's airborne pail. The small boy, balanced on his hands and knees, stared out at him through the bars of the cot. Then he yawned widely and overbalanced.

"Where my mommy?" his first woken words

LIKE

"I know all about this," she sputters indignantly. "The writer who hasn't got a story so he writes about writing. Well I think it's abysmal!"

She flings the pages at him and bangs the door behind her. The walls shudder around him as she rackets down the stairs and he hears the distinct crack of her neck as she hits the bottom.

He calls this one, *The Writer's Vengeance.* Outside the night is truculent, leaning against the roof so that the beams protest, whining at the front door

Some stories are like the wind, he thinks as he ruminates over the precise com-position of his midnight snack in front of the open refrigerator. They swoop down at your back as you sit before the monitor with poised fingertips, tearing open all those prissy paragraphs of calculated diction and syntax. They blow right through your head, swirling and tumbling in your senses, whistling up your trouser legs and plucking the shirt out of your pants. They forge an instrument out of your ribcage, your vertebrae; they nip you at the nape and coccyx and swing you up through the thermals.

Better let the simile out the front, it's getting difficult to contain, he decides as he glimpses the Cheese Spread behind the Yoghurt. In the side rack there also happens to reside – having recently relocated from the supermarket – an unopened bottle, the Gherkins, whom, he surmises, it would be interesting to introduce to the Tomatoes two racks below, perhaps at the invitation of those mutual acquaintances and well-known social brokers, the Salticrax, who have also recently moved in at the grocery cupboard on the opposite wall.

The wind swoops down the street outside, a muscular blustering wet north-west-erly that actually knocks about the street lights and traffic signs and wrenches the plates of street poles in sudden spates of renaming so that when the city awakes it no longer recognises itself. Anyway, labouring down this street at an angle of hunched and obdurate exertion is a man in a rather dull brown suit, let's say, which is marginally too short at the wrists and shins. He's late from the office again – unpaid overtime drudgery – and it's the end of the week and one of his shoe soles is cracked and he can feel an unpleasant creeping wet grimace through his sock with each left step, let's say, and in the right knee there is that dull rheumatic ache which will get to know him more keenly as he persists through the years, his tucked chin spreading like cheese on his bumpy collar, his pate-redeeming strands of browny-grey slapping back against his red scalp. It is the circumstances surrounding his nose and its emissions, however, of which he is most miserably aware. This nose, its little purple veins beginning to fan at the flares, numbing from the tip, is dripping, unfortunately, let's say, and, because he is holding his umbrella in one hand and his briefcase in the other, he has no way of diverting the drips before they congregate and process down the little aisle at the centre of his upper lip. This incipient snotti-ness reminds him of his two children whom he constantly rebukes for a madden-ingly limp and listless passivity. They seem to waft through their primary school years like empty crimped packets of crisps through underbrush, sticking nowhere, catching nothing but air while nevertheless racketing insufferably. *Do you have no ambitions in life? What is to become of you? Are you destined to pickle in the vine-gar of mediocrity for the rest of your days?* (No, he would not say that, thinks the writer, reaching for the bottle.) Sniffing is of no avail; it serves merely to contain the phlegm while it continues to gather expectantly in the arches. Stopping to put down his briefcase and retrieve his handkerchief and unfold it with one flapping hand and hold it up against his nose while the bells finally gong and then reversing the entire rigmarole would not only delay his homecoming but also disrupt his momentum against the wind. Anyway, to get back to the wind, it lunges around low all of a sud-den (the writer makes a mental note here to click the beginning of a new paragraph).

The wind lunges down low all of a sudden and with a gusting uppercut upends his umbrella, whipping his arm up and backwards so that he feels the individual but-tons of his jacket pressed into his abdomen and hears his lapels flapping as his knees buckle and then lock and the wind straightens him up and inspects him through his clothes and in his ears and wipes his dripping nose and takes him. He, back-peddling, leaving with a scrape of his heels on the pavement, lunging away, does not panic for who, after all, can answer the wind when it calls? There is the matter of gravity and, given the terrestrial disposition of the species, one cannot deny a certain background apprehension, but for the moment there is the abrupt release from muscular travail. He is free. No longer a hunched and ponderous recluse, he is a full citizen of the elements. Wingless but aloft, he crows between his teeth, grinning. Although he remains low, he is certainly in flight, and, craning his neck, he can see below him in the rushing sheen of the road the letters of the names of the streets, flashing up, and he begins to rearrange these letters and to string them into words and in no time at all he is telling himself a story which, he suspects as his umbrella burgeons overhead, has some cryptic link to his destination.

So much for stories like the wind, which blows where it wills, concludes the writer, who has introduced Cheese Spread and the Tomatoes to the Salticrax, all of

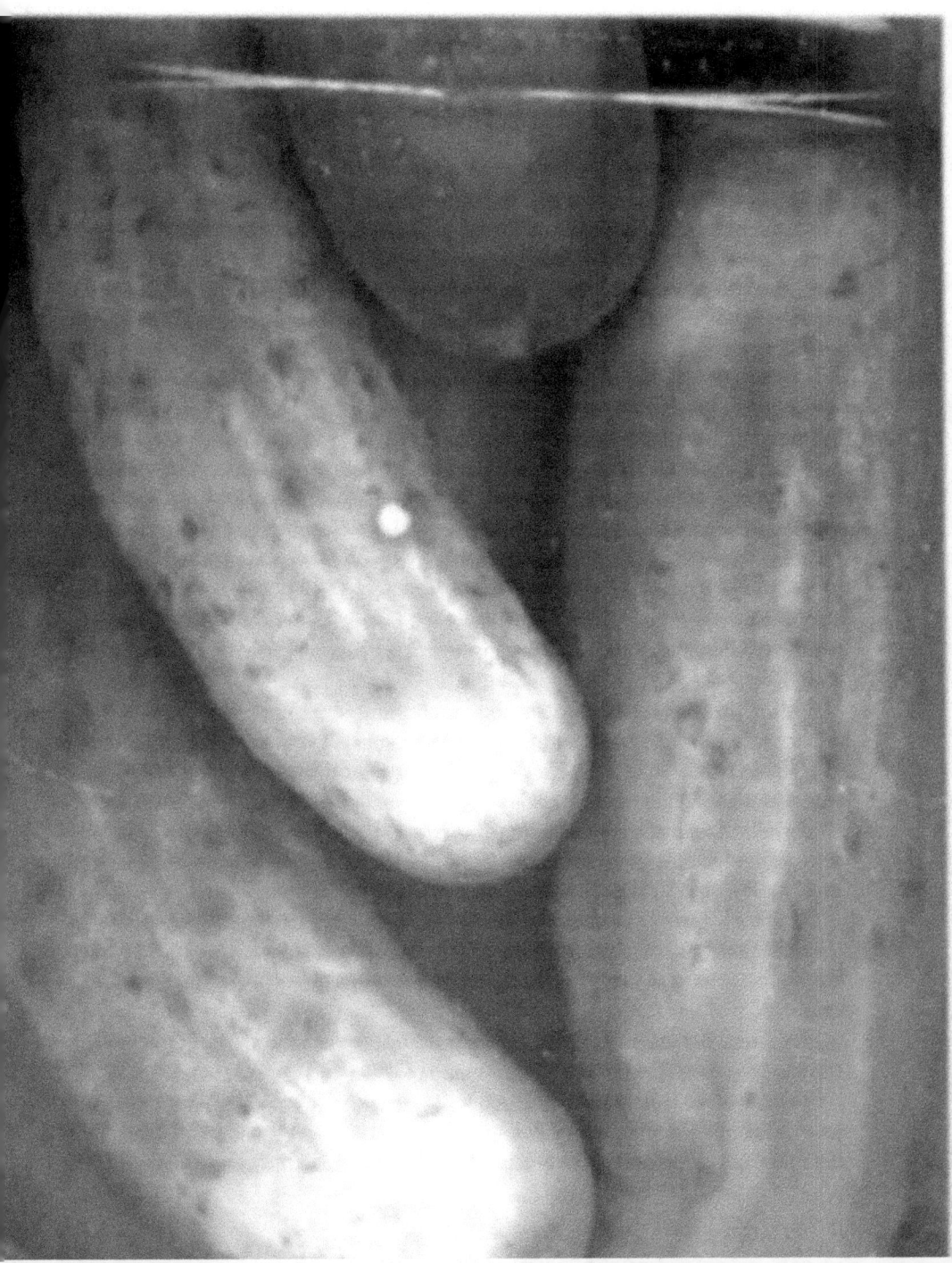

whom now eagerly await the arrival of their new neighbours, the Gherkins, so that they can get more intimately acquainted in the conviviality of the Writer's Palate. He feels little ducts of saliva opening at the prospect and a kind of tingling at the edges of his tongue.

However, some stories are like a new bottle of gherkins with a tight lid. Some stories reveal themselves all at once, he thinks as the contents quiver in his straining hands, but remain sealed. Like spermatozoa thrashing in false alarm in the scrotum. Some stories are fully and immediately awakened in the imagination but will not allow themselves to pass into the materiality of sound or print. They resist, gleaming like tadpoles that touch tails intuitively in a creviced rock pool, limpid and beyond reach.

He holds the lid under the hot water tap and wonders if the change in temperature minutely transforms the composition of the gherkins, at a molecular level, so that they will taste different when they finally reach his palate. Different to what? Is there some essential quality of taste, abstract and tongueless, that resides there in the pristine environs of sealed vinegar? Without the tools of appetite, without teeth and tongue and palate, without human concupiscence, would gherkins possess the characteristics of taste at all: flavour, texture, crispness? And since the very notion of the gherkin is at least partially constituted by an association with pungency, would the gherkin as such exist at all in the absence of the sense of taste? This, ponders the writer, beginning to sweat, casts a disquieting circularity on the proposition that we are what we eat.

He slumps down onto the kitchen stool, tries once more to wrestle off the lid, once more in vain, and stares at the insensate members through the glass. In what sense do you exist without my palate? – he poses rhetorically. Why not allow me to realise your authentic being in the ontological immediacy of significant others, inter alia, Cheese Spread, the Tomatoes and Salticrax, with the prospect of others joining in as the party gathers momentum? He drops his head in a moment of solipsistic anguish: How can I attribute to them volition if I deny their ontological priority?

Breathing heavily, he strains at the lid. He uses a dry cloth and a wet cloth. He places the bottle on the floor and exerts downward pressure with his foot. He shakes the bottle. He turns it upside down for several minutes. He considers placing it on a hot plate.

At a particular moment, as he strides frantically between the sink, the fridge and the stove, he drops the bottle of gherkins onto the tiled kitchen floor. A cracking and a swoosh and the suddenness of the odour of vinegar. There, among the shards and wetness they lie, curled and glistening. Like slugs. Like scaly slugs that have crept out of the dank green darkness of their natural habitat under the passage carpet and embarked on their nocturnal migration across the smooth aridity of the tiles to the fecund cracks under the grocery cupboard. But ... pulverised by a deluge of light, they have been arrested by the writer who, awakened by his stretching intestines, seeks refreshment.

He stoops swiftly, or perhaps lunges is the word, for, like a bird of prey, he sees his own shadow grow suddenly near as he plucks up a large specimen and lands it on his tongue and bites it with the honed keenness of incisors.

From simile to sensibility. His eyes water. With great care he retrieves the gherkins, rinses them off, then sweeps up the glass and wipes the floor.

With a handful of gherkins in his anorak pocket, for replenishment, his umbrella under his arm, he ventures out into the windy night, pausing for a moment on the doorstep to notice how his shadow multiplies under the street lights, and then craning his neck upwards, let's say, looking for a story.

THE SEASON OF FIRES

A cool July winter morning. The season of fires is here. Yesterday, on my afternoon cycle up the Richmond road, with the Msunduzi valley falling away to my right, Pietermaritzburg spreading behind me, I saw the plumes of smoke at a distance, and later the broken yellow-glass glitter of fire on the hillside. I ascended a steep hill, over the hump of the summit, and suddenly it was at the side of the road, acrid smoke spilling into my eyes. I could hear the beast in the undergrowth – hissing, cracking, cussing, bursting. It was not the brazen dance of the devils with their tall spiking tongues that lit up the sky last winter, armed multitudes crossing the hills, roaring with the sap of the earth, reflecting in faces and eyes for miles around. This winter, because the June rains have left some moisture in the grass, the fires are a low fury, a partial devastation, leaving some yellow stalks standing, thin widows of the smouldering earth. A season when tiny tails of ash, caught up in the grave of the air like feather spines withered in flight, find rest on the hairs of your arms, your lips, dissolving into taste and touch like intimations of the deceased.

MakaZanele wrapped her eldest daughter in a blanket and carried her to Edendale Hospital on her back, unable to afford the taxi fare. A nineteen-year-old, her daughter was as light as a child but she could feel the bones sticking into her, these bones of her own bones but with no modesty of flesh to cover them and hide them from the world. "I am burning, mama," the child whispered to her. "I ask for water." She stopped to fetch her a cup of water from one of the houses and the people watched her as she helped the child to wet her lips. "It is a cold morning and you are trembling, my child," she said, almost to herself, seeing and trying not to see the emasculated hands that gripped the cup around her own.

"She is carrying a fire inside her that is eating her up," said the fat woman from the house who was still in her dressing gown, the small children and their flagrant eyes crowding around her skirts, her arms across her chest like a shield. "She must be bewitched."

MakaZanele did not reply but, thanking the woman, heaved the child onto her back once more and continued on her way. There were more people in the street now, hurrying off to work and to school. The smoke lay over the streets like a pall and the sun was weak, the thin yellow of cold chicken soup, but she felt the weight of their eyes as they fell on her. Some looked at her first with surprise and then with a kind of accusation, as if she had said what should not be said, while others looked at her while trying not to look, as if she passed them before they could turn their

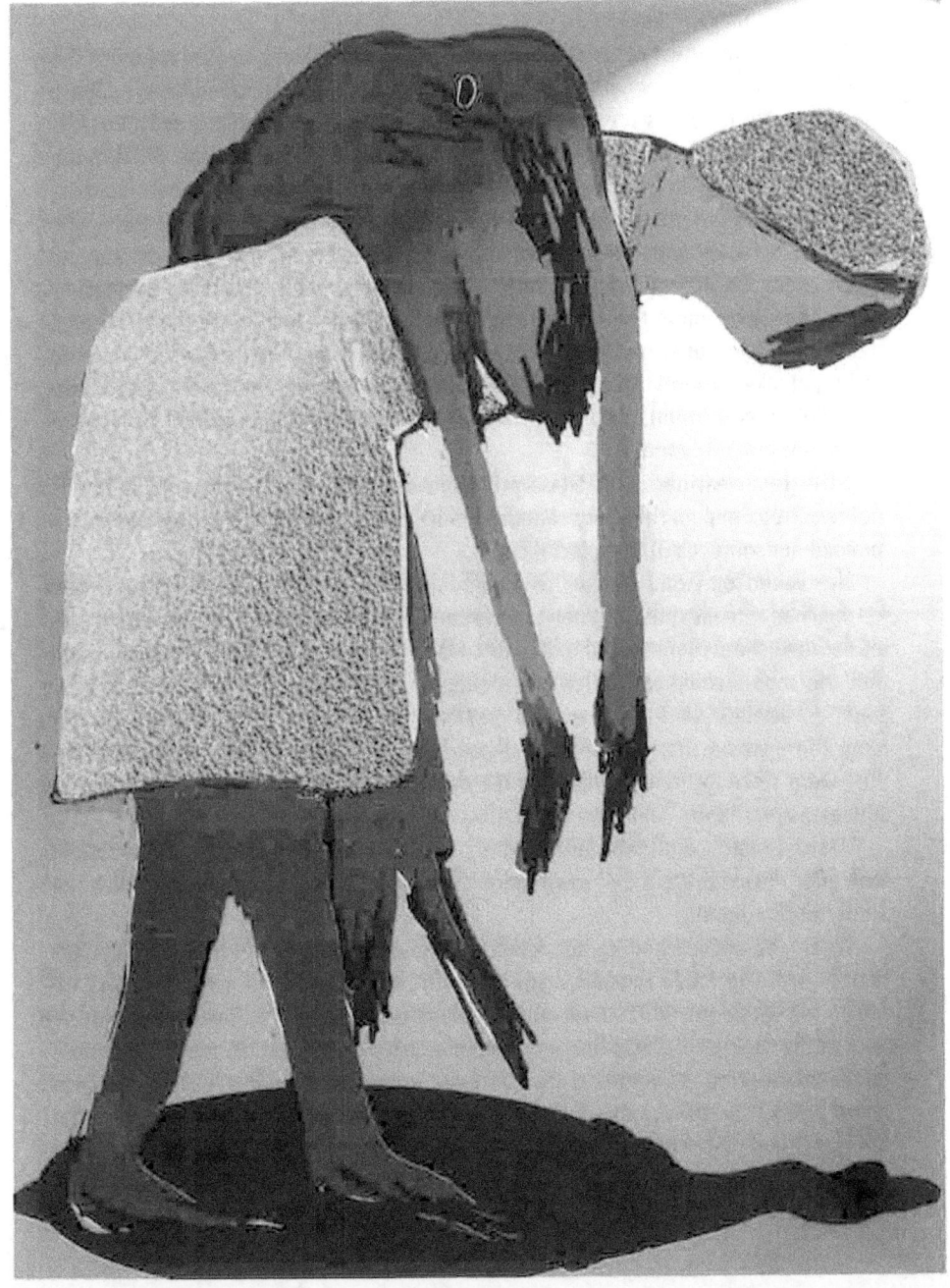

heads away. She walked slowly, bent over with the burden of her years, the dull sound of her heart in her ears.

Perhaps it was the mother of Jabulani who had bewitched her, the mother of the child from down the road who had grown into a man and then faded away, staying out of sight until he was seen no more, leaving behind her daughter and three children. Perhaps it was Jabulani's mother, the one who had stood outside shaking the gate on its hinges and hurling her words at the windows about how her daughter had poisoned Jabulani, killing him slowly so that no one would suspect her – she could not be fooled and she knew who it was who had stolen away her son, the joy of her eyes, the strength of her years, the sustenance of her old age, leaving her alone. She felt no anger towards Jabulani's mother as she reached the hospital gates and the young security guard with his old eyes greeted her and helped to wrap the trailing blanket around the child. After all, it was the mothers who were left to bury the children they brought into to world, and who had to become mothers once more of the children left behind.

With great weariness, she felt now that she would like to sit down with Jabulani's mother, stretching out their legs together in the sun in the front yard. She would like to make her some tea in the special cup.

She waited for a long time at the hospital with her daughter, but she was relieved for the chance to sit still. And then she waited in a queue to take the child to the toilet because she had messed the blanket and needed to be cleaned. The nurse said that she should come back after two nights because there was nothing much they could do besides calm the fever and dress the sores. They could not keep her for long. There was a shortage of beds. It was best to look after them at home where they were close to their families. "Come back in two days, mama" said the nurse, squeezing her hand. "And have a rest. I can see you are tired."

"Have a rest?" said MakaZanele with surprise, almost to herself. "And who will look after the children in the mean time? The time I lie down for my rest is the time I will not rise again."

When she arrived home, the children were playing down the road in a neighbour's yard. She made herself a cup of tea in the special china cup that was still intact, the white one with small yellow flowers around the rim that she kept at the back of the cupboard. It was the one remaining from a set that she and her late husband had received as a wedding present twenty-nine years before. Then she washed it and dried it carefully and put it away. At least, when he had died on the night that the impis had rolled down the hills into the township in 1985, they could afford a funeral. At least it had been the children who had buried their parent and not the other way round. She fetched the spade from next door and began to dig in the veld behind the house, next to the mounds of her son and daughter-in-law, the smell of the earth rising into her nostrils.

Zachariah Rapola

Graphics by Ike Mboneni Muila

A SOOTHSAYER'S DEPOSIT

"*Ousie*[23], hey, ousie, give me a hundred rands and I will tell your future," the malnourished stranger said to Karabo.

"*O s'ka nhlanyetsa wena*[24]," Karabo responded.

"W-what?" he stammered, his eyes shifting from the hem of her skirt to her handbag. A potential bag-snatcher or serial killer, she concluded.

"Such a cheap future doesn't need telling," she snapped and carried on walking.

"Please, *ousie*, I'm serious. Listen, I see you touting a vase for sale. The vase is filled with your future husband's blood," he whispered, sauntering behind her, his right hand extended to receive payment.

"*Uu!* shame. Try somebody else. If I were you, I would concentrate on seeing potential jobs in my future ..."

Karabo was amused by her response to the hustler. That's what he was, a deceiving rogue and a parasite. But what can you expect, with all the unemployment and hunger around, conniving charlatans were hard at their trade. But later, when she had given greater thought to the prediction, she was infuriated. How could the demented fool make up such a scurrilous lie? She, Karabo, the groomed and cultured daughter of Rre Thekiso and Mme Kagiso Makgatho?

"*Ka mma ruri!*[25] A twisted upbringing does indeed affect the brain." That was added to the refrain days later. She realised it was one's moral duty to sympathise with such souls. Nonetheless in the days that followed her indignation grew. She went out into the streets in search of what she now referred to as her 'charlatan' to give him a dressing down, but her friends advised that that wouldn't be enough.

"Take the bastard to court! Sue him."

"My dear, your humility is scandalous. You should be more assertive. None of us can stand such pretentious fraudsters."

"A lazy one at that."

"If he were driving a Merc, I mean, that would be understandable," another added with bravado.

However, her search in the streets proved unsuccessful.

"Mokgotsi! Set a private detective on him. I tell you we shouldn't let him get away with that insult."

To Karabo it was not only an insult but also a riddle. Judas ... Judas Iscariot, the name echoed in her head, the man recorded to have traded Jesus' love for silver coins. She was no Judas. "Me put a deposit on another human being's life? What nonsense."

She abhorred violence so much that she would curse people who killed rats and mice, be it with poisoned bait or mouse traps, or who trampled on ants or took swipes at flies. Eventually she started using a catapult with pebbles on beggars who crushed fleas and bugs. That was twelve years ago. Looking back she realised that her abhorrence of violence had intensified. Her only recourse would be to join an order where meditation and fasting would provide ammunition against sliding into madness.

The riddle intensified when Chris came into her life while she was still in mourning. Eight months earlier, her lover, Tiro, had died in a car hijacking. Of the three who were in the car, only her little boy survived.

Now and then Karabo would chastise herself. Those vile thoughts, what was their source? How come she sometimes wished her little son had perished with the others? How to deal with his nightmares and piercing screams ... Every Friday towards dawn he would repeat the same word: "Noooooooooooooo!" She knew that even in his sleep he could not bring himself to finish his pleading: "Don't kill my father." And she would cuddle him, her tears mingling with his sweat which seeped down like Tiro's blood.

"Your child is haunted," a sangoma told her family and the late Tiro's when they went to inquire about the boy's disturbed state.

"That's rubbish! Our son was a Christian," Tiro's mother snapped.

"*Aowa, Mma,* I am ..." the sangoma tried to interrupt Tiro's mother.

"Listen, even if he never burned candles in church at Easter it doesn't mean that he was not committed," the furious mother continued. After protracted argument along these lines, Tiro's mother calmed down. What sacrilege! Dead Christians don't roam about haunting the living, and that was what the sangoma was insinuating.

The sangoma was forced to clarify his statement: "The child is haunted by fear. Fear that all male figures in his life will be killed in hijackings."

The paternal grandmother grudgingly accepted that.

It was only later, when she was alone, that the sangoma's warning struck Karabo as peculiar. She regretted not having challenged him there and then to clarify his divination. Had she done so, she would not have worried afterwards. And we all know that 'Worry' is addictive, like cocaine, morphine, ecstasy and all other drugs.

Because she was preoccupied with raising her son, she never had time to ponder the possibility of a connection between the sangoma's words and the soothsayer's prediction. Another reason was that she saw life as a bed, a smooth bed on which you stretched out to enjoy a good night's sleep. At times, you really did enjoy it, while at other times it felt like bits of gravel had found their way into your sheets.

During your sleep you'd scratch your skin, kneading it with rough massages, so that you woke up with all sorts of little pricks and pains. And sometimes nightmares crept into your sleep like nimble fingers of pick-pockets, and you woke with a nagging feeling that all was not well. Or worse still, nightmares would storm in like stampeding buffaloes until you jumped from bed, screaming.

If life was like that, especially if you were Karabo, what would you do? You simply carried on with the business of getting the best out of it and dumping the bothersome rest into the nearest dustbin. That was seven years ago.

From the outset, when he first came into her life, Karabo was convinced that Chris was her God-chosen partner. That is, after Tiro. In fact, a disembodied male voice would frequently urge her to embrace him with all her heart. And eventually she started associating that voice with Tiro. It seemed as if Chris was hand-picked by her late fiance to partner her in shouldering the burdens of life.

Chris was her opposite. To him, life was a menu of repulsive dishes with a serving of some tasty dessert now and then. But for the rest – "I swear, it is horrible. All the degrading human ailments like runny stomachs, dripping noses, headaches ...." In arguing this way, he was, in fact, quoting a farewell statement attributed to Queen Mamahola on her deathbed in 1903. "I swear, Karabo, these might look like minor irritations, but they sure are permanent reminders of our mortality."

Yet despite this drawback, as Karabo termed his negative philosophy of life, he had the potential to make a fine husband. Then what was the noose hanging over her head?

Though she didn't believe in soothsayers, sangomas and other such people who tamper with the future or the supernatural, Karabo was becoming increasingly convinced that the dead could, and do, engage in dialogue with the living. Certainly Tiro was busy grooming Chris as his successor in his affections. Having reached that conclusion, she was in the mood for celebration. But all she managed to have was an unpleasant dream.

She dreamt of an intriguing encounter with a man from up north. The man telephoned to inform her that he had stolen her husband's manhood. In trying to understand this message, she recalled how, when she was a girl, reckless boys would assert their masculinity by stealing cars, and how writers bridge their creative blocks by stealing ideas from others. She had heard stories about old people who prolong their lives by stealing those of young people. Maybe then there was nothing absurd about the stranger's craft – he offered to restore the stolen potency on condition she consented to sleep with him.

"*Yebo Mkhatsi, wena* shleep wid me. Mi give bag you husiband's shing."

It was an unsavoury bargain – she sleep with him so he would restore her hus band's manhood? Never! That you will never get, you filthy scoundrel! I would rather give any other ransom you demand. Anything but that! But what was 'anything'? Anything was anything. I am prepared to do whatever you wish to save my marriage. The nightmare might have continued, except that in trying to grab him by the scruff of his neck and wring it, she fell from the sofa. She sighed with relief after that.

However, her relief was short-lived. The noose tightened. The dream's spell was not broken. She had to conquer her enemy in the land of dreams for that to happen. Once again a half-baked solution ... It was like moving her feet forward only to have the ground shift back underneath them. She realised that she had to reassess her situation. Fortunately there was another source of relief: she had a child, this was comfort in itself, definite proof of her fertility, a boy – triumphant progeny of her loins.

The dead, when they speak, say, 'Habahabahaba' or mumble similar unfamiliar sounds. It is a cryptic language very few people can understand. Maybe that is why diviners and spirit mediums are needed to decode that occult talk. And that was why Karabo resolved to consult a spirit medium to inquire from the dead about the soothsayer's prediction. Illusions do bring comfort at times. Like her friends, neighbours and colleagues, Karabo was no exception in liking to be told she'd live to a thousand years, or that in her next life she'd be reincarnated as a billionaire. But the spirit medium took her into a future of horrors, a future infested with brothels selling private parts for sex transplants, restaurants and take-aways serving streaming human blood, butcheries pawning and offering lay-bye purchases of human embryos, sperm and ova. More twists in the labyrinth – that prophecy foresaw everything except what she wanted to know: how should she, Karabo, a God-fearing Christian, put a deposit on her future husband's life? Could it be that she would be paying lobola instead of him? Or maybe he would die before her and she would have to bear all his funeral expenses?

Fervently resolved to find the answer, she decided to consult another medium. He was sympathetic to her situation but, like the famed Greek emperor Alexander's sorcerer, demanded that she present him with a jewellery casket in order to unseal the lips of the dead. They could be exorbitantly expensive, the dead, she cursed. To think that in their time they may well have subsisted on a few head of cattle and goats and prided themselves on being frugal. Moreover, their agents – soothsayers, sangomas, spirit mediums and a few charlatans – seemed determined to undo that injustice by living in opulence.

The third spirit medium was far, far better. Like all such professionals, she first took Karabo on a detour. She led her through a future where nursery schools offered tuition in pick-pocketing, bag-snatching and other petty crimes; a tomorrow in which the lower grades offered courses in hijacking, kidnapping and extortion. The medium shrieked, sneezed and belched repeatedly before uttering the damning warning that the four Horsemen of the Apocalypse were frantically grooming and harnessing their wild stallions, sharpening their swords, preparing for the final battle. It was then that Karabo felt convinced that her Chris would not survive .... And that she was similarly fated. She thought of Lot's wife turned into a pillar of salt. Her destiny was dim, cursed like Jocasta's or Medea's. Unless ...

Karabo grew up believing that Good triumphs over Evil. Or was supposed to. Because of this faith, she prepared herself to overthrow the bad omen. She started giving more alms to the poor. She rationalized that if beggars could sustain themselves, the whole economic equation would be balanced, secure people wouldn't scour the pavements for coins.

Like pigeons gathering round their feeders, legions of beggars would swarm round her in Joubert Park, pecking and nibbling at ten cent pieces. To nourish them, she started collecting coins in her pockets. This didn't worry her banker: "Never mind the young lady, our vaults can hardly cope with the mountains of small change. Let her take them all." But they became alarmed when she started drawing from her retirement and pension investments.

♪ *Beggars and muggers,*
Beggars and muggers,
Give me beggars and muggers.
Give me one, two, three coins,
Beggars and muggers,
Beggars and muggers.
Round the corner, somewhere,
Round that alley, one, two, three, ♪
Give me beggars and muggers! ♪

Karabo had a tuneful voice. She would sing out loud as she sat feeding the assembled crowds. All who heard the refrain would be so taken with it that they unconsciously began singing it themselves. Including beggars and muggers. Within a short time it hit the top of the radio and television charts.

"*Beggars and muggers, round the corner, somewhere ...*"

The beggar is king of the concrete jungle, ruthlessly hunting for coins; muggers come after him to scrounge for leftovers. She reasoned that with the removal of beggars, society's cancer would be cured. Then vicious species like car hijackers would not endanger her Chris. So, as time passed, emboldened, she thought: how pathetic are the medium's diatribes! If the medium had any decency, she should take it upon herself to throw her witchcraft into the sewers — where it belonged.

But Chris threw her back into confusion by winning a top of the range Mercedes Benz in a charity competition. He further roused her ire by insisting on keeping it.

"Please darling, sell it ... swop it for money instead. Please! Anything but that car. I don't want the whole township queuing to rob us."

"C'mon, dear." She so hated it when he put on that American accent. "You can't be serious, Karabo. You really mean we should give away a gift from the ancestors?"

"Please, dear, for my sake!"

"What about their sakes?"

"Chr-i-s!" She stopped, shock on her face. Was it really her screaming at her husband? "I'm sorry, sweetheart, I didn't mean to. But you know the danger such things expose us to."

"They gave it as a present. They will most probably look after it."

"But Chris, are you serious? There are car hijackers everywhere, whereas your ancestors are long rotten under ..."

He hit her. For the first time, Chris hit her. She was so stunned she could not bring herself to speak to him. And because of his naivete, like most men, he was convinced it was out of anger or because she resented his curbing her freedom of expression. So he pleaded with her, saying he would never hurt her again, vowing to do anything to please her, even forfeit his life to make amends to his angel. Throughout that period he maintained his vigil, kneeling before her, entreating her to have mercy on her chastised little devil. And his remorse touched her, though she could not utter a word to him for days; such humility and remorse left her speechless. But he kept the car all the same.

She started having dreams of him driving a car with defective brakes. Sometimes the car would topple over a cliff, sometimes it would plunge into a speeding train at a level crossing or, like a powerboat, it would streak over water; it wouldn't stop at robots. Without consulting any spirit medium, she recognised the omen.

This time she visited a private detective. The detective passed her on to a colleague who sold car security systems. He told her about new advances in technology; the advantages of satellite tracking devices.

"With those little chips you would be able to monitor your husband's exact movements."

"Don't misunderstand me, it's not his movements that interest me but those of his car."

"Come now, lady, don't be shy or guilty about it. It's common these days for spouses to spy on each other. Who can be blamed? With so much unfaithfulness going around. Add the high tax levies on single divorced parties and it's perfectly legitimate that we all take precautions."

"My husband is not that type, the divorcing or deserting kind ... You see, I need to be on the alert about his security. Install a warning for him to avoid certain roads, like a bleeper, a panic-button, or some such thing. Of course, I want it done anonymously. I mean it must sound like ... you know the thing about traffic reports. But this one should advise against using certain routes because of the danger of hijacking."

"Lady, I don't know what you re talking about. You certainly are looking for some high-tech gadget. Are you in the espionage profession?"

"Look! Can you install it? And for how much?"

"I certainly can. But unfortunately we don't have such a gadget at this stage. Come and inquire a decade from now. Hey! In the meantime, talk it over with your Neighbourhood Watch."

Having considered the matter for some months, Karabo found she couldn't bear to sit by idly and wait. So she revisited the crusader of merriment and good cheer to sign a contract for a custom-built device. The technology was highly rated, supposedly used only by the CIA. Because of that the crusader demanded a hundred thousand rand advance payment.

"Christ! Where do I get that kind of money?"

"How much is a human life worth? Tell me, lady. How much would you say your spouse is worth?"

"It's not how much he's worth. You've already put a price on him."

"Come on, lady. It is an arbitrary figure. I could have said a hundred rand. and you most certainly would have felt insulted."

"I just can't afford so much money right away ..."

"Put down a deposit then. A couple of thousand now, say ten, and the rest later. How's that, hmmm? I see you look relieved, hmmm! I'll be damned if we don't have a deal."

That Friday at dawn her son never screamed and she had one of the longest and most relaxing sleeps she had ever had.

"ALLEY, ALLEY, WHERE IS MY LOVER?"

That was the lament of almost every girl in our township. Lerato was one of them, one of the loners whose potential lover had skipped the country. Sadly, hopes of being reunited with him were bleak because those strange lands seemed to be infatuated with our young men. And who could blame them? Those young men were dreamers. They dreamt aloud, talked confidently about the future when they would be ministers, deputy ministers or diplomats. Some were even bold enough to predict that they would be ministers of finance. And those foreign women would marvel at the prospect of playing personal assistants to their husbands as they signed and balanced treasury cheques.

Lerato knew that in her case the privilege of cutting ribbons at official functions was remote. Her only salvation lay in disappearing into exile for a few months. Once there, she would publicise herself as much as possible, strive to meet one or two ministers-in-waiting. There was also the possibility of changing her surname and accent. With those, she would be assured of affluent returnee status.

Now her friend, Thandi, was a different matter. She enjoyed the chat of local boys. Sometimes she would drag Lerato out for a stroll.

"Let's go meet the *outies, mhlambe unga thola e ou encha*.²⁶" And Lerato would reluctantly accompany her. Then they would go about teasing all the boys they met. On these excursions it was Thandi who managed to get additional telephone numbers and addresses in her diary.

Lerato thought all that demeaning. She believed in finding lovers at decent places. Yet time was running out for her. After failing to meet any at soccer matches and music shows, what other places were left? There were street corners, shop stoeps and alleys. These were far safer than venturing into shebeens.

"Would you mind coming with me to First Avenue?" Thandi asked one day.

"Wena! I'd love to, but isn't it too late?"

"Come on, lovie, it is only half past five."

"Remember, my mother comes back from work at six. And she likes things to be ready."

"Ashee, never mind. We will be back by then. A little walk might earn somebody a 'prospective'."

"Please, Thandi, promise that we will be back by quarter to six."

They set off. On the way Thandi continued her fun of teasing boys.

"Hey! look at that one. See the thin lips. No good for delivering a good kiss."

"Uuuu, what about that one? Small feet, probably his thing is small as well … I'm sure of it. Won't be able to satisfy you or make a baby."

"Yoo, Thandi, sies!"

"Do you want to prove it? Hey, sonny, come here. What's your name?"

"*Ke Lesiba, ousie.*"

"How old are you?"

"*Ke na le fourteen, ousie.*"

"Have you ever had … it?"

"What?"

"A girl … has any woman ever given you?"

"Er … *ousie*, they refuse."

"You see, Lerato, take him and go try it. Hey, sonny, ousie ona would like to give you."

"I'm afraid."

The fun continued through the evening. Lerato only managed to get home by quarter past twelve. She was in a bad state. Her face was bruised and swollen.

"Lerato! What … where have you been? What happened to your face?"

Lerato responded with a blank stare, tears rolling down her cheeks. Her mother tried to press for an answer, but couldn't get any.

"Lovie, come for a walk," said Thandi several weeks later.

"I'm sorry, I'm too busy."

"Why, what's wrong with you? By the way, how did you go last time?"

"Thandi, we'd better not talk about that."

Meanwhile, Lerato's mother asked herself over and over what had happened. She finally came back to Lerato.

"Don't be ashamed, Lerato. Tell me …"

"Mother, I know I shouldn't have gone along with Thandi."

"What about her? Tell me everything."

"We started off at the Red Flame Tavern, then ended up at Mapetla's. She insist-ed on ordering beers even though we didn't have any money. She banked on one of the gents footing our bill but when no-one paid … you know …"

"Hmmm! So they *moered* you?"

"Sort of … ."

Soon afterwards Lerato's longings turned into a dream. And the dream produced a young man. The dream would slip into her sleep at odd times, during the night while she was asleep and by day while she was awake. She saw herself in his arms.

Through frequent recurrence, she became familiar with his features. If she were to meet him, she would most certainly pick him out in a crowd. But supposing the dream did not materialise? Would she have to settle for some lousy loafer?

As time passed and the sun rose and set with relentless, dull regularity, she realised she had to do something. That meant going out into the streets where she scouted around for months. Still her dream prince refused to appear. In desperation she ended up jolling with different young men.

Her mother always scolded her: "Hey! *Ngwanenyana ke wena?* Can't *kuku eo ya gago*[27], stay without boys for a while?" Or, "Where do you think all this changing of boyfriends like underwear will lead you?"

These words would always strike after she returned home from seeing one of her casual pickups, when she was already feeling dejected and abused by their methods. After a couple of minutes, the men were exhausted; hurried, ungentle, at times even hostile. Their major concern was to dash off the moment passersby approached; their unwashed mouths couldn't spare any tender words, only an acrid, nauseating smell. Not even a thank-you-kiss for her favour. That always left her shattered.

She reflected and concluded that no sane young men were left. All potential partners who would have staked their matrimonial future on her were married to either foreign lands or foreign graves. Who was left? A marauding bunch of pick-pockets, rapists, bank robbers and child molesters.

"That's a shame, Lerato. I mean, there should be some exceptions," her white cashier colleague at Checkers said.

"You don't know them. The ones around are only interested in S.S.B.S."

"Oooh, what's that?"

"Sex, soccer, beer and score ... that's robbery."

At this point the colleague advised her to join singles clubs.

"Who knows, maybe that way you might meet your ideal."

But after a few months of trying those, Lerato gave up. Her colleague then advised her to join voluntary organisations.

"You know, doing all that work keeps you occupied. You skip the loneliness part of life. And there's a plus – you might meet some really nice gentleman in one of those programmes."

Lerato endured voluntary work for a couple of months. Night after night, she came home dejected.

One day her mother said: "Why not visit a friend?"

"I'm fine here, mother."

"No, Lerato. It's a sin for one your age to sit brooding every evening like a widow."

Lerato forced herself to the door. Then gave her mother that vacant look of hers. Seconds later, darkness enveloped her.

She walked the streets. Big dogs greeted her with their hollow, booming barks, little *brakkies*[32] echoed shrilly and bats welcomed her with their haunting whistles. She turned a corner into an alley adjoining Fifteenth Avenue and saw a group of four men standing there. When she drew closer, their profiles took on grotesque shapes. What if she invited one, would the other three force themselves on her? What if they were zombies or restless spirits of the Msomi gang?

Still, she resolved to move on, edge forward, one step at a time. It was only when she was opposite them that she could guess at their ages – men long past their prime, without interest in women. Yet the fact that they were men fuelled the flames burning in her heart and loins.

She kept moving, leaving these tired, spent out things. Somewhere in the streets and alleys she was bound to meet someone younger, eager to get 'it' for free. Then, twenty metres ahead of her, she saw him.

A solitary man in his prime, that she could tell from his firm, confident steps. He was solidly built, tall and well fed. He walked on, his shoes ruthlessly crushing the gravel. No girl ahead of or behind him. As he drew closer, her eyes fixed on his profile. She dared not move them lest he disappear like her dream.

"O, tch!"

A split second and he would be gone and lost for ever. He was already one step past her.

"*Dumela, Oubutie,*" she whispered, her voice coming out in a choking rasp.

"Hello, *Ousiki.* Saying anything?"

He paused and turned to her. Her panic was mounting. Then she saw his smile and was reassured.

"Er ... er ... I was only ... I said *dumela.*"

"Come, Ousikie. I can see you are not in a hurry, ne?"

He came and stood in front of her. She felt her body go into a spasm. He looked at her face for a while; she felt like a commodity being assessed for its value.

Then he gently took her hand and led her to the alley corner next to a derelict wall. Unhurriedly he laid her down. There, on the rough and filthy ground, the act was done. The traffic of passing male voices did not unsettle or disturb him. Afterwards, he rewarded her with a cuddle and a kiss. She stood watching him as with delicate care he dusted his clothing with a white handkerchief. There was a lingering passion in her.

"Have ... er ... do you have a girlfriend, Ouboetie? I would like to become your ..."

"Don't you think it's a bit rushed for that?"

"But just now we enjoyed each other. We could continue seeing each other."

"I don't know. Maybe ... Okay, let us meet next Thursday, around five in the afternoon."

On the Thursday, at four o'clock, Lerato was already waiting for him, trying to visualise what he would look like in daylight. Hopefully he didn't sport knife scars and the like. She wondered what kind of dreams filled his sleep. Did he experience those that came to other ordinary dreamers? Or were his dreams filled with stolen cars fleeing from flashing blue lights?

Suddenly she saw him coming. He was young and gay. She laughed with pleasure. It was easy to understand the source of the energy he had displayed on the night of their first meeting. As he drew closer she could feel her body responding, a burning surge emanating from her loins. His eyes fixed on her, stripping her naked with longing and lust. Only three steps from her ... two ... one, he turned his head away and passed.

She was stunned. How could he behave like that? The son of a bitch, the shameless piece of donkey dung, the sperm-filled skull! It was only when she paused to think of worse, more fitting curses to heap on him, that she realised he wasn't her alley partner.

She bowed her head.

When she raised it again, it was five-thirty. She looked around. The township streets were emptying, stretching themselves for a temporary rest until young lovers invaded them. Her mother was probably already home preparing supper.

Lerato sat waiting. Her head slumped into the ridge of her breasts. Tears streamed down her cheeks. She didn't care any more whether he came or not. She didn't care about anything else either.

When she lifted her head again, it was ten at night. She tried to raise herself, but couldn't. Her head dropped once more. Dogs quietened down. Sounds of speeding cars faded.

At dawn the next morning, early risers and workers passed her still in that posture.

LETTER FROM THE DEAD

It was on the third day of the incident that we braced ourselves for something sinister. Not that an itchy palm was a riddle, something to shame the beards of our wisdom. We knew, though, that it was an omen. Even describing it as an incident might not be appropriate. But then, having chased the same sun behind the same trees and mountain shadows for the better part of our lives, we were prone to hyperbole in our descriptions of things merely to give our monotonous lives a semblance of significance.

And it was inevitable that we, individually and collectively, should bear grudges against Pontsho. Who was she anyway, to pour scorn on our communal pride? Pontsho ridiculed everything: our jokes; our indulging in sorghum and marula beer; our marabaraba games; and the habitual lounging in the shade after midday meals. All the while we kept reminding her that these are just diversions to ease the drudgery of our lives. She countered by accusing us of ineptitude and laziness, all the while spitting out a stream of insults. Bearing this in mind, you will understand our triumph at what we later collectively referred to as Pontsho's affliction.

Pontsho grouchy, strumming her minute guitar because of an itchy palm. Pontsho continually scratching and scratching 'like a mongrel or a pig with *lekker krap*[33]'. In making this observation, the speaker earned himself a gourd of frothing sorghum beer. Our triumph was not gratifying, though, because Pontsho treated our making an issue of her palm-itch with scorn.

"Come off it, you illiterates. None of you invented a fart or a belch, so stop pretending that my itchy palm is a countdown to the end of the world."

Shock prompted us to consult a *ngaka-ya-ditaola*[28] for we all agreed only one bewitched could degenerate into such a bad neighbour. But Pontsho's palm was not the only village issue. She was beautiful as well, the kind of bewitching beauty only angels or she-devils possess. What else could we term it? At a time when women's worth was measured by the number of babies their wombs could produce or the number of menial tasks their arms could carry out, she chose to parade the pain beauty was capable of inflicting.

All the mothers in our village used to advise their marriageable sons: "*Mosadi ke tshwene, o lewa mabogo*[29]." Prospective mothers-in-law pointed out that her kind of beauty relished feeding only the eyes while sucking out men's guts, leaving them zombies. We thought the mothers' warnings were motivated by female jealousy, until we began hearing about the bizarre behaviour of some of our brothers.

Boys, married men and even bent over grey beards were so besotted with Pontsho that they would wander about the streets or in nearby woods at moontide crooning, chanting or whispering her name and then fell into stuttering and swooning spells in her presence. These afflictions were known to disappear when she withdrew.

That was why we started believing sermons by some preachers that Pontsho was a she-devil incarnate, bent on corrupting Christian youths who, tantalised by her beauty, were convinced she was the madonna. Kgwedi, the village *boemelaar*[34], nearly started an interreligious blood bath between Catholics and Protestants by insisting that the waters of ever lasting life flowed between her legs – the idiot Protestant deserter forgetting in his drunken stupor that the guzzler on his left was the local Catholic priest!

From those before us, we had learnt that when your palm itched it was an omen of receiving money, that is, if you were owed, or if a rich uncle on his deathbed forgot you were worse than a piece of dog shit and decided to bequeath his entire estate to you; or you might shake someone's hand in greeting, that is, if your distant acquaintances far outnumber your enemies.

We also learned of the body's different codes and their interpretation. Itchy soles foretold travel possibilities, or being soaked in rain. A palpitating upper eye lid meant seeing a long lost acquaintance; an itchy lower eye lid foretold crying or mourning for a loved one. Best of all was choking on saliva, which foretold a coming feast. Most of us liked this last sign. How could we not, when meat and other delicacies were scarce? It was only the occasional death that brought us those treats. Collective panic would set in if none of us reported such an omen. Then we would set about lamenting. It was at such times that our palates would get only fried termites and locusts as substitutes for real meat.

As tradition demanded, we passed the codes on to our grandchildren, particularly because there was little else we could show off to them as proof that we had harvested and suckled from Mother Nature. But it wasn't as if our grandchildren appreciated our wisdom. Words hitchhiking on the wings of bats and owls reached us about how they condemned us as a generation of failures. We knew, and were powerless to reverse that. For we knew only too well that had we but left them herds of goats and cows and mealie fields as an inheritance, our stigma as failures would be erased.

In time we became convinced that Pontsho was the prophetess of the generation of ridiculers – all the young ones were starting to adopt her attitude. Over frothing sorghum beer we plotted counter strategies. We made light of the young by pointing out that they conducted themselves in that way because they were conceived during daytime. Yea, only dogs and donkeys mated by day! Not surprising, then, that the offspring of drunkards and day-time fornicators behaved like animals.

After those strategising sessions we would turn to our favourite songs, like;
Couzy-motswala is for sale,
buy her and fill our bellies,
tswang-tswang motswala.
Couzy-motswala is for sale,
bed my wife, I'll bed yours ...
A new refrain added to the popular ditty:
Tswang-tswang motswala,
motswala-ka ngwana malome,
kare ntsee oa gana.
Tswang-tswang motswala,
motswala-ka ngwana malome.
Kgomo di boela shakeng.
(Merry, merry, sweet cousin,
cousin child of my uncle,
have me for a spouse ...
Let dowry cattle remain in
the family ...)
Our days were spent on such humorous sentiments until Pontsho came with what she referred to as 'poor old women and men's tales'. Did you hear that little witch? She rubbishes our warning regarding her itchy palm with such nonsense!

And anybody daring to echo her blasphemy would be cautioned with: "Stop right there, before a curse follows you up to the seventh generation!" We all pointed out in detail what would befall her, but Pontsho, being Pontsho, chose to defy our collective indignation, if not that of the ancestors. From that day onwards we waited with bated breath to witness Pontsho reaping the bitter rewards of disrespect for our customs.

Our anticipation reached fever pitch when we heard rumours that her palm was getting itchier by the day. We reasoned with her that if she wanted to dispel the omen of death – maybe her own or that of someone close to her – she needed to act quickly. When it appeared that she was going to do nothing, we resolved to act.

Our first action was to send children, little ones whom we reckoned had not yet committed any sin. Their task was to scratch her palm; that was the remedy we all applied when our palms itched. When that failed, we exclaimed: "You call those children! Miniature monsters, no manners or shame in them! With the bad influence from those moving pictures they see, *kare ruri*, you get little playground serial killers. At the age of three they're already expert at torturing frogs, ants and dung beetles. Then they learn to push sticks, stones and all sorts of funny things up the rear ends of domestic animals."

"*Ka mma ruri*, with chickens born with four legs! The world is truly nearing its end."

At a village *kgotla* we resolved that a virgin was our next best bet. Though we were all equally jealous of Pontsho, we were united in our efforts to shield her from any possible destructive fate. Secretly we knew that if she were to die from the curse, our obsession with ogling her, and eventually seeing her humiliated and humbled, would come to nought.

After patiently waiting for one parent, at least one, to volunteer his or her child, panic broke loose. We were all shocked to realise that the level of decadence in the village was at such a low point that not a single virgin could be found amongst approximately ten thousand children and teenagers. Some churchgoers jumped in, enthusiastically citing this fact as the reason why the village was experiencing such a terrible drought of late.

We would probably have sat there the whole day, but then Mme-Makgatho came dragging her mentally retarded eighteen-year-old daughter. Relief loosened our tongues. The customary riddles, jokes and anecdotes followed. In our excitement we formed a guard of honour for both of them as we led the drooling girl to Pontsho's compound.

"Why abuse the poor thing?" Pontsho jeered.

"*Homola wena*[35], be grateful that we share in your suffering."

"What! Call an itching palm an affliction? You backward natives!"

In fairness we might indeed be called 'backward natives', but to be called that by a woman — a girl really, and an unmarried one at that — was too much: trampling, trivialising and spitting on the manhood hanging between our legs.

A group of men were about to let their tempers descend to the level of their ridiculed manhood. But we pointed out to them that, as in previous instances, arguing with Pontsho was like pissing in our own sorghum beer, spoiling not only the beer but your day as well. We all agreed that our time should rather be spent productively, guzzling our beloved wives' brews.

Some of us enjoyed provoking her, especially during a ploughing season when the sun was in the habit of conspiring with our limbs to usher in yet another harvest shortfall. Nonetheless, we got Mapule to scratch Pontsho's palm. That night we never slept as we raced the hours to the new day. While we kept vigil outside her house, Pontsho had a good night's sleep.

Despite warnings by a fellow village elder that the sun would rise encircled by an unusual red halo, the third day of our suspense dawned like any other. The cocks

crowed at the usual time, the dawn breeze sprayed our roofs with dew, calves demanded sustenance at the usual time. And we were reminded of Nongxawusi and her dream-interpreting uncle, Mhlagaza. We dreamt that the mealie fields would tend themselves, that benevolent spirits would do the reaping, grinding and cooking for us, that our enemies would turn into cow dung so that we could manure our fields. These dreams were fed by our desire to spend more time competing with ants, beetles and flies for shade.

Our disappointment at seeing the sun rise and set without any extraordinary red haloes drove us dejectedly to our different compounds. Then we started counselling each other:

"Patience, patience, *bathong*. The day is still young. Who knows, irresponsible midwives might still sour our celebrations with news of a still birth." That was the kind of language we all wanted to hear, a promise that all was not lost, that something dramatic might still happen.

Our dread of continuing boredom was relieved at midday. News reached us that Pontsho's palm was itching again. Like bees heeding the call of their queen, we converged on Pontsho's compound, an umbilical cord threading its way from her navel through her palm to the core of our brains.

Once again we united in laying blame for our failure to eradicate her affliction. Indeed, how could a community of old men – constantly chewing the cud of experience, heads bald to allow the sun to radiate Solomon's wisdom on their brains – fail to deal with such a trifling matter as Pontsho's affliction?

Our condemnations were piled on Mapule's mother. Some of us recalled having heard rumours of her selling her retarded daughter's womanhood to supplement their meagre family income, her old age pension. Some recalled earlier stories that the daughter was the offspring of the mother's incestuous relationship with her brother. That was said to have happened after the death of her husband a few months after the marriage.

It was inevitable – this was clear to those of us who knew Pontsho's attitude – that she would lose patience with our interference. She berated us and told us to go swop our trousers for skirts because, as she put it, real men would find worthier employment than counting goat and chicken droppings. Really, had respect for one's elders – and male ones at that – dropped so low that unmarried girls could allude to men's anatomy in public? To those who were circumcised or not, and those who had a big or small organ? We knew then that male dignity was eroded. Later we wished we had taken offence, that would have showed that we still had pride. It was as if she had cast a spell over us. Some said anyone who stood close enough to her to inhale the smell of her armpits always behaved strangely afterwards. One old man went even further: he said the eyes of those who had crossed her path or touched her during her menstrual period became glazed forever, blind to any sight except her. Had it not been for his age, we were certain, younger men who were constantly wooing her would have burnt him alive. How could they not? His insinuation was that their potential bride was a witch. What was not known, though, was that Pontsho would one day marry Death.

The saga of Pontsho's affliction finally came to a head when she received a letter from her twin brother. He was known to have died at the age of twelve from an accident – a fall from a bicycle, How changed things were becoming these days! In our boyhood we used to fall from tall trees but only bruise our knees, break the occasional rib, finger, leg or arm. Really, fancy dying from falling off something that creeps on the ground! What punishments are the ancestors meting out, and for what?

Once again we converged on her compound. We trampled and crushed each other as we vied to see, touch and smell the envelope from the dead, because Pontsho refused to let us see the contents of the letter itself. Each of us scrutinised and sniffed it for signs of proof that it was indeed from Beyond.

"Say, how much postage did it cost?"

"Did it take two months to deliver like all other letters?"

"I don't know ... I don't know ... " Pontsho mumbled.

"Was it an owl, a white chicken or goat that delivered it?"

"Does he say if there is plenty of beer, meat and shade?"

Most of us salivated when we posed the last question. But Pontsho frustrated our curiosity about the other world. Poor Pontsho. It was the first time that we saw her tongue-tied, her eyes darting about, appealing and searching for volunteers to provide answers.

"What does he say, what does he want?" we asked in chorus.

She merely looked at us and hid her face in her palms as if praying.

"Hahaa! *A reye*, go on like you always do, invent ridicule for this one as well," we thought secretly, passing around the yellow dust-stained envelope.

"Relax, Pontsho, it's probably one of your suitors playing tricks on you."

"Patience, the drunkard behind all this will emerge!"

"That's just a prank by besotted *tampus*[30]."

Some of the womenfolk tried to soothe her. But Pontsho started crying, ranting and tearing her clothes. Oh! Such a beauty gone mad. Bachelors, young and old, bemoaned this potential loss of a fine wife. "What can a man do with a mad wife, regardless of her beauty or skillful hands?" potential mothers-in-law wondered. Older married men were depressed, too. Of course, for them, it meant losing out on a potential second, third or even seventh wife. But no, it was not yet time for jealous spinsters and witches to celebrate – Pontsho stopped her wild behaviour.

She gathered herself, went into one of the huts and collected a hoe, a gourd of beer, some one cent coins, two candles and a plate. Then we knew where she was going. We followed her at a distance. It was only at the cemetery gates that we stopped her. Sounds of a cock crowing from the village could be heard. We reminded her it was taboo to enter graveyards during daytime except for burials.

"You can't, Pontsho, you can't go and tend your brother's grave at this time of day. That will bring bad luck. You will have to come before sunrise," Mme-Makgatho told her.

We heard the distant cock crowing again. Without arguing Pontsho let herself be led back to the compound by the old woman, and our procession followed at a safe distance. When the cock crowed the third time we could only wonder who was being betrayed this time.

The letter marked the transformation of Pontsho. While she did not go out of her way to be polite, she stopped ridiculing things. As if in reaction to that, our banter, jokes and marathon beer-drinking sessions lost momentum. Men walked like zombies or instead of gulping down the contents, sat with eyes fixed meditatively on their calabashes. It was as if the whole village was in mourning for the chief's heir or an *imbongi*.

Contrary to the norm whereby our ears quickly picked up and interpreted whisperings on the wind, it took us four whole months to learn the contents of Pontsho's letter from her late twin brother. That those sketchy dribs and drabs came through Mapule, Mme-Makgatho's retarded daughter, irritated us the most. Did Pontsho have to stoop that low to show her contempt for us, confiding in a dribbling, drooling human waste? That made us swallow our pride. Reluctantly, we also found ourselves forced to censure those who persisted in ridiculing the retarded girl.

One Wednesday morning Mapule surprised us by informing us that we should prepare for Pontsho's wedding party. The village entered a period of pandemonium. Most men neglected *kgotla* and village council affairs to busy themselves sorting cattle, goats and hens as possible lobola for Pontsho. But then the retarded girl infuriated us by saying that none of us, despite our vast wealth, was a match for Pontsho's husband-to-be.

"What conceit!"

"What a presumptuous insult!"

"What disrespectful gibberish!"

"Which upstart is that?"

"From whose womb did he come?"

We were convinced that the impostor was not from our village. No, he was certainly not – ALL the young men turned on us, accusing us of stealing their bride, while we in turn pointed crooked forefingers at them. Then they ducked or hid behind tree trunks and logs, for they feared that which would strike them from our vengeful spite and muti-soaked fingers.

This time chewing our beards did not offer any comfort. How could it, when we were being robbed of a young thoroughbred – a mount to rejuvenate our blood?

"Fragile old beards cannot substitute for brooms when cleaning out soiled huts. Why then do young and old poke each other's eyes with dirty finger-nails? Pontsho belongs to those who reside amid shades ..."

We all turned, mouths and eyes wide open, palms glued to our cheeks, as we listened to the retarded Mapule. Gathering ourselves, we hastily pulled away from the girl. Then, like chastised children, we huddled together.

"Mourn for yourselves, lost men. In your prime, armed with impatience, you charged ahead to find infancy in old age. Retreating, you will find infancy in childhood. Pontsho is loved by spirits whose shadows are mist ..."

That finally convinced us that Mapule, apart from being retarded, was, in fact mad. Young men jumped forward and started tying her up with ropes. Dead tree trunks and logs were hastily brought and a bonfire made. We retreated and had to cover our noses as the burning witch filled the air with nauseating odour. Days after the roasting, we went about comforting each other.

"Yaa! I always warned you that Pontsho's conduct was that of one bewitched. But who could have known that the witch was a retarded girl?" one old man said, repeatedly stroking his beard.

"Indeed, indeed, your words strike the very tip of the cow's horns. What can we say?" another agreed. In former times those words would have been downed with well-brewed sorghum or marula beer. But not now, only a few days after the frying. Our stomachs could not retain anything.

Early one morning, not long after Mapule's death, Pontsho once again collected snuff, sorghum beer and grave-cleaning tools and left for the graveyard. And that was the last time we ever saw her. Rumours later reached us that she had eloped with this or that old or young man; those who were named would spend days cursing and wishing that our accusations were true. Another rumour was that she had dug open her late twin brother's grave.

"*Aowa, lena*, then how did she manage to refill the grave?"

Almost thirty years have passed since Pontsho's affliction, but we haven't forgotten it. This is because Time hobbles along in the village like widowed old men and women continually resurrecting their spouses with the aid of marula and mokgope beer that sticks in obsessive devotion in their gullets.

Our grandchildren felt it their duty to offer reminders of the incident. They invented a new game called 'great-scratch' which entails each player pretending to meet the other for the first time. As is customary, they shake hands, and that is the climax of the game: both extending their hands, but just before clasping, each would pretend the hand was itching and start scratching vigorously, first with the same hand's fingers, then with the other hand. Then both would pretend surprise to see each other thus engaged in scratching.

"*Mokgotsi*, what is poverty doing to me? Me receive money! *Hao! batho*, are the ancestors mocking my suffering?"

"*O ra nna*, everything repossessed, including relatives and friends. But who will shake my hand in greeting? *Aretse*, maybe the cold and bony palms of the dead?"

And the children would laugh so heartily that some would roll on the ground.

WHEN A NAME AWAKES

Though he looked forty, Tutankhamen was in fact thirty. He had a slight stoop, bowed legs and a face hardened into a mask of wrinkles and furrows. What interested me, though, was not the face. For in our part of the world there were many faces like his: faces defaced by suffering, distorted by the merciless hand of hard labour, faces on which the tortures of life were drawn.

In some, the loss of loved ones was written in the eyes; loss of children, loss of friends. Because there was no more room in their hearts to hide and harbour it, the pain seeped out and ended up etching its hideous signature on the flesh. In a way Tutankhamen's face was like those – a cracked, dilapidated wall on which nature chose to paint its saddest murals.

These murals complemented the ones painted by the political masters of our land in the early sixties.

What interested me and others about him was that precious yet dispensable noun we call a name. There was much speculation about its origin. On several occasions he was asked about his hereditary name – the sacred one that is passed from one generation to the next, serving as a link or as testimony to one's allegiance to one's tradition; the name that is usually accompanied by totems and praise poems.

Tutankhamen told me his family were descendants of the great Khazimola. After that he looked at me sternly, maybe because he thought I would chuckle or giggle as most people did. But I could not laugh at the bearer of that name while a tormented face was staring at me.

Long established legend had it that Khazimola, meaning 'the one who always yawns', received the name for his renowned fatigue: every emotion was expressed by a yawn. He was known to spend days without uttering a word. His wives were always ready to testify to that. His drinking friends reported that he could share beer calabashes for hours on end without laughing at even the most amusing of jokes. It was also said that he was incapable of shedding tears, not even over the tragic loss of four of his five wives. Then the deaths of seven of his children followed. Again it did not make his tear ducts relent.

A seven-year drought followed. Everybody, including the chief, was desperate. Khazimola's only reaction during those days was said to be fits of yawning. Then the chief's only son and heir died. Khazimola would have yawned as well, except that as the village's chief muti man, his honour and wisdom were now in question. Then he wept, a seven-day wailing that is said to have disturbed the repose of the ancestors.

After that he was given a new name, Nyembezi. He could not bear the ridicule of that name ('the wailer, the lamenter, the tearful one') and he opted to do what all disgraced men do – he drank a potion of crocodile's brain. From that day on, the village entered a period of revival as they went about initiating a new chief muti man. A few tears were shed in mourning for Khazimola, but everybody knew it was merely a civil ceremony to bid an unregretted farewell to a failure. For how could a great muti man have failed to protect and shield the chief's son?

That is how the Khazimolas ended up being called the Nyembezis. Reluctantly the family had to live with the latter name, which served as a reminder of their fall from grace. That was until Tutankhamen's grandfather returned from the Great War, having been one of the few black troops that faced and survived *Mjeremane*[31] in the Great War. It was there, in the vast desert, that Tutankhamen's grandfather first heard about the mummified Egyptian pharaohs. His fascination with them was great. He asked and gathered information about them. And he vowed that should he survive *Mjeremane's* fierce bullets, he would erase his family's imposed servility and restore it to greatness.

On his return from the war he was one of the few local heroes. He was held in high esteem. Crowds hung around him as he narrated his adventures. Everyone was awed when he talked of the great dry land where sand and sky embrace; where wind storms and heat are partners that squash humans between them. As time went by, his experiences became longer and more varied, but no-one could argue with him. For in the village most men chose to hide in the caves and mountains rather than face up to the challenge of fighting the great witch-doctor from the north. That was how that noble name of Tutankhamen struck root at the foot of the Hlabati mountains until the second-generation Tutankhamen profaned it thirty years later in Alexandra township, Johannesburg.

Tutankhamen was to blame for this. But then the times and the world he lived in weren't that innocent either. Had he been someone else he would have led a happy life. But Tutankhamen chose to be ambitious in a land where ambition in someone with a dark skin was sacrilege. There were many times that he wished the gods had endowed him with a lighter skin. A skin that would have ensured him the warmest sun rays in winter, the coolest shade in harsh summer. He remembered growing up amid stories about Santa Claus who distributed beautiful goods not only in white households, but in their dust bins as well.

That he was one of only two surviving members of the 1959 sub A class at Ikageng primary school was enough achievement. But he made the terrible mistake of thinking that all humans are equal. He thought that because all incubated in a woman's womb for the same duration of time, sucked from her breast where warmth and tenderness flowed, everyone would be warm and tender to each other. But no, these feelings, nurtured from conception onwards, were soon wiped away by greed and ambition. Wasn't that why he and his older brother were now estranged — locked in bitter rivalry to inherit their late father's possessions? Or was it because those who started kicking violently while still in the womb, or those who took savage bites at their mother's tits while sucking, were destined to be equally savage in later life?

It didn't take long before rumours started circulating that Tutankhamen was the direct descendant of the great Pharaoh himself.

"You are a liar!"

"Hey, mamela ... why do people always name their children after somebody in the family? Usually somebody who is deceased. Hee, tell me!"

"Life is a circle. We sleep in death and wake again in birth. Fools! Can't you see, the great man himself is back!"

"Liar! Where is your kingdom?"

"Hey! *Kgosi, re botse*[36], where are your subjects?"

"*Ba-gaetsho! tlang le bone se-tsoga bahung*[37], *Kgosi Tutankhamen*," people joked and laughed.

At the same time, Tutankhamen's life did not change. Indeed, he plunged deeper into his suffering. To flee that and the inhumanity of his tribesmen, he sought solace in the bottle. He embraced and wrapped his solitude in its acids. It was only when boasting about being the reincarnation of Tutankhamen that his sense of self-worth returned. And so he relentlessly peddled that story.

Township gossip-mongers gave it wings with which to fly. In their re-telling, new narrators added fresh plots to rescue it from becoming stale. Soon these versions, all of them studiously keeping to the same central theme — Tutankhamen's reincarnation in Alexandra — started reaching him at his different drinking spots. He would roar with laughter, buy beers and offer toasts to the narrators. Soon the stories became known throughout Alexandra, from First to Twenty-second Avenue. They spilled over and were recounted at garden parties on the East Bank. Then they invaded Lombardy East. New settlers from Alexandra related them to their white neighbours across pre-cast fences. Eager and inquisitive children built platforms next to the fences to hear their elders better. Curious dogs burrowed and dug fervently to flatten the walls of division. Most people thought they were after some treasured bones, but it soon became clear they were pioneers of destroying borders between neighbours.

Youngsters from Lombardy East started relating the story to class mates from other suburbs. From then on it soon spread to Linksfield and Fourways. Innovative essays that surprised English teachers with their poignancy followed.

"*Huwiii*! Tutankhamen in Alexandra, hahaa! What a shame! Of all places."

"But, dear, they say it is true. Several newspapers are said to have assigned their investigative reporters to look into the rumour."

"*Huwii*! What a waste, *kana*, those illiterates like over-blowing their worth. And for newspapers to buy such rubbish!"

It didn't take long for a local newspaper to run a front page blurb:

HOAX OR EIGHTH WONDER?
Alex man claims to be reincarnation of Pharaoh Tutankhamen.
PAGE 2

"Shame! Unscrupulous reporters out for a cheap scoop." That is how one newspaper responded to their rival's lead. But then they, too, saw fit to send their chief reporter to investigate the rumour. And Tutankhamen found himself enjoying a remarkable measure of attention. He was wined, dined and chauffeured around by different newspapers, each determined to outbid the other for his exclusive interview.

This was a major reason why he believed he was superior to Rambane. The latter was the only other surviving member of his 1959 sub A Class.

"*O-hwoo*, don't bother to mention that one. The alcoholic, the gobo, the idiot!"

"Who? Rambane, *e'sbotho leso*[38]," Tutankhamen would say dismissively whenever people mentioned his former buddy. Still, there wasn't much difference between them.

"Of course there is, Rambane has never had his picture in the newspapers."

"Except that time when he appeared in the Community News section for relatives to come identify a near frozen hobo found in a donga."

That was despite his having once challenged members of the Young Ones gang after their kidnapping of his younger sister and a girlfriend. That was also despite his telling the story over and over and storming the local newspaper and insisting they publish it. His audience would always ignore his animated gesticulations, frothings and swearings. Worst of all was when they dismissed his offer of money. He realised that prosperity had destroyed humanity when time-honoured gestures like honorariums were so easily spurned.

Tutankhamen started telling everyone that a large reward was coming his way. He would contentedly stroke his beard and rub his belly. He added that he was going to marry Sis Phuti. Everybody envied him, for Sis Phuti was one of those elegant beauties on the shebeen circuit.

The stories reached Sis Phuti. She stopped going to shebeens with us. Her face lost some of its furrows. Even the bitterness around her mouth disappeared. A robust

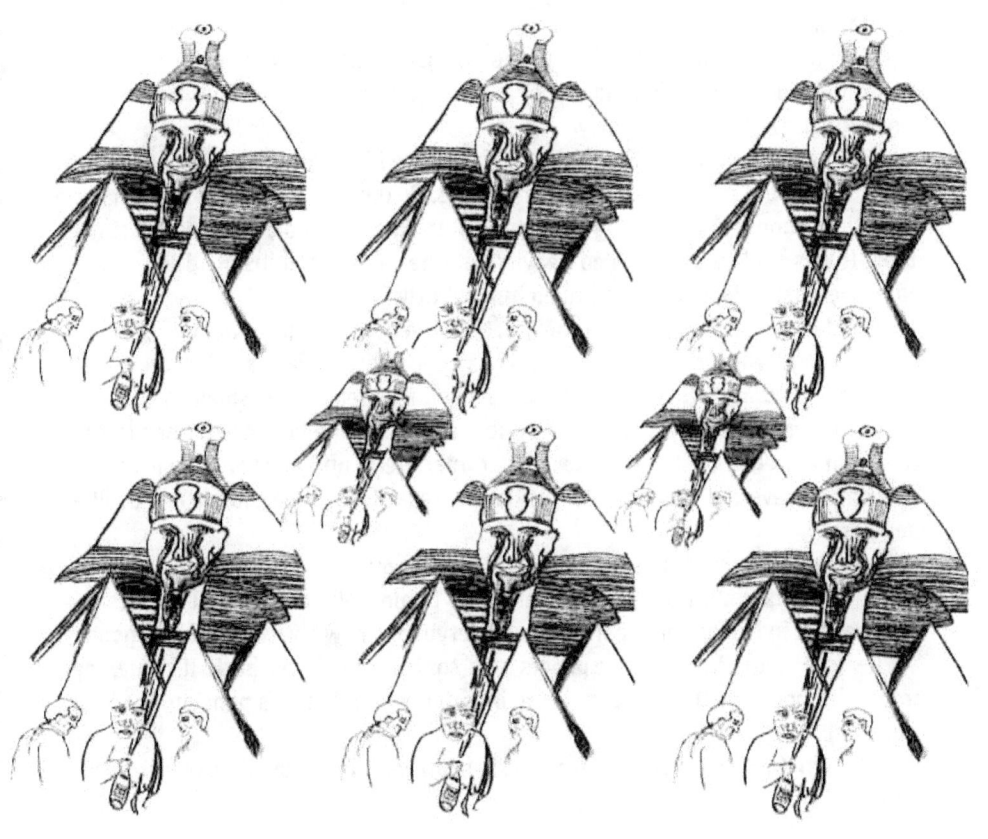

gait replaced her habitual slouch. Her female friends said she was now grooming herself for an expected life style on the East Bank or in Lombardy East, where the couple was naturally expected to live. She was also said to spend most of her Friday and Saturday nights practising new drinking manners: the delicacy that was reputed to go with wine sipping, tilting of the head when talking, throwing back of the neck, thrusting out of the bosom and gentle flapping of the hands when chatting and laughing with important people.

With concealed envy and overt wishes of good luck, we waited for the cash reward to be delivered. After months of patient waiting it became clear that somebody's tongue had slipped terribly.

Word passed round that Sis Phuti now frequented little known and remote shebeens. It was said she only stayed for brief visits. By the time we caught up with her it was three months later. During that period Tutankhamen had developed a distinct stoop. It was said to be weighted heavily with her abuse and insults. I was there when she finally slapped and ridiculed him publicly.

"S'botho tena! ... hmmm? Am I cheap ... hmm? Where is your Lombardy East? Sis! nja ena. Futsek with your cheap beers ... cheap babalaas. ... cheap smelly socks ...Seazi abanqono thina[39]. Not cheap dogs ... smelly underwear. ... sis! smelly armpits."

In stunned silence we watched. Despite the effect of the beer on our heads, the lessons of our elders hold firm: "Never ever interfere in affairs between a man and his woman. Never!" That is why to this day we regard marriage counsellors as idle meddlers.

Then I saw Tutankhamen's wrinkles and furrows pull tighter under the weight of that silence. Sis Phuti stood up and walked up to him. Without a moment's hesitation she spat in his face and marched out. Everybody knew she was gone for good.

"It's true ... ka Rre, the newspapers said so. Please call her back. It's true, my brother is gone. I am the sole survivor to inherit my grandfather's pension," he kept repeating.

At four in the morning, when I left the shebeen, he was still doubled over, bewailing his misfortunes.

Michael Vines

Graphics by Michael Vines

CONDITION ONE

A LOVE STORY

"All you need for a movie is a gun and a girl"
Jean-Luc Godard

There is an image that will remain forever in my mind. An image that is stamped indelibly on my unconscious. I swear it's true. You may not believe any of this, but I'll tell you. I bet anyone would love to claim this image as their own, have it in their head every morning to wake up to.

Here is my memory:

A girl, with mussed blonde hair and pink heart-shaped lips, points a gleaming silver gun at me. One eyebrow is raised, and fine blue veins stand out in her wrists as her finger tenses on the trigger. I notice, not for the first time, how her arms are impossibly smooth. She is lit from behind. The fine blonde hair on her arms shine. I look deep into her relentless eyes, eyes that have seen death many times before. Despite an underlying sense of terror, I can't help but feel turned on. There is a sharp noise from behind her; I see a couple walk into the bar. One of them – the girl – screams, and they back out, their shoes squeaking on the polished floor. The blonde girl twitches, pulls the trigger. The gun jerks and a hot white light flashes from the muzzle. I feel a shocking thrust at my chest, an invisible force pushes me back and to the floor. My body is numb, useless. There is no pain. At least, not immediately. I hear no sound after the bullet hits me, no sound except a song playing in my head. Mick Jagger sings *Sweet Black Angel,* and I spin, my arms flailing, the lights above me turning, and my head hits the ground.

Whoomp.

"I love you," she says from above.

But wait.

I'm getting ahead of myself here.

I met her at the all night store in a Caltex garage off Louis Botha Avenue on a quiet Saturday night. I was on the way home from a friend's place. It was about half past one in the morning and I was trembling with caffeine overload. I'd had so much coffee that night my eyes felt as though they'd been stapled open. My mouth was sour and my spit had turned to paste. If I hadn't stopped at that Caltex shop for some mineral water and chewing gum none of this would have happened.

I thought it odd that the Select store was so still inside. It had the strained, hushed atmosphere of a public library. I smiled at the cashier and said hi. She stared at me and said nothing.

"Okay," I said and turned down an aisle. I picked through packets of gum, examined the brightly-coloured packaging. I found some Clorets, tore open the green packaging and tossed a piece into my mouth straight away. I looked over to the cashier.

"I'll pay for these just now, all right?" I said, in case she thought I was stealing them. The last thing I needed in the early days of my law degree was a conviction for theft. It would look terrible on my CV. The cashier said nothing. The wide whites of her eyes freaked me out.

My Buffalo shoes shrieked on the polished floor as I made my way to the refrigerators that lined the far wall. I felt very aware of myself and made up my mind to get out of there as quickly as possible. I grabbed a bottle of mineral water, and walked swiftly to the counter. As I placed the bottle onto the counter, I saw that it was sparkling water, which I disliked. Glancing again at the cashier I decided not to replace it, just to get the hell out of there. She made no effort to serve me. I had the impression she was melting. Rivulets of sweat ran down her face from her hairline to her chin, where they gathered, and dripped to the counter. I looked at her red name tag and leaned forward.

"Can I pay for these, Gladys?"

My voice sounded louder than it really was. I should have known something was wrong. After a few long seconds, Gladys reached for my bottle of Schoonspruit and lifted the scanner with her other shaking hand, her eyes still fixed straight ahead. I realized I was still holding the torn-off bit of wrapper from the Clorets pack. Again I leaned over the counter, looking down at Gladys' feet.

"Do you have a rubbish bin down there?" I asked. "I need to throw this away."

I heard Gladys fill her lungs with air and a lithe figure leapt from the floor at Gladys' feet, belting her across the face with a shiny metal object. I fell backwards, bringing a stand of Mars Bars crashing to the ground with me. I lay still. My glasses were beside my head. One of the lenses had cracked.

"You fucking idiot!" someone was screaming, "You had to look behind the count er, didn't you?"

I opened my eyes and saw a face directly above mine.

"Get up!" shouted the girl, kicking me in the ribs with a pointed black shoe. "Get the fuck up."

I lifted myself up from the floor. The girl was roughly the same age as me. She had bleached blonde hair and thick lips painted a rich magenta. She wore a sky blue vest that sat an inch above black leather pants, revealing a sly strip of tanned belly. On her feet were expensive black leather boots.

"Nice shoes," I mumbled weakly. My attention turned to the silver gun that she held in her hand, casually pointed in my direction. The best thing would be to stay calm, I told myself, just don't babble.

"Why did you hit that lady?" I asked her. Shit, I thought. I thumped my thigh with a tight fist.

She examined me in silence.

"You're a nerd, aren't you?" she said.

I opened my mouth to reply, but she held up a hand. "It was a rhetorical question, dummy."

She strode back to the other side of the counter and tapped the CASH button on the till. The drawer slid open, rattling the coins inside. She grabbed handfuls of money from the drawer, a couple of two hundred Rand notes, but mostly fifties and tens. She pushed them into a plastic packet and dropped some five Rand coins in there as well. I stood motionless. I had no idea what to do. I thought it better to let the girl carry on. She seemed to know what she was doing. I would do whatever she told me, until the police came and rescued me.

I looked out the door, hoping to see a flickering blue light. Reading my thoughts, the girl said, "They're on their way, don't worry. Gladys touched the panic button when you came to the counter."

Nervously, I joined her behind the counter. Gladys was sprawled out on the floor. Her face was a mess. Blood streamed from her nose and her mouth. Several packs of cigarettes were scattered over her inert body. The blonde girl knelt beside her, took a pack of Gitanes from her lap and ripped at the cellophane. She flipped the box open and offered me a cigarette. I shook my head. She shrugged and lit hers with a lighter from a rack on the counter.

"Is she dead?" I looked at the prone cashier leaking blood.

"No. Her nose is broken, though. And maybe her jaw."

My stomach twisted, I could feel the gallons of coffee I had consumed earlier rise. I began to salivate, which happened whenever I was going to puke. I swallowed repeatedly, forced my stomach to settle.

"Where are the rest of the staff? And the petrol attendants?"

"I locked them in the toilets," she said. "You fucked everything up. Gladys was about to open the till for me when you arrived. It was the easiest robbery I'd ever done, I was thinking. No violence, just a neat in and out." She rested her elbows on the counter.

"You fucked it all up," she said again. "And now I'm going to take you hostage." She smiled and gestured towards the door with a wave of her gun. "C'mon, let's get going."

"Why?" I asked in alarm. "The police aren't even here, you don't need a hostage."

"I need some company," she said simply. "Put it that way. And you're cute and you look unhappy."

"I'm not unhappy. I'm fine." I managed a grim smile to show her just how happy I was.

"If you're so happy, then what are you doing buying fucking mineral water at 1:30 on a Sunday morning? And sparkling mineral water, at that. Gross. You should be out, having fun, or with your girlfriend."

"I don't have a girlfriend."

"You see?" she said, tilting her head. "You're unhappy."

She poked me in the ribs and her tone was harsh.

"Get a move on."

"My parents will worry about me," I told my abductor. She sat in the passenger seat with the gun in her lap. I drove her beat-up Toyota fast, obeying the directions she barked at me every now and then.

"Stop looking at my breasts," she grunted.

"I wasn't," I said, taking my eyes from the road and looking at her. I was indignant; her body was the last thing on my mind. "I really wasn't."

"Oh," she said vaguely. "Good."

"My name is Joseph," I told her.

"Okay. I'm Angelique."

"It's nice to meet you."

"Is it?"

"Well, I think so. I'm not sure yet. Maybe nice is the wrong word."

"I hope so."

"Maybe it should be life-changing. Angelique, it's life-changing to meet you."

The excitement I had felt earlier was gone, leaving fear and uncertainty in its place. I had no idea what she planned to do with me, and I had no desire to become embroiled in a shoot out between her and the police if we were stopped. I had a terrible image of my corpse being discovered in the boot of the Toyota sometime that afternoon, and I felt a rush of panic.

"Blue is the colour of freedom, Joseph," said Angelique suddenly. "Look at the sky."

The sky on the horizon was tinged a fiery pink, which collided with the receding black night. In between, blending the two colours, was a deep indigo. We had been driving for several hours now, and had left Jo'burg far behind. The sweet smell of fresh air rushed inside the car from Angelique's open window. We were in the flat dull landscape of the Free State, and dawn was about to break. Something shifted within me, and I grinned at my kidnapper. She smiled back. I remembered a trip to Durban as a child, leaving home in the early morning, falling asleep in the car and waking to a similar sky. We were probably halfway to Harrismith now.

"What are you going to do with me?" I asked.

"I'm going to buy you breakfast," she replied, tucking her gun into the back of her pants.

"Is that loaded?"

"Of course."

"Will it go off?"

"It shouldn't. The safety's on. It's the best way to carry it, especially in my circumstances — cocked and locked." She pulled it out and showed me. The hammer was pulled back, but the safety was switched to On.

"Easy to use in an emergency, you see."

She pointed at an approaching truck stop. "Pull in there," she instructed me. "There's a Golden Egg there, we can eat."

"Yummy," I said.

"Don't fuck around, Joseph. Remember, I'm the one with the gun, and you're the one with the piss-stained Calvins."

I felt stupid again. I had only noticed I'd wet myself when we'd been driving for about an hour. Angelique had found it hysterical. She'd snorted with laughter until I'd had the courage to point out that it was her car seat I had dampened.

At a picnic spot a while later, outside Villiers, she made me stop the car. She found a pair of jeans in the boot, and told me to put them on. They were a little long for me — she was a good two inches taller than me — and the waist was tight, but they were dry. She threw the damp Calvins I'd bought on my mom's Stuttafords account over the barbed wire fence that bounded the hard shoulder. She sat on the edge of a concrete picnic table and lit a cigarette. I sat in the passenger seat with the door open, breathing in the sharp night air and watching her swing her long legs.

"Turn on the radio," she hollered. I twisted a knob on the radio face, and found the Rolling Stones halfway through *19th Nervous Breakdown*.

Over the crackling reception, she asked me, "Do you like the Rolling Stones?"

"Not really. My dad does though, so I know most of their stuff."

"They're my best," she said. Her lips moved with Mick Jagger's voice: Here it comes, here it comes, here it cooomes! "What do you like?"

"I don't know, really. The Beastie Boys?" I said, examining my broken glasses. The left lens was cracked along the top rim, so I found that if I bent the frame a little, I could see out the bottom of it.

We sat opposite one another in red plastic seats bolted to the floor in the Golden Egg. She ordered a filter coffee and a burger, and I asked for a toasted cheese and tomato sandwich and a Coke.

"These places are shit," she said when we got our food, "but I love their burgers. God knows why. The coffee's good, too. It's frothy and milky and it makes you nauseous if you drink too much of it."

She wore a dark brown leather coat to disguise the bulge of her gun. There was a smear of blood on her sleeve. I glanced at the smattering of clientele at the other tables. I finished the last sip of Coke and wiped my mouth with a napkin. Music I vaguely recognized began to seep from somewhere. It was the Stones again!

"Oh my God," I said, in mock-surprise. "Is that blood on your sleeve?" I pointed to the patch of dried blood. I remembered Angelique picking up her coat from the counter after belting Gladys in the face.

A black waitress who stood nearby looked at me.

"Don't be silly, it's tomato sauce," said Angelique quickly.

I got up from the chair. "It's blood!" I said, louder now. People were beginning to turn towards us, pay some attention. A thickset hick with a mullet and a check shirt seemed particularly interested. He put down his coffee, scratched at his shadowed chin.

"Sit down," warned Angelique, her eyes like needles. "Sit down and shut up."

A heavy bass line, drums, guitar.

"She's got blood on her sleeve. It's blood. She killed someone!" I yelled, moving slowly away from her. "Help me!"

I got nasty habits, I take tea at three, said Mick Jagger.

She dropped the half-eaten burger to her plate. Tomato sauce spattered the table. She reached behind her and tugged the gun out from her pants. She slammed it on the counter, upsetting the hot cup of coffee. It spilled into her lap.

"Everyone get down on the floor!" Angelique yelled, her eyes darting about the place, taking every detail in, but not rising from her seat.

"Help," I said. "Help me!"

I watched the hick, his eyes were fixed on the sleek gun she'd pulled out

... my best friend he shoots water rats and feeds them to his geese ...

Angelique was up on her feet, her gun describing a threatening curve across the room.

"You've opened the gates of hell, Joey," she said to me under her breath.

I think that was when I fell in love with her.

The hick hit the floor, rolled. His hands went to his feet. I caught sight of a leather holster and a gun at his ankle. Waitresses wailed, they dropped behind the kitchen counter.

... don'tcha think there's a place for you, in between the sheets? ...

Screams, a woman screeched: "Oh my God, omigod!"

The music was growing louder, it was almost deafening: *C'mon now honey, don'tcha wanna live with me?*

The hick was on his feet, his own gun aimed at Angelique. "Sit neer die geweer, lady. Lady, put your gun down. Put it down."

He was so calm. And it struck me that I didn't want her to get hurt. I scrambled across the floor and stood in between them, to shield Angelique from him.

Piano.

... they got dirty necks, they're so Twentieth Century ...

She dived left, dropped to her knees, and there was a hideous explosion. A cartridge clinked almost delicately to the floor. My eardrums felt as though wads of cotton had been thrust against them.

A saxophone in my dulled ears.

A wet thud as the bullet hit the cop in the gut. There was a small magenta circle in the centre of his stomach. He gasped, made a throaty noise like a burp.

Piano, drums, bass, guitar, voice all building to a crescendo.

... the cook she is a whore, the butler has a place for her behind the bedroom door ...

Angelique grabbed a clump of my hair and pulled me towards the door. There was another explosion. The hick, I thought. A sheet of plate glass shattered right beside my ear. I cried out as shards of glass pricked at my face, my arms and my chest.

... don'tcha think there's a place for us right across the street? ...

... don'tcha think there's a place for you in between the sheets? ...

We sprinted across the car park, I was shouting and I could feel the warm muzzle of her gun in my back. Her boots thudded on the tarmac. It was a beautiful morning. Cars beeped at us as we ran in front of them.

"Hey!" someone shouted.

... don'tcha wanna live with me? ...

She bundled me into the passenger seat and I got a Colt across the bridge of my nose.

For days after the Golden Egg incident, we didn't speak. I was unconscious for nearly twelve hours, and when I woke up, I kept quiet, just watched her drive. She'd pass me beers, gum and take-away burgers, which I would accept without a word.

She had a medical kit, from which she gave me shots of morphine for the pain. My nose swelled to twice its normal size. I had a nasty cut on the bridge that should have been stitched. I still have the scar – it's quite impressive, I am often asked about it. My parents have even suggested plastic surgery to me, but it's a part of me now, I'm quite proud of it, and it's the only physical thing I have to remember her by.

The morphine knocked me out, but when I came around, the pain was there, always there. A blinding pain that seemed to have been building as I slept, gaining strength, ready to pounce as soon as I regained consciousness.

"Why," I asked her later, "can I always hear music when I'm around you?"

"It's my soundtrack," she told me, her white teeth bared in a grin.

"You have a soundtrack?"

"Mmh hmm. It gets annoying sometimes. Especially when I'm in bed with someone. You can only listen to Barry White for so long."

"I've only heard Stones stuff so far."

"Well, they're my best. I told you that."

And, as if on cue, the woozy strains of Neil Young's *Heart of Gold* washed through the car. We were crunching down a dirt road forty or fifty kilometres off the N2, near Pongolapoort Dam. The police were almost certainly after us, and though we couldn't remain on the main roads, we couldn't stray far either because we relied on the stopover garages and motels for food and accommodation. Bourgeois kid that I was, I couldn't go long without a bed or a shower. Angelique, if anything, looked better when she hadn't bathed for a couple of days, hadn't slept comfortably or eaten properly. She blossomed when covered in grit and grime from the road, living on fast food and beer. At night, she'd lie back on the bonnet and stare dreamily at the sky.

"D'you know any of the stars, the constellations and stuff?" she asked me once.

"Please be serious. I'm from the suburbs."

"Thought not," she grumbled.

"I can divine water, though," I said, but she didn't laugh. I suppose it wasn't that funny.

I climbed up onto the bonnet beside her. "You know," I said, "I wake up every morning and generally, I'm not in a very good mood. I mean, I don't think I'm very happy, and ..."

"And?"

"And I've never done anything about it. But you have. You've made a difference for yourself. I've never had the courage to do anything like what you've done."

She was looking at the stars again. "Maybe," she said. "Though somehow I don't think my parents would share your enthusiasm. Armed robbery isn't a widely respected industry. Though the money is tax-free."

I reached out to touch her hair, but stopped. Instead I said that I was tired and climbed into the back seat of the car to sleep.

I spent those first few days drifting in and out of sleep, watching her drive. She drove well, skillfully, unselfconsciously. It was sexy watching her drive. I fell in love with her during those early days. At first I thought it was the morphine, but that soon wore off, and my growing attraction to her remained, in fact, I was as dizzy and calm as I had been when I was under. I felt full, warm and safe

There was never a rainy day. The sun shone for the full six weeks I was with her. I smiled dopily all the time, the world was tinted in a rosy, Prozac sheen.

— that's not a good metaphor, Prozac suggests a thinness to the sensations she aroused in me. It was deeper, more ... whole than that.

Being with her was like chewing bubblegum, only better because the flavour never left my mouth. Bubblegum with which I could blow bubbles so big I floated away inside them.

But then, as I said, she had fed me a load of morphine.

We stopped at a little roadside cafe. It was a white windowless box set just off the hard shoulder in a field of rippling gold. A Coca-Cola sign and a board that said 'Sangeeta's Cafe' were all that decorated the exterior.

"We have to stop here," exclaimed Angelique, her eyes glowing, "It's the best place! I know the owner. She's so cool!"

INT. SANGEETA'S CAFE – DAY

The cafe is dull and comfortable. There is a bar counter along one side of the room. A few tables are scattered about the place. Weird Indian spiritual artwork hangs on the walls. Bare red globes light the place, hanging from the ceiling. The floor is concrete, decorated with rugs. Sunlight drifts lazily into the room from the open door highlighting the dust in the air. Three girls sit at a table drinking Sol beers. They look as though they are from the Northern Suburbs of Jo'burg, they are wearing expensive clothes and three cellular phones lie on their table. Their presence seems incongruous in such surroundings.

The place is totally Angelique, she fits in there like it was built for her. She is happy and relaxed, though aware of the girls.
Sangeeta knows Angelique. They are obviously old friends.

ANGELIQUE

Hello baby!

SANGEETA

Angelique, my darling. Who is this beautiful boy? Your lover?

ANGELIQUE

Not quite.

CU – Joseph's face. He seems upset by her answer.

JOSEPH

I'm her hostage. She kidnapped me.

SANGEETA

You don't look like an unwilling hostage.

FLASH ON:

Joey pointing the gun at a cashier in a snack shop.

BACK TO:

JOSEPH

Oh no, I am.

ANGELIQUE

He's Mick, I'm Keith. We're the Glimmer Twins. It's a beautiful relationship.

FLASH ON:

Angelique pulling Joseph by the hair from the Golden Egg, after shooting the cop.

Back to the cafe. The two seat themselves at the bar. Sangeeta puts a bottle of tequila on the counter and sets two tot glasses down in front of Angelique. The girls at the table are silent, they have been so since Angelique and Joseph arrived. They watch the two of them closely.

ANGELIQUE

I'm gonna teach you to drink tequila slammers.

JOSEPH

I'm not that much of a nerd, I've had tequila slammers before.

ANGELIQUE

Not like this.

She fills one tot glass with tequila, and the other with lemonade. Sangeeta, grinning

*expectantly, hands her a straw cut in two. Angelique pushes the glasses together
and puts a half straw in each glass. She bends over the glasses and pushes the
straws into her nostrils. She snorts the liquid up noisily and falls to the floor almost
immediately, coughing and spluttering.*

JOSEPH

Ja, you're right – never like that. But I've been quite happy with the more tradi-
tional form of drinking, using my mouth.

(he looks at the entrance to the toilet with mock interest)

Is that the bathroom? Excuse me for a moment.

ANGELIQUE

(getting up from the floor)

Wow! That's rad! Wait, wait.

(she rubs her nose, which appears to be bleeding)

Okay, it's your go.

*She fills both glasses again, and proffers Joseph the straws. He looks at her pour-
ing nose and shudders.*

JOSEPH

(laughing)

No, really, I'll er, have a Coke.

ANGELIQUE

Come on, man. Do it. You gotta do it, it's a rush, like eating chilies.

JOSEPH

Well, that's not something I make a habit of doing, either.

*Sangeeta fills one glass with tequila, the other with lemonade. Angelique hands him
the straws. The girls across the room are spellbound. A cellphone rings, they ignore
it.*

Okay, I'll do it. But just the one, alright? Fuck. This is insane. What's wrong with
drinking beer, for fuck sake?

ANGELIQUE

Ha! You said 'fuck'.

(to Sangeeta)

He said 'fuck'! Twice!

Sangeeta nods. Joseph focuses on the tot glasses, bites his upper lip in apprehension, sniffs to clear his sinuses, and takes his tequila slammer.

JOSEPH

Jesus Christ!

He leans over the counter, cupping his nose with his hands. He looks as though he's praying.

OKAY! Hot damn, that feels good!

Angelique bursts into hysterical laughter at him. They are both already trashed. She claps her hands, and orders another round. They snort it up together, and she ruffles his hair in a sudden rush of affection.

ANGELIQUE

You're doing well, baby!

She pulls her gun out, and spins it on the end of her index finger like Billy the Kid. Sangeeta winces.

JOSEPH
(uncomfortably)

What are you doing, Angeliqe?

ANGELIQUE

Chill, baby, chill. It's time to prove yourself. Rites of passage, Joseph.

She hands Joseph the gun, which he accepts awkwardly. She gathers up all eight tot glasses that lie on the counter in her hands, and nods towards the door. Her face is flushed, and snot, blood and tequila stream from her nose.

Come outside with me, kiddo.

They stumble out together, giggling. The girls at the table follow.

EXT. SANGEETA'S CAFE – DAY

CU – Eight tot glasses stacked along the bonnet of Angelique's Toyota, glinting in the late afternoon sun.

ANGELIQUE
(off)
Okay? You hit all eight glasses, and I'll let you kiss me.

Angelique's eye fills the screen. We see it close and then open again in a slow wink. Joseph holds the gun in both hands. Taking his time, and with intense concentration, he takes aim and squeezes the trigger. Nothing happens. Angelique leans over and flips the safety off.

JOSEPH
(sheepishly)
Sorry.

Angelique shakes her head.

ANGELIQUE
Don't be. Try again.

Joseph takes aim again. This time, when he pulls the trigger, one of the glasses explodes.

Well done, man! You're a regular outlaw!

Joseph grins broadly, but doesn't take his eyes from his target. In quick succession, he picks off the next six glasses. However, the final glass he misses. A bullet ricochets from the whitewashed wall of the cafe. One of the Northern Suburbs girls squeals.

JOSEPH
Shit.

He drops the gun to the ground. There is a pause, and Angelique throws her arms around him and kisses him anyway. He kisses her back, deeply. They are unaware of anything else around them. Her coat is lifted by a gust of wind. She wraps a leg round him. The chicks from inside have followed them out. They cheer. The camera spins round the embracing couple from a low angle. A glow of sunlight encircles their heads. There is the whine of a ricocheting bullet. It's the bullet that missed the last tot glass! It whizzes past our heroes, and smashes the glass to bits. They smile at one another, and begin to kiss again.

"You should have a cooler car," I said. It was late at night, and so dark that the world seemed not to exist outside of the Toyota. The only evidence of the world was the road lit up in front of us.

"What would you like me to have, Joseph?" She only called me Joseph now when she was irritated. "Something really inconspicuous, like a red Porsche, perhaps?"

"It would be great if you drove me around in a red Porsche."

"Hey, at least it's a silver Toyota. It's quite glam."

"Ja, a silver Toyota, that's lank rock 'n' roll," I sighed.

An hour or so later, a Golf overshot a red robot right in front of us. Angelique braked sharply, as did the black woman driving the other car. We narrowly missed colliding. She glared at us, angry that we had gotten in her way. Angelique stared blankly back, before opening her window and shooting out the chick's tyres. We rocketed away.

"*Shoch*," I muttered.

"Huh?"

"Oh. It's Yiddish, it means the same as *kaffir*," I explained, guiltily.

"That's not very nice."

"What? You mean, it's okay for you to blow away her tyres, but as soon as I show a hint of racism, you tell me I'm not being nice?" I sighed. "You're out of your tree."

"I didn't think you'd be a bigot. You're Jewish, aren't you?"

"What the fuck is that supposed to mean? Jesus, when did you switch into 'asshole' mode?"

"Sorry, man. All I mean is that Jews complain about being discriminated against, and then you call that lady a *kaffir*."

"You are a deeply sensitive person, Ange. Anyway, I called her a *shoch*."

"You said it means the same thing."

"You kill people, Angelique, I only called her a name."

"Ja, but I kill indiscriminately."

"That's admirable."

We traveled in silence for a while.

"Tell me some more Yiddish words, I want to learn some." Angelique still had the bubble gum going. She blew a bubble so big it stuck to the windscreen and burst, leaving a big pink splat there. "Shit."

I gave her another piece. "Okay," I said, "there's a *schnorrer*."

"And what's that mean?"

"It's a cheapskate, a sponge. A *nebbish* is like, an idiot, but it's more a term of endearment, and *meshuge* means crazy."

"They're very cool words. They sound like what they mean. How do you say 'fuck off'?"

"Um, I dunno,

"Ah, it's my best song!" She turned the volume up. It was a song I didn't recognize.

"And?" She started to blow another bubble, this one bigger than the last. She breathed into it slowly and skillfully so a shape began to form. A heart shape. She pinched the membranous pink bubble where it met her lips and passed it to me.

"And then there's *haish*," I said, looking at her out of the corner of my eye. I let the heart-shaped bubble out of the window, into the rushing wind, and watched it float into the sky.

"Mmh," she said. Her mouth widened into an evil grin. "I think I know that one." She pulled the car off the road. "Let's see if I'm right."

We were speeding up the R37, between Sabie and Nelspruit. It was a stiflingly hot afternoon. Angelique was driving, humming along to a Sly and the Family Stone song on the radio, an open bottle of beer in her lap. I sat with my bare feet up on the dashboard and one hand stretched along the back of her headrest, tickling the nape of her neck. The atmosphere was hazy with the heat and the road ahead looked as though it was melting into sticky pools of tar. On either side of the road were fields of green, green grass spotted with purple-blue cosmos; it was a beautifully pastoral hippie landscape, a relief from the otherwise dry countryside we encountered.

"Pass me some gum, won'tcha?" Angelique asked me.

I twisted around in my seat, picked through the piles of empty beer bottles, chip packets and creased map books that littered the back seat. I fished in a plastic bag of groceries we had bought from a supermarket in Nelspruit. Grabbing a pack of Bazooka Joe bubble gum, I glanced out of the rear windscreen. My jaw dropped and I grew queasy.

"Uh, Angelique."

"Ja?"

"Did you know there was a police car behind us?"

"Ja." Quite relaxed. "It's been following us for about twenty K's now. Don't worry about it, we've done nothing wrong."

"Nothing wrong? Are you kidding?"

"He doesn't know that though, does he?"

"Maybe not."

She lifted her foot from the accelerator a little, took the Toyota down to a sensible sixty km/h. I gave her the gum, she unwrapped it and passed me the wrapper.

"Read the cartoon and relax, kiddo," she told me.

I looked at the badly registered comic strip on the tiny oblong slip of paper.

"It's in Hebrew I think."

"So, read it to me."

"I can't read Hebrew," I snapped.

"You're Jewish aren't you?"

"Ja, but that doesn't mean I can read fucking Hebrew. It could be fucking Arabic, for all I know. I'm English-speaking, Angelique."

"Yes, I'd noticed that, Joey," she said in a voice steeped in sarcasm, "but I thought maybe you could read it, that's all."

"Well, I can't," I snapped.

Angelique pushed her lips together in annoyance, showing the dimple in her cheek.

"Look, I'm sorry," I said, feeling bad immediately, "I'm really hot and sweaty and tired, and—"

"Fuck you," she said under her breath.

"WHAT?"

"Not you, retard. The cop's got his lights on, he's right behind us. Shit fuck BAS-TARD," she said.

"Do you have to swear like that all the time? It really bugs me." I glanced up at the rear view mirror, and saw the shaky reflection of a traffic police car with its blue lights flashing. "You'd better pull over," I told her.

"Hey, that's a good idea." She slipped the heavy gun into the tray in the door, and slowing down, pulled off the road. She kept her eyes on the rear view mirror, half-listening to me.

"And that's another thing," I said. The beers I had drunk during the afternoon were bubbling to the surface of my system. I was on quite a roll. "You must do something about that sarcasm thing. I can't take you to meet my parents if you shout and swear and get cocky with them."

The cop got out of his car, and walked with deliberate ease to the Toyota's driver's side.

"Meet your parents?" yelled Angelique. "What the hell do you think this is,

Joseph? Did you think that that was what's going on here? She threw the door open at the very moment the cop stepped beside her. It caught him in the chest, and he bent double, his face an angry red.

"Vok!" he gasped.

"Sweet Jesus, Joseph, we're different. Can't you see that?" She stepped calmly from the car, the gleaming Colt in hand.

I knew what she was about to do, but I froze; I couldn't stop her.

Dimly, I watched as she fired into the policeman's chest at point blank range. The bullet knocked him off balance, and Angelique pushed him to the ground with a kick to the groin. A cloud of dust rose from around his twitching body. She stood over him and fired repeatedly into his uniformed bulk, holding the gun side on. The slide slammed back over her hand when the magazine had emptied. She flicked the release, and it clicked back into place.

"Joey," she said, "I love you. But I don't want to come home with you. I can't, I just can't." She stared dispassionately at the corpse, barely taking it in.

I couldn't believe what I was hearing.

"You what?"

"I love you," she said clearly, standing in a growing puddle of the policeman's blood, her shoulders slumped wretchedly. Glistening beads of tears fell like diamonds from her eyes, mixing with the blood in the dust. I scrambled from the car, slid across the bonnet to where she stood. I pulled her close to me and held her tight and kissed her tears away.

Taking her hand, I led her over the roadside gravel to a field of flowers. I kissed her again, hard, and pulled her to the cool ground, carpeted in sweet blue cosmos and soft green leaves.

And as we made love, I heard the unmistakable sweet soul groove of Mr Barry White.

We never stopped for long. There was the occasional night we spent in a motel, but generally, we slept in the car, or just drove, catching infrequent naps on the back seat. We were pretty certain that the police were after us, but their presence was hardly noticeable. Angelique and I only had a few run-ins with them, and it seemed quite safe to show our faces from time to time.

In one cafe, somewhere in Mpumalanga, I found an ancient Atari arcade game called *Captain Mookie*. As Angelique shopped for gum and beers, the staple diet on our six-week run, I played *Mookie*. The machine required two old twenty-cent pieces to play.

"Ange!" I shouted. "Have you got two old bits?"

From across the supermarket, she tossed me two silver coins. I caught them both in one hand, inserted them into the machine and began to play.

(split screen)

For me, playing video games has always been a talent. I think it comes from always having the things in the house. In *Captain Mookie*, I started out as a little rookie in a smart blue police uniform collecting ammo, bribes and bravery medals and killing crackheads and serial rapists, before being promoted, at level three, to a detective who did the same things, just with bigger guns.

"Get the bastards," commanded the voice of my superior back at Control throughout the game, "blow them away!"

It was evidently a game produced long before the more politically correct games of today, with their anti-drug stances. *Captain Mookie* was a good guy with a dark side. The game manufacturers were intelligent enough to understand that there are shades of gray in the eternal battle of good vs evil. *Mookie* was a good cop with a conscience, who made a little extra on the side. Where's the harm in that?

Angelique emptied a red plastic basket of groceries onto the counter, in front of the elderly man who owned the cafe. He smiled at her breasts.

"Good afternoon, lady."

"Hey. Can I get a pack of Gitanes, please."

He placed the cigarettes in front of her, and rang up the gum, beers, biltong, chips and chocolates.

"Forty-three seventy-five," said the man, watching the rise and fall of her bosom.

Angelique reached into a pocket in the front of her pants, slowly retrieving a box of tampons. "Oh, and these, too. Sorry, I nearly forgot about them." She held them out to him.

He coloured slightly, and took them from her, bowing his head. As he did so, she grabbed him by the ears, and slammed his head onto the counter. His nose burst, and he gave a gurgling cry through the blood that poured into his mouth. Angelique gripped his chin, and twisted his head around until she could see his face and his neck had broken with a wet snap.

"*Hello,*" she sang to him.

The gentleman slid off the counter, leaving behind a messy trail of blood.

"You could use one of these yourself," said Angelique, tossing the tampons onto his crumpled form. She wiped her bloody hands on his kakhi safari suit shirt as he grunted his last breath, and pressed the CASH button on the till.

"That character in the kinky uniform went on to form the Village People, didn't he?" said Angelique from behind me, licking an ice-cream.

"Did you buy that King Cone, or shoot someone for it?" I asked her, my eyes on the screen.

"I *bought* it," she replied, fluttering her eyelashes like a naughty girl to her dad.

"I'm very proud of you, kid. You've managed to spend almost ten minutes in here, and you've not pulled a gun on anyone."

She grinned at me. "A girl's allowed a day off, isn't she?" She looked at me oddly, as though seeing me for the first time. Neatening my collar, which had somehow twisted itself at the back, she said, "This shirt looks lovely on you." I had found it in a second-hand store the day before. It was a cool shirt, dark blue, with a wide Seventies collar. Angelique smiled at me again and kissed my forehead. She breathed into my hair. "We'll find a nice, comfortable bed in a motel tonight."

"Where'd you find the money?"

"Forget the money."

When I turned back to the arcade game, a mammoth gorilla kingpin pimp beat *Captain Mookie* to a pulp, and the screen flashed 'Game Over - Loser'.

"Shit," I said. "Level five, and I was almost Police Commissioner."

"Bad luck, geek boy. C'mon, we'd best be going."

We spoke as she drove. I found I wanted to tell her everything. And I was sure she felt that way about me.

"... and this dick said some shit, like, "Howzit babe, come boogie" and he kept pushing his dick into my leg, so I flicked my coat back and showed him the gun."

She had gone on the road just over a year ago, after shooting this guy in a club in Braamfontein.

"Cool."

"God, thank God I'm away from all that shit. Jo'burg drove me mental. I hated all the slang and the smart clothes, creeps in their matching outfits, and worrying about what crowd you belonged to."

"So you do come from somewhere."

"Of course," she said primly, "I went to Waverley, buddy."

I laughed. "And look what private education did to you. I bet you aren't on the past pupils board."

We sat without speaking for a while, watching the road in front lit up by the Toyota's headlights. The beams of occasional cars coming from the opposite direction merged with ours, connecting us with them for a few seconds. It reminded me of those secretive glances Angelique and I had begun to exchange. Those glances when, for a moment, I knew just what was on her mind. There was an intense silence, I was sure she was thinking something similar.

"What are you thinking?"

"I'm thinking we should get moving," she said, after a pause.

"Why?" I asked.

"It's the next scene."

"Scene?"

"We must move from set piece to set piece. Don't get bogged down in the mundane details of life, Joey, you'll go insane if you think too much."

"A marksman and a philosopher!"

She was in the car, revving the engine. "Don't get smart, four-eyes," she shouted over the engine's howl.

cut!

"Miss?" said the barmaid.

"Oh," said Angelique, "Can we run a tab?"

"Yes, you can pay later. But there's a call for you."

"Thank you," she replied, unflinchingly.

I stared at her. "Are you expecting a call from someone?"

"Of course not." She walked slowly behind the bar. I watched her, my knees bouncing up and down in agitation. I wondered who could possibly know that we were at this anonymous shit hole of a bar on the outskirts of Gauteng. It had to be a wrong number, I decided. That was it. Whoever was on the phone had to have asked for a blonde lady, and the barmaid had assumed it was Angelique.

"Yes, that's me," I heard Angelique say into the mouthpiece of the phone, shattering my theory.

Angelique turned her back to me and put a finger to her other ear to block out the noise of the gambling machines that pinged and hooted merrily. She nodded every few seconds, which seemed a little pointless to me. I wondered if this was some elaborate practical joke that she had arranged. I ordered another beer, and watched her back tersely.

She hung up and walked back to her stool, shaking her head in disbelief.

"What was that?" I whispered piercingly. I took a sip of beer, spilling half of it down my front.

"It's over," she said. "It's all over." She lay her head on the bar, and ran shaking

fingers through her hair.

"Over? What's over. Who was that?" I reached for one of her Gitanes, and lit the fat cigarette. I choked uncontrollably. My throat felt like it had been doused in petroleum and set alight.

"Mmh, nice," I said, holding the cigarette up to Angelique. I stubbed it out impatiently. "Please. Who was that?"

Angelique didn't reply. Instead, she snapped her fingers to attract the barmaid's attention.

"Can we have another round of beers and a round of tequila slammers, too." She turned to me, her eyes shining, heavy with tears. "It was a man called Allen Klein. He holds the rights to most of the Rolling Stones' songs from the Sixties. Apparently, since I have not been given the rights to use Rolling Stones songs on my soundtrack, I cannot continue doing so, and I have to disappear or he'll sue. This happy little phase is over, baby. We have to pretend it never happened. It's the end. I have to go."

It was like she had slapped me again. My nose ached sympathetically. "What? Why? How does this affect someone like you? You break the law all the time, you kill people, why should a threatened lawsuit frighten you? Are you fucking crazy?"

She let my questions fly past her like stray bullets. "He said that he would turn me in to the cops if I continued unlawfully using material that rightfully belonged to his company. He says he knows where I am, my movements, every last detail about me." She looked over her shoulder suspiciously. "Apparently, someone's on their way already as a little taster of what's to come if I persist in my illegal activities. I'm paraphrasing here, it was all a load of corporate jargon I could barely understand."

"Maybe I can iron this thing out. I'm studying this stuff."

"Joey, your parents are on their way here. I have to make it look as though you've resisted me, and then I can escape. I can't go to prison. And it's really time you carried on with your life."

"What?" I had lost my grasp on the situation, if indeed I had ever held it in the first place. "What?" I said again.

She held a hand up to me and looked at the tequila slammers that had been laid in front of us. "Hey! Who makes the drinks in this flophouse? No straws, and in one glass? What is this?"

"I love you," I said dispiritedly.

"Sssh," was all she said. "Sssh." She held her tot glass up to me. "Cheers."

I took my tequila, and we downed them together.

"I love you, too," she said.

And then she shot me.

If you trace the places we visited – as I have, hundreds of times – an interesting pattern appears. I think she was trying to tell me something. I have spent hours hunched over road atlases of South Africa, scribbling notes, plotting sketchy maps on draughting paper and acetate, based on half-remembered place names and sign-posts, vague memories of scenes in this and that town. I had thought, during our journey that Angelique was just driving. Driving from place to place, not caring where we ended up. But I now think she was trying to tell me something; she knew I would dwell on our weeks together.

Jo'burg down the N3, heading East at Harrismith. The R103 to Ladysmith. Up to Dundee, Utrecht, to Piet Retief, along the Swazi border, over the N4 and Nelspruit, through Sabie, heading North to Pietersburg, down the N1, veering off at the R520. A deep curve into what was Bophuthatswana, sensibly avoiding Pretoria and then hitting Rustenburg, re-entering Gauteng from the West.

You have to use your imagination a little, but it's there – an unbroken heart shape. The place names are less than beautiful, but join them in a particular way, and you've got true love.

And where's the harm in that?

I'm pretty sure she killed all the staff in the petrol station the night I met her and, in the reflection of the Atari game screen, I saw her break the cafe owner's neck that day in Graskop, but she never denied her homicidal tendencies. She remained true to herself, and to me, and that is what I learned from her, this blonde girl who wore the same clothes for the six weeks I spent with her, who chewed gum instead of brushing her teeth, who, in a mini-golf park, shot a man because he laughed at the blue bowling shirt she'd bought for me. A girl with ruffled blonde hair kept in place with pink Barbie clips who shot me in the gut with a Colt Delta Elite.

roll the credits

BLACK AND WHITE DISASTER (1997), OR: ANDY AND ME IN THE NEW AGE

Some love is fire: some love is rust:
But the fiercest, cleanest love is lust.
"The Wild Party"
Joseph Moncure March

there was light and then dark, dark and then light. Consciousness came and went with the quiet calm of the tides. Light and then dark, black and then white.

What I recall is hazy, like a picture so over-magnified only meaningless pixels remain

and consciousness returns slowly, naggingly. There is light, then dark; movement then calm. The old world washes over me tauntingly, daring me to slip back into its dark, churning waters. A constant pain radiates through my body, beginning nowhere and ending nowhere. I can feel it has been there for some time. I have grown accustomed to my body's dull ache, and drift listlessly inside myself. I dream of footprints in loose dry sand. Two pairs of footprints – hers and mine. Her hand is warm, and her smooth tan calf muscles pull attractively as she walks. She is an angel and she glows like neon

white starkness surrounds me, and there is a faint antiseptic smell in the air. I am sore, so sore, and I whisper Andy's name. I want to look around, but my head is held fast by a brace of some kind.

–Would you please hold your head still, a female voice instructs me.

–John, I'm only dancing, I say, and laugh.

Hovering through cramped corridors, I stretch my long body out. Strips of neon light flash above me, making the silver clouds that ricochet off the walls and ceiling shine. Four, maybe six faces appear and stare down at me. They execute a beautiful-ly improvised dance routine, and I smile in appreciation.

–Doctor Cunningham, I say, –that was wonderful!

i am naked, I realise. Naked in front of strangers. Andy peers through a gap in the curtains pattering through bright corridors, I draw sullen glares. A gown – once white, now grey – drapes my body, hanging just above my knees. I've always been so tall. The gown is open at the back with two flaps tied loosely at my shoulder blades, leaving my arse bare and cold. I sit on the edge of the bed and the gown rides up my thighs, revealing my groin for everyone to see. I find this oddly arousing, and now I understand how she felt in her short dresses, crossing her legs, hiding her sex with only her naked tan thighs

she lies back in my bed, parting her legs. She is naked, I am not. I move over her, covering her body, and our lips meet. I stroke her chin, her neck. I squeeze her small breasts, trace a circle over her flat stomach. I tangle my long fingers in the triangle of dark hair between her soft thighs, pinching at her skin. I relish the feeling of her skin against my fingertips; the contrast between the curls of her pubic hair and the fine skin of her thighs. She draws my hand closer to her vagina, and her breathing deepens gloriously. Blood thunders in my ears

on a stiff grey blanket I lay, willing the agony to leave my body. I pull my skinny white legs up to my pale belly, and catch a glimpse of my white Nikes. The police have taken the laces, and the thick leather tongues flop helplessly. My trainers were expensive, I saved for months to buy them. They are very cool shoes, but looking down at them now they seem wretched, robbed of any value bestowed upon them by the blue swoosh up their sides.

Andy sits beside me, propped against a rolled up blanket and smoking a filter-tipped cigarette.

—I didn't know you smoked, I say.

—I don't, Andy replies. —But you do. He pushes the moist cigarette between my dry lips.

I smile weakly

my ears ring, and Andy swoops past me through the corridors on a hospital cot, his arms spread wide, whooping gleefully. I watch him from the edge of my bed, swinging my legs, and clapping my hands in delight. His dark glasses flash under the fluorescent strips that line the ceiling, like a windscreen reflecting street lamps on the highway. A nurse turns the corner, moving directly into his path. I close my eyes and wait for the impact

she and I sit silently together on a black leather couch in the vastness of the Karoo. We sip red wine from crystal glasses and blow smoke rings into the hot dry air. Pointing at the desert floor, she whispers, —look!

I stare down, following the direction of her finger, and see two copper coins in the dust.

—Lucky pennies, she says, passing me one and pushing the other into a pocket in her black leather jacket

andy ruffles my hair gently, and gestures towards the man who occupies the cell I have been locked into. He stands rigidly, holding a cutthroat razor and a cupful of frothy water. I look up at him and ask, —What happens now?

—That's up to Andy, he replies sturdily. —Have you been charged yet? he asks me.

—No, I tell him. —Why are you here? I ask.

—Armed robbery, he tells me, wielding his blade menacingly.

Something unpleasant occurs to me. I turn around. —Did he steal her? I inquire of Andy.

—No, he laughs, — she wasn't stolen from you. You lost her along the way. Andy shakes his head, and his silver hair flops over his high cheekbones. —You disappoint me, he says, pushing back his fringe. Bangs. Andy calls his fringe 'bangs'

i run my fingers over her cheeks, along her chin, and down a pulsing vein in her throat. I tilt her head back, and lean against her, pressing my lips against her warm neck. From the pit of my stomach there rises a desire to bite into her, drawing a rush of blood. I imagine her hot coppery blood running over my teeth and onto my tongue

at the base of my bed is a large brown envelope. I crawl across snowy mountains of sheets and pillows to reach it. On opening it, I find an acetate sheet of x-rays. X-rays of my head, my head from every angle. Dark clouds, black troughs, and cloudy depressions fill the white shape of my skull. My eyes are visible in one section of the sheet, and I study them carefully. I swear I can see lucky pennies in the centre of both my eye sockets

andy holds my hand, leads me to a kindly nurse in a crisp white uniform.

—Excuse me, I say, —I've not been permitted any phone calls, and I would really like to call my mother. Andy taps me tentatively on the shoulder in support. The woman frowns, and tells me in Afrikaans that it is not permitted for me to make any calls.

—What's she saying? asks Andy. —Is there something wrong with her?

The sister turns away abruptly, but then looks back and says with slight hesitation, —Ja, ek kan seker 'n oproep vir jou maak. She smiles sympathetically.

I am a pathetic sight, black-eyed, cut and bruised. My effeminate and self-pitying demeanour can be of some use, I think. I give the woman several numbers. She studiously takes them down, and asks me what message I would like her to pass on to my family.

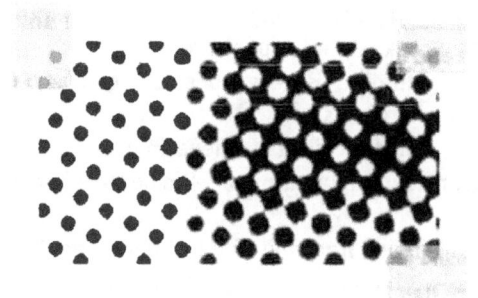

—Ask for some cigarettes, I slur.

—And some candy, says Andy. —Get me candy.

—And some candy, I dutifully repeat.

—*En wat van skoon klere en 'n tandeborsel*? she prompts me, helpfully.

—No thanks, I say. —Just the cigarettes and the candy.

Andy gives a fey smile, and standing on one foot shines a boot on the back of his leather pants

a young Jewish doctor and several interns stroll across to my bed. He peers indifferently into my dilated pupils. It's weird, I have discovered, the way people react to me once they learn I have attempted suicide. My very presence is ignored. I may as well have succeeded, the way people treat me now. Perhaps, in their eyes, I have lost — or lost the right to — my soul.

—How are you feeling this morning? the doctor asks me quietly.

—Cool, I say.

He gives an uncertain smile. An attractive blonde in a white uniform laughs silently behind her hand. I pull a face at her. She stops laughing. Andy is sat on a pillow beside me, peeling shell from an egg. —I'm sooo bored, he whines limply. He studies the clean white egg and pops it into his mouth.

—Can you remember what happened to your face? asks the doctor. —You're very badly cut and bruised.

—No, I say honestly. —I don't remember anything.
—Did the police do this to you?
—Dunno.
—I think that we can safely discharge you now, continues the doctor, earnestly. —The abrasions will soon heal.
—I'm going back to the cells? My head feels heavy, and my palms begin to sweat. —Could you prescribe me some Vaseline? I ask, and Andy falls off the bed onto the cold floor. I can see only the toes of his pointed black boots. He gets up.
—Ouch, he says ruefully, dusting himself off. There is a smidgen of yolk at the corner of his mouth

andy, sitting on my chest in the police van, tells me of love:
—Couples you see walking down the street hand in hand, licking strawberry ice-cream, they do it all for comfort; for the sake of convenience. It's all so false. There can never be love in a healthy relationship. And I should know, he says bitterly. He lays a hand on his chest and winces. I notice his black sweater is stuck to him. —I must be going, he says softly, staring down at himself.
Thin windows line each side of the van. Andy slides one open smoothly and squeezes out. When he is gone, I finger the rubber trim. There is something warm and sticky there. I examine my finger curiously. It is stained a deep red

busy people surround me. Blood seeps from my ears. Noises reverberate at an indescribable level, punching holes in the walls. A steady stream of white noise has ruptured my eardrums. Mouths move wordlessly. I am on my back; I smile up at the ceiling. Andy kisses the top of my head, and passes me a Love Heart. I read the inscription on the pastel pink candy. Someone is thinking of you, it says.
I lift the sweet to my mouth, but someone knocks it away, and I can hear it shatter, even above the uproar that surrounds me. I look up at Andy, watch his lips.
—Aw, geez, he says, frowning

andy takes yet more Polaroid's of my battered face.
—Please stop it, Andy, I beg meekly. Desert sand scours my throat with every breath. My chest aches and my ears ring. —I look like hell. Wait for me to get better.
—Oh, c'mon. There'll be no point. You'll look normal then, and it'll be so mundane.
I give in, exhausted, and settle back into my pillow. I watch him move about the cramped ward, cooing and mumbling appreciatively to himself

my friend crushes heroin the colour of earth into the black tip of a glass pipe.
—I knew you'd give in sometime, he says. I nod.
—Hey, you should try speedballing with me sometime, he enthuses. —It's lank

cool! You see, the coke takes you up. He raises his hand above his head. —And then the brown chills you out. His hand settles at chest height

we stand in the arid vastness of the desert. It is dusk, and in the sun's late glow, we watch the silhouettes of other lovers, walking hand in hand over the harsh landscape. She smiles at me over her shoulder and feels for my hand. I am surprised at this rare show of affection, and grip hers almost immediately. We stand holding hands, taking sips of pink champagne straight from the bottle, until the sun has all but disappeared. I push the bottle into a nearby wine cooler, packed high with sparkling ice, and begin to move my cold hands up and down her arms. She edges closer to me, thrusting her ass against me. I slip my frosty hands into the back of her little cotton dress, and feel around for her breasts. We watch all the people walk by. Her nipples stiffen

i am lying on my side, a hand brushes my gown softly from my shoulder, and cold fingers slip down to one of my nipples. I feel hot breath against my neck. Flapping a skinny arm lazily, I send Andy's glasses spinning from his big nose. He leaps back in shock, and picks up his shattered glasses. —Sorry, he whispers, —I'm so sorry. He runs from the ward, his arms swaying

—why are you here with me? I ask Andy. He is perched on a plastic visitors' chair, sketching my ugly feet.
—Don't draw my feet, I say, —I hate them.
Andy ignores my protest, and continues drawing. —I'm not here by choice, he laughs lightly. I was sent here to do some work.
—Like a guardian angel? I ask in disbelief. It's my turn to laugh. —God hires out dead celebrities as guardian angels? My stomach is still so sore, but I can't help laughing.
The other patients in the ward glare at us. Andy gives another fluttering chuckle.
—It's a cool concept, huh? One of mine, he adds thoughtfully

she kisses my unshaven cheek, her full lips make faint smacking sounds. Our hips grind together restlessly

—but why were you sent here, Andy? Please tell me, I beg, growing frustrated. The policemen in navy-blue uniforms are steadily approaching my cot to take me back to the cells, and I must know the truth.
—Forget it, he says, a little sharply. The cops have guns that glint in the artificial yellow light, and Andy sits glumly, filing his neat fingernails

damp thighs grip damp thighs. Hot hands wipe glistening foreheads. Shallow breathing, a fumbling of dry lips and tongues. Ruffled hair and cold air

heroin tastes like burning plastic. I draw a lungfull of smoke from the pipe, and feel an immediate rush. As I corkscrew into unconsciousness, I can hear my friend laughing at me. When I wake up he is gone. I leave his flat, pausing only to vomit in a plant pot in the hallway. Everything is water. The light bends and twists. I breathe in thick heavy air. In my car I take a gulp from the whisky bottle I find on the passenger seat to rid the sour taste of bile from my mouth

—what time is it? Andy asks me. I look up at him sitting on the window ledge. It seems an age since he has last spoken to me. I shrug and return my gaze to the sterilised floor, avoiding the eyes of the other patients. I am in a room full of criminals, black criminals, I think. Never before have I been in such close proximity to black people. I am terrified of making any mistakes.

The man in the cot directly opposite me attracts my attention and raises his fingers to his lips. —*Ugwayi*? he says. Cigarette?

I nod nervously, and he tosses me one across the ward. I give him an uncertain but grateful smile

i light the cigarette and inhale luxuriously. A welcome cloud of smoke plunges into my pink wet lungs. I breathe deeply and nicotine washes numbingly through my system. I hold the smoke deep inside for longer than I should, like she used to do with me.

—That's enough, snaps Andy, snatching the cigarette from me before I've even exhaled. He hands it back to the black man in the cot opposite.

—Do you want to get yourself killed? hisses Andy violently.

—What, again? I giggle, pulling his hand to my mouth and tenderly kissing his fingers one by one

it's the first time I have seen myself in God knows how long. I stare at my battered reflection in the bathroom mirror dispassionately, poking at every bruise and gash.

—Careful, shudders Andy.

—You've taken pictures of this? I ask him.

—Don't worry, he says vaguely, —I'll paint all that out in the final portrait. I always cover zits and blemishes in my portraits.

—These are a little more serious than blemishes, Andy, I say.

—Jane Fonda, continues Andy, ignoring me, has terrible skin. Simply awful. He puts a hand to his face.

—So why not take photos when my face has healed?

—There's really no need, says Andy quietly. I look at him, trying to see through his sunglasses and into his eyes, but he turns his back to me

she stands quickly, as soon as I've withdrawn from her. Gathering underwear from the cold tiled floor, she says impassively, —I have to go.

—What? I say groggily. A dream had already begun to wash itself across the inside of my eyelids.

—I'm leaving, she says again.

—Stay, I say, waking quickly. —Lie with me.

She sits down awkwardly on the rumpled bed. I hold her, stroke her clammy shoulders. She pulls away, frowning. A tear slides down her cheek and drips onto the bed.

—I have to go, she repeats. She gets up and walks to the door, waits for me there. I pull on my pants and patter over the icy floor to where she stands. She leans down slightly and gives me a quick kiss. She opens the door and steps out into the night.

I go back to bed, straighten it, and fall into a strange and fitful slumber

—you are the sign of the approaching millennium, Andy tells me calmly. I look up at him in alarm. I did not expect such words from him. Andy drifts above me, arms open wide. His black turtleneck sweater sleeves hang over his fingers. An eddying light radiates from behind him, making his wig twinkle like a fibre optic lamp.

—Marilyn Monroe was a sad, beautiful individual, he says, —you, with your battered face, your body pumped full of sedatives and heroin, your shattered ego and your self-pity, you represent the new age. An age of a sheltered, pampered generation incapable of coping with responsibility. Welcome to the new age, a giant Screw up. You are within everyone, and the world must recognise your qualities, those that are within them, too.

—You aren't really going to remove the blemishes in my portrait, are you? I ask him, still trying to come to terms with Andy's radical metamorphosis.

—Of course not, he says, a wry smile momentarily touching his mean lips. —Disasters are no longer rare, shocking events. Disaster is everything and everywhere. Normality and goodness are now only rare, shocking moments in this frenetic ruin of a world. You are disaster, and I see your face in everyone else's.

I begin to cry. Warm, salty droplets run over my cheeks and onto the hospital pillow. And this shocks me, shocks me more than anything that has happened since I arrived in this twilight world. I haven't cried for so, so long. I have quite forgotten how it feels. My throat is tight, I cannot swallow. My nose bubbles with snot, and my chest heaves. I don't understand, I don't think I ever have.

—Andy, I say. —I thought you were my friend, Andy.

Tears run into my mouth.

—Oh, please, he growls. —How do you think I became immortal? Fragility? Don't fool yourself. I don't have time for pathetic bullshit like this

sitting in my dirty white car, I drain the last drops from the bottle of cheap whisky. I stare out the windscreen at the light in her bedroom window. The light shifts in and out of focus, streaking this way and that through my line of vision. The heroin I smoked hours before still rushes through my body. I throw the bottle to the floor, and scoop up a pile of sleeping tablets that litter the passenger seat. I cram them into my mouth, simultaneously chewing and swallowing. I gag at the taste. They remind me of the bitter quinine tablets I had to take as a child whenever my family visited my aunt and uncle in the Eastern Transvaal

i hang from a steel girder high above the city. She stands towering above me, her heavy black shoes crushing my fingers. A howling wind threatens to wrench me from the scaffolding, into a sky the colour of slate. Rain falls heavily onto the empty streets far below me, every drop reflecting light from the swirling neon Coca-Cola signs that cling to the sides of almost every building.

I stare down at the slicked streets, and her face appears before me. She glows with a light more piercing than a thousand flashbulbs popping at once.

—I love you, I tell her.

But her eyes show a deep cavernous rage, her pupils burning red and so dilated they eclipse her irises.

—You are nothing, she whispers softly to me. —There is nothing you can give me. I feel nothing for you. I never have. She moves closer to me; our noses touch. —Feeling comes from within, she murmurs venomously, —from somewhere inside you, not from your fingertips, or your groin.

She spreads her wings, and drifts into the clouds

i stop my car at the side of the road. Falling out of the open window, I land on sharp gravel, cutting the palms of my hands. I kneel, my back against the front wheel for support. Hunching over, I jam a filthy, bloody fist into my mouth and poke at the back of my throat. I retch hard, but nothing comes up. I try again, stretching my lips so wide that the corners of my mouth split. Vomit erupts from my mouth onto the gravel and up my car door. The headlamps of a passing car illuminate the spatters of vomit. The car doesn't stop. I fall forward, retching and shuddering. Silvery strings of saliva hang from my lips. Wiping the back of my hand against my mouth, I rise slowly and clamber back inside my window

and there is someone in the passenger seat. I screw up my eyes in confusion.

–Hi! says the shadowy figure, passing me an empty whisky bottle, –Looking for this?

Concentrating, struggling against the grip of the pills that dissolve gradually in my heaving stomach, I see the stranger more clearly. He is wearing sunglasses, despite it being a particularly dark night. A line from a trashy film I watched as a kid pops into my head: –*When you're cool, the sun shines on you twenty-four hours a day.* He is dressed all in black, and has white – no, silver – hair, mussed like he's just woken up.

–God, you smell, he says, sniffing at the air distastefully. –You have baaad BO

He smiles warmly. –My name's Andy, he tells me.

–Hi Andy, I say, managing a wan smile

And then Andy's dark form seems to bleed from its edges, like an ink blot on a page, slowly filling my vision until I can see nothing else

(fade to white)

BATHTUB

"Shall we bath just now?" he asked her.

Maisie nodded. "Just now."

She was making a salad: spinach, small cubes of soft mozzarella cheese, tinned tuna, fresh plum tomatoes with olive oil and balsamic vinegar.

"Did you get a magazine today?" she asked.

"Ja." Alan stood behind his girlfriend, holding a bottle of beer. He put his hand on the small of her back as she twisted a pepper grinder over the bowl of salad. He walked through to their lounge, noticed that the music had stopped. He returned the CD to its cover and put something else on. Maisie didn't recognize it, she thought it might be something local, it was jazz and had a tinge of township to it. She moved her hips from side to side, placed a loaf of bread in the oven. She wiped her nose with the back of her hand and drummed the kitchen counter, trying to remember what it was that she had been thinking a moment ago. *Wine!* She found a box of wine in the fridge and poured herself a glass. She took a sip, glad for its coolness. It was late November and the nights were becoming warmer.

She looked from the kitchen out through the lounge and couldn't see Alan. She saw a movement out on the balcony and joined him there. They had hung out a strip of small red lights shaped like chillies, and they stood beneath them, watching over the street below. They lived on the first floor overlooking a street filled with restaurants and bars. The nights were busy and noisy, but quietened down by about twelve, and it was surprising how much noise they could block out by simply closing the sliding door that linked the lounge to the balcony. The other tenants of the block were mainly young, like Alan and Maisie, but had Playstations and smoked weed. Constant electronic bleeps and squelches and the smell of dope floated over their balcony in the evenings. Most of the other tenants seemed to work in advertising or, like Alan, as journalists. An up-and-coming photographer who was in the papers the week before last, dead in a car accident, had lived two doors down on the same floor.

There was the sound of loud voices below them. They looked down to see a young guy pushing away a stoned beggar, then get into a yellow sports car and screech away. He drove up and down the street several times, the engine roaring. Then he parked it where it had been before, directly below them, only facing the other way.

"That's the new Saab," said Maisie, who knew about these kinds of things.

"Oh?" said Alan, who didn't.

"He's the guy who owns that new bar on the corner, next to the Italian restaurant.

Leon. My brother was at school with him."

"I thought I recognized him. He looks familiar."

They watched him walk back into the café beneath them, smoothing back his ponytail with the palms of his hands. He walked with an exaggerated roll, as though his shoulders were too heavy to move both at once.

"I didn't know people still had ponytails," said Alan.

"Only Lebanese gangsters."

"He's a gangster?"

"Something like that."

"Did you see what he did to that street kid?"

"Ja, I know. He's a dick, you shouldn't let him bother you."

She touched his arm.

"Should we eat now? The bread will be done in a couple of minutes."

"Okay. I just want to have a cigarette."

"Get one for me, too," said Maisie.

He went inside and got his cigarettes and a lighter. He lit one for her and then one for himself.

"Thanks," she said. She took a drag and, with her other hand, rubbed her nose again. "I think I breathed in some pepper. It's driving my nose crazy."

"You're going to win some money," said Alan.

"What?"

"Isn't that it? An itchy nose?"

"Oh. No that's itchy palms. An itchy nose means that we're going to fight."

Alan smiled. "We never fight."

"We might. We have to do pinkies."

"Pinkies?"

"Ja." She held her small finger out. "Now hold my pinky with yours. There, now we won't have an argument."

"Good," said Alan. He tossed his cigarette onto the road so it bounced off the yellow car and onto the street in a small shower of sparks. A young black boy, a beggar, looked up at them vacantly and hissed.

"Alan!"

"I didn't mean to do it."

"Ja, right. Come. The bread'll be ready, I'll get it out of the oven. You go run a bath."

He lit candles in the bathroom, the short fat one on the cistern and the tall ones that Maisie had melted into place on the pine cabinet beside the bathtub. He lit a stick of sandalwood incense – the smell of which he hated, but she enjoyed – and turned the taps on. He poured a generous amount of herbal foam bath into the running water and removed his clothes. He sat on the toilet seat naked and breathed in the sweet smell of the incense. The steam rising from the tub diffused its smell, and he thought it not too bad.

Maisie came in and closed the door. "Mmh, that's nice," she said. She took off her clothes and placed a foot in the water. "Ow! It's too hot."

Alan said, "Pour in some cold water. I just want to get another Castle." He got up from the toilet and opened the door again. Maisie studied his thin body, usually pale, given a healthy glow in the candlelight. She didn't like his body much; it was far too skinny, although he had a nicely defined stomach. But she loved him. He was kind and he made her happy. He walked through to the kitchen.

"Get the other towel from on top of the washing machine," she called.

"Okay."

"I'm just getting the magazine," he said.

She heard a loud banging at the front door.

"Shit," she said, and heard Alan echo her a moment later.

"I'll get it."

"But you've got no clothes on," she shouted.

"It's okay, I've got the towel."

There was a quirk to the design of their flat. The front door didn't open straight into their flat, instead it was set at the end of a mystifyingly long and narrow corridor that intersected their living room. As she heard Alan patter down the corridor, Maisie thought of something.

"Don't open the door! It'll be that guy from downstairs—"

But she heard the door open and him say, "Hello?"

She heard a thick voice say: "Hey, you fucking poes. Did you throw that cigarette?"

"Uh, ja," said Alan. "Sorry about that. It wasn't intentional."

Maisie stood, wrapped a towel round the top of her breasts and crept to the door of the bathroom, put her head around the corner. At the end of the corridor, she saw Alan standing in front of the Lebanese guy from downstairs, who was angry and drunk. A small crowd of his friends stood unsteadily behind him. She had no idea what to do. He was sure to beat Alan senseless.

"Shit," she muttered. "Shit."

"Don't be sorry, cousin," said the guy, whose name was Leon. "You're in kak now." He grinned nastily and pushed at Alan, hitting him hard in the face. Alan fell back and to the floor, actually skidding over the polished wood. His white towel fell from

around his waist, exposing his penis. He looked down at himself, at the floor and then up at Leon, who towered furiously above him. There was a pause, a few moments in which everything seemed hushed and still to Maisie. Then Alan licked his lips. He made no effort to cover himself. He simply stood up, nude, and gave Leon a soft smile.

"Why don't you come in?" he asked gently. He began slowly to walk towards Leon.

Leon stood still. He opened his mouth and closed it again.

"What?" His voice sounded strange; there was a quaver to it. He screwed his face up into an expression of confusion and what looked to Maisie like panic. His friends stood behind him, jeering. A grimace briefly touched his lips. He threw a fist at the air in front of Alan.

"Fucking faggot," he said. "Faggot!" he screamed.

His friends laughed loudly. One of them dropped a glass. The smell of whisky filled the air. Leon turned around, punched at the front door and left. They all marched off, shouting and yelling. Alan stood naked in the passage, staring straight ahead, his blue eyes dark. His hands trembled slightly. A woman appeared at the door. She stared at Alan, glanced down at his dick. "Oh my God!" she said and giggled loudly. She rushed away.

Maisie stepped quickly over to Alan, and put her arms around him. "Are you okay, babe? Are you alright? He hit you so hard."

"I'm okay," said Alan quietly. He reached over and slammed the door shut. He chuckled. "I deserved that, I suppose."

"No, you didn't." Maisie was almost in tears.

They sat in the bath, facing one another. It was hot; they both loved hot baths. They heard it was raining softly now. The bathroom window was open and cool air filled the room. A heavy blanket of steam rose from the water. The bath was filled with white foam from the bubble bath Alan had poured in. The water turned their flesh pink and their fingers wrinkled almost immediately. Alan sat against the taps. He held a knotted dishcloth filled with ice cubes to his cheek. It was swollen, already beginning to show a purple bruise just below his right eye. Maisie held the Virgin Ass magazine up out of the water and said: "Okay. Which story do you want?"

"What are the options?" he asked, relaxing a little.

She shifted herself up. Her bottom squeaked over the tub. "There's 'Fuck My Face', 'Finger Banging', or," she leafed through the magazine, "'Wild in the Cuntry'. That's 'cuntry' without an 'o'."

"I thought so," grinned Alan. He drank the last of his beer. "I think I'll go for 'Fuck

My Face'. It sounds the most promising, artistically speaking."

"Okay. Good call." She cleared her throat and began to read. "My pussy is so small that I am scared of big dicks. Don't get me wrong, I love big cocks and one of my biggest fantasies is fucking the hugest cock I can find."

"She's a girl with ambition," said Alan, nodding. "I can relate to that."

He watched Maisie as she read the story. She was concentrating fiercely through the steam. Every now and then she'd pick up her glass of wine and have a sip, still looking at the page.

Maisie giggled. "Wait. There's a good bit coming up: He looks back at her and starts fingering my pussy, but there's no way I'm going to let him fuck me with that big dick ... "

"This is like poetry, babe," said Alan. He was on his third beer. He felt light-headed and though still shocked from his encounter with Leon, felt good. He brushed a piece of damp hair from Maisie's forehead and settled back against the soft towel that hung from a rail behind him. Their nights at home together made him happy, though he often worried that Maisie would tire of staying in so often.

" ... sure enough, after a couple of strong jerks with my fist and some more mouth on his knob, the fucker blows his load straight down my throat and that makes me the happiest little whore in the whole neighbourhood. The end." Maisie looked up at Alan and grinned. "Evocative stuff, hey?"

"It moved me," he said solemnly. "I cannot believe it is a work of fiction."

She laughed and leaned towards him and they kissed.

"We should eat now."

"Ja," he said.

They ate supper watching the news on TV. There was a news item on violence in Kwazulu-Natal, they saw footage of some flooding in the Cape. There had been a volcanic eruption in the Far East; almost ten thousand people had died.

"I like this bread," said Alan, mopping up the remains of his salad and olive oil with a thick slice.

"It's great. I got it from Pick 'n' Pay. It's only half-cooked, so you have to put it in the oven and it's like, freshly-baked when it comes out."

"Won't you pass me the wine?"

Maisie refilled his glass for him. She watched him as she did, spilling some wine on the table. Her mouth opened and closed again. He raised his eyebrows at her.

"What's wrong, babe?"

She cleared her throat and had some wine.

"How come you invited Leon in like that?"

Alan laughed softly. "I didn't know what the fuck else to do. I was shitting myself. Guys like that never know what to do when they're presented with a situation that might make them seem gay."

"How did you know he wouldn't come in and hit you again?"

"I didn't."

"I'm sorry I didn't do anything."

"Don't be." He moved over to her and held her. "There was nothing you could have done. I shouldn't have thrown that cigarette onto his fucking car. It was a ridiculous thing to do."

Her head was on his shoulder. She looked up at him. Her eyes were pretty, dark and appealing.

"I could have spoken to him," she said.

"That would have done nothing. And it would have blown my cover."

"I did pinkies with the wrong person. If I'd gone downstairs and made him do pinkies, none of this would have happened."

"I somehow can't see Leon doing pinkies with anyone."

Maisie laughed. "Sorry," she said, but she kept laughing. *"Do you want to come in?"* She laughed even more. Alan laughed too. He looked around the room, at their things, the paintings a friend of Maisie's had given them; at their furniture bought from second-hand stores or handed down to them from parents; at the windowsill that served as a bookshelf, housing their sun-bleached books and at the damp patch in the corner of the ceiling.

"I like living here," he said.

"Me too."

"It's our place."

"Yes; ours."

They watched a margarine advert and went to bed. Alan read for a while, propped up against the pillows and Maisie sat on the floor by the bed, smoking a cigarette and playing with a thread that hung from the sleeve of the thermal vest she slept in. She watched Alan as he read, his eyebrows arched in concentration behind his buckled glasses, his lips twitching slightly every now and then. When sitting up in bed, he liked to wrap the duvet around his long body, tucking it under his back and thighs, making him look rather like a literate worm in a cocoon.

"I love you," she told him.

Alan peered down at her myopically.

"I love you, too."

Phaswane Mpe

Graphics by Patrick Rorke

LERATO'S ORDEAL

It was not very bright in the bar. The main lights were switched off. The only lighting came from the TV screen. Lerato and two fellow students sat close to the TV set. Jack stood behind the counter, where he was selling the beer, and from which he was watching the TV as well. They were all arguing about who was the player of the day in the rugby match.

Refentse walked in, greeted them all with his usual cheerfulness. Lerato did not need to catch whiffs of lager from his breathe to realise that he was a little excited. Excited, for he had always refused to call himself drunk. The two exchanged a few pleasantries. Refentse then approached Jack. Lerato's eyes wandered back to the TV screen, while her ears were divided between the TV sound and Refentse's voice, the voice of the secret bone of her heart.

"Two cases of cans, please," Refentse said. Jack asked what the occasion was.

"We have won, brother! That's it. Those New Zealanders thought that they owned this game of rugby. We have won!"

Lerato smiled to herself as Refentse praised the Springboks for winning the World Cup. She knew Refentse did not care much about sport, especially rugby. His praise could only be a joke, made even lighter by its feebleness as a justification for swallowing so much lager.

Lerato knew that Refentse would have come to buy large quantities of beer, any-way. In the early days when they first got to know each other, when they did their first year in the university, Lerato used to wonder when Refentse did his studying, with so much drinking. She discovered that he usually bought beer and drank while reading. Unlike most students she knew, who indulged in taking these waters, Refentse had never submitted a late essay.

"Time management!" he had told her when she suggested that perhaps books and drink did not go together.

She knew, at this moment, that Refentse bought the beer, if for nothing else, at least to keep him company while he worked on the assignment due soon. Rugby could be no reason for deterring him from his work.

As Refentse turned around to leave, he found himself facing the mouth of a gun, behind which was a balaclava, so that he could not see the face.

"Face down!"

Jack, Lerato and the other two students threw themselves down immediately. Refentse remained standing. Lerato's heart missed a beat or two. She wanted to shout, "Refentse!"

"Come out from behind the counter!" Instructions spat out from behind the balaclava.

And to Refentse: "Face down!"

The balaclava was slowly approaching him. As this second order hissed between
the lips, another balaclava appeared at the slightly opened door. It shifted somewhat
to allow a third to appear, also pointing a gun at whoever might be in the bar. This
third invader retreated as soon as he had appeared, and gently closed the door
behind him.

The first invader was still approaching Refentse. Lerato could see the dim form of
the gun pointing at her best university friend, who could have become her lover had
he initiated a discussion to that effect. Lerato had for a long time wished that he
would, sooner rather than later.

The man came closer. Lerato's fear created visions of her friend's stubbornness
taking him to the grave. She heard voices singing the familiar funeral song, "We are
just passers-by on this earth".

Refentse had often talked to her about the importance of being stubborn. He had
first raised this point when she was intimidated in class by their lecturer. She had
thought of de-registering. She meant to spend the rest of the following term at
home, weighing up whether she really wanted to have a degree if getting one meant
cruel exposure to lecturers' whims. She would have left the university had Refentse
not talked about respecting herself and not letting anyone trample on her.

After a lengthy talk, in which he cited many examples of people who were nearly destroyed, and some were indeed destroyed, by careless comments from their
seniors, Refentse concluded: "If you leave, you can be sure that Dr Lewi's opinion
that you are not university material will be vindicated."

He had given her a mission to prove to herself that she was worth more than Dr
Lewi reckoned.

But, as she lay there on the carpeted floor, she could not persuade herself that
stubbornness should be pushed to the very limits the way Refentse was doing. She
raised her head a little, thinking of standing up and pulling Refentse down to the
floor. She thought about what might be going on in the mind of the man in baracla-
va. Pictures of her miserable friend who had been raped in an ordeal involving car
robbery cut across her mind with sharp strokes. They mingled uneasily with visions
of Refentse's corpse and the mournful tones of "We are just passers-by on this
earth".

She remained glued to the carpet, claustrophobia stifling her attempt to call out
to Refentse to do what they were all doing.

The man in the balaclava neared them.

"Don't try my patience ... I said, Face down!'"

The voice sent a tremor down her back. She could also feel cold sweat trickling down the valley between her breasts.

Refentse seemed to have come back to his senses but not as quickly as Lerato would have wished. Unlike Jack, he did not hurl himself onto the cold tiles immediately. He walked toward the area that was carpeted, where Lerato and the others were lying. Lerato's visions of Refentse's corpse and of men in balaclavas topping her friend were becoming sharper by the second. With startling bends of the imagination she would substitute herself for the gang-raped friend.

"Where is Jack?"

"Here." Jack's voice was faint.

Lerato's thought patterns followed the aggressive questions and the timid replies. She thought about Jack. She could not decide what Jack could have done to deserve death by shooting. It was not just that he was a good soul that Lerato could not understand. No, it was more than that. Anyway, she loved Refentse far more to keep her attention on Jack for too long. Lerato told herself that Jack would be the first victim who would be lucky enough not to experience the mounting pain of waiting for his death by watching others go before him. Then it would be Refentse. Or the two chaps lying on either side of her on the carpet.

"Where are the car keys?"

"Here." Again faintly.

"Throw them in front of you!"

Jack used the car occasionally, on weekends, to carry beer from the brewery to the Parktown Village bar. On these occasions he would also take advantage of the car to visit his girlfriend and often bring her along to the Village. For her sake, Lerato was thankful that she was not there with them this time. .

Jack threw the keys in front of him, sliding them towards the invader. The second invader picked them up. Deciding that the students were entirely harmless, he curtly said to his companion, "Keep order!" and went out.

The first invader stayed behind. Jack moved a little in order to make himself as comfortable as was possible. The gun instantly pointed in his direction.

Lerato shut her eyes. She opened them just as quickly. She coughed. A stifled kind of cough that she hoped would not irritate the man. She could not forget that she was the only woman in the bar. She saw herself melting into pictures on the following day's newspaper and TV headlines. She listened to the haunting echoes, as if originating from within her own skull, of voices of people in the streets, singing "Amabokoboko aya phumelela ..."

Then the gun pointed at Refentse. Again Lerato shut her eyes quickly, with a pang she had never imagined she could experience. His impending death forced her into severe self-reproach. She had let cowardice reign in her heart. She would have told Refentse how much she loved him, had she not overwhelmed herself with the thought that, when they got to know that she had initiated their potential love life, people would say that she was a whore. Now, in the fragmented, tormenting review of her own life and her relationship with Refentse, while she lay there on the carpet, she wondered if whoredom did not lie in the failure to pour unreservedly the deep passions of her heart into her beloved's ears.

"Switch that shit off!" The gun pointed to the TV set this time.

Refentse stood up, slowly. In Lerato's mind the slowness of his movements made his death a certainty. He switched off the TV. Guided by the dimness from the lights outside the bar, he went back to his former place.

"Not there, cheeky bastard! Come over here."

Refentse stood up. He went down again, right at the feet of his tormentor this time. Lerato's mind went blank as the gun pointed at his skull. The gunman moved backward until he reached the window. He lifted up the corner of the curtain ever so slightly. He then moved closer again, toward Jack this time.

"Take off that shit over there!" – pointing with the gun at the telephone in the bar.

With one mighty attempt Jack pulled off the handset violently, so that it and the cord were in his hand while the boot remained there by itself.

Lerato coughed again, a suppressed cough. She waited for the gun shot. But just as worrying was the thought that something was sure to be done to her before the gun went off. The tormentor went back to the window and repeated his exercise, but whatever was happening outside did not progress at a speedy pace. He returned to his old place and opened a can of the beer that Refentse had just bought.

The door opened slightly. Something was thrown into the bar. The man picked it up. Must have been a signal of some sort.

"You remain as you are until I come back. Which could be anytime! Any silly movements and you will serve as an example to the rest that I'm not here to play."

He went out, and just as soon came back before Lerato could whisper to Refentse to obey orders as they came, if only for her sake.

The man seemed to be satisfied with their behaviour.

"Good students!" he observed on his return. "Do not worry. As long as there are no monkey tricks, you will remain safe. All we came for is the university car. Just be good students. Do not die for things that do not belong to you. We only want the car that belongs to whites. Or is there any white student here?" he asked rhetorically.

Lerato felt more uneasy. Her male companions might not be shot dead, but the man's words echoed what had announced the beginning of her friend's rape ordeal. She saw her friend's violation taking place in this university residence, which she had always thought to be entirely safe. Or at least much safer than the streets of her township, Alexandra. Now it was clear to her that guns could be brandished anywhere.

Lerato could not swallow the huge lump that stuck in her throat, making breathing almost impossible.

REFENTSE'S ORDEAL

Refentse wanted to laugh. That was before he realised he was in grave danger. There was something rather strange about three men in balaclavas, pointing guns at him. He had never thought his existence could threaten anyone.

It was on the day South Africa won the Rugby World Cup. Refentse and his friends watched the match on TV that afternoon at a friend's flat in Hillbrow. None of them was a great fan of rugby. But there was something thrilling about identifying with Amabokoboko, as the team, the Springboks, was sometimes fondly called, even if temporarily. A team that, where sport was concerned, was more than any other associated in their minds with the apartheid era. Now, with the government's rhetoric of a rainbow nation, Amabokoboko was supposedly one of the most important symbols of reconciliation and goodwill, and Rolihlahla Mandela could be seen in an Amabokoboko jersey when they played for the country. Refentse and his friends were drunk then, having bought loads of dumpies so that they would not have to go out while the game was still on.

After the match they decided to join the noisy crowds in the streets of Hillbrow. Once outside they decided it would be even better to go to the Johannesburg College of Education where many rugby supporters – real and those feigning – had been watching the match on big screens. But while on their way to the College, Refentse separated from his friends. He meant to buy meat. He invited them to join him for the usual supper of maize meal, meat and sauce – and, naturally, more drinks – when they were tired of the noise at the College. On arriving at his university residence in Parktown Village, only five minutes' walk from the College, he prepared the meal as he had promised. While the maize meal was cooking on the stove he dashed out to the Village bar to get the beer.

That was where the whole problem began.

It was not very bright in the bar. The main lights were switched off. The only light was from the TV screen. There were four fellow students in the bar. Lerato and two others whom Refentse did not know well sat close to the TV set. Jack stood behind the counter where he was selling the beer, and from which he was also watching the TV. They were all arguing about who had been the player of the day in the match.

Refentse greeted everyone, and after exchanging a few pleasantries with Lerato, approached Jack.,

"Two cases of cans, please," he said.

Jack asked what the occasion was.

"We have won, brother! That's it. Those New Zealanders thought that they owned this game of rugby. We have won!"

Jack smiled as he served Refentse. He could read from Refentse's tone that the match was not such an important occasion, if it could be called an occasion at all. Or maybe it was not that he could read into anything that Refentse said, but that he knew Refentse would anyway have come to buy large quantities of beer. Some people said the main reason Refentse did not have a girlfriend at the university, which was unusual for his age, was that in the depths of his heart, books and beer came first. Women came second. Or did not count at all. Some said that was why he had no love relationship with Lerato, despite the fact that, so the word went, she was clearly in love with him. Jack could not say for sure that Refentse's life could be explained so simply. But he could certainly testify to the number of times Refentse visited the bar. He could also testify to the large quantities Refentse usually bought, in most cases when there was no event to justify such spending.

As Refentse turned around to leave, he found himself facing the mouth of a gun, behind which was a balaclava.

"Face down!"

Jack, Lerato and the other two students threw themselves down immediately. Refentse remained standing.

"Come out from behind the counter!" Instructions sprayed them from behind the balaclava.

And to Refentse: "Face down!" The balaclava was slowly approaching him.

As this second order slipped out, another balaclava appeared at the slightly opened door. It shifted somewhat to allow a third to appear, also pointing a gun at whoever might be in the bar. This third invader retreated as soon as he had appeared, and gently closed the door behind him. (Well, at least they all looked like 'hims' to Refentse.)

The first invader was still approaching slowly, as if tiptoeing — maybe he was, Refentse was not quite sure — toward Refentse. He came very close. He then patted Refentse on the shoulder.

"Don't try my patience ... " I said, "Face down!'"

It was only with the combination of the cold feel of the hand on his shoulder, the brutality of the voice hissing between the lips of the balaclava, and the sharpened vision of the reality of the gun that Refentse's brain began to do its work. Even then, it was not as quick as anyone who loved him could have wished. For, against the odd presence of his impending death, Refentse found himself asking himself, with a sense of disbelief, whether all the wrongs he had committed in his life justified this sight.

Unlike Jack, he did not hurl himself onto the cold tiles. He walked, as if in an uneasy dream, toward the area that was carpeted, where Lerato and the others were lying. He made himself comfortable, at least as comfortable as he could, not knowing how he had earned his impending death.

"Where is Jack?"

"Here."

Jack's voice was faint.

Refentse's thoughts shifted to Jack. He wondered what personal grudges Jack, who was the quietest person known to him in the Village, could have with these gun-toting thugs.

"Where are the car keys?"

"Here." Again faintly.

"Throw them in front of you!"

Refentse looked at Jack as he stood up on his knees, feeling in his pocket. He was relieved for Jack's sake, though not without the gnawing misgiving that that was not all.

These, Refentse thought, were no ordinary robbers. How did they know that Jack had the university car keys? Did they organise with someone from within – a fellow student, maybe, or, better still, a more knowledgeable university staff member? Maybe they even knew exactly who Jack was, and were merely asking questions for fun?

Jack used the car occasionally on weekends to ferry beer from the brewery to the Village bar. On these occasions, he would also use the car to visit his girlfriend and, often, bring her along to the Village. But she was not with him this time.

Jack threw the keys in front of him in the direction of the invader. The second one picked them up. Apparently having decided that the students were entirely harmless, the second invader just said to his companion, "Keep order!" and went out.

The first invader stayed behind.

Jack moved slightly in order to make himself as comfortable as possible. The gun pointed in his direction instantly.

Refentse's stomach tightened ...

Lerato coughed, a stifled cough that brought no soothing thoughts to Refentse's already sweating brain. It would be her turn now, he thought. Then he found himself reviewing his life. It just flashed, whole, in the speed of lightning. And even in that brief moment of review, he found a chance to regret that she was going to die, and that he would follow suit before he could tell her how much he loved her. His sober state – it was as if he had not drunk a thing not so long ago – did not make his fears and regrets more endurable.

He listened with dismay to the jubilant voices in the street, as people sang "Amabokoboko aya phumelela ..."

The gun pointed at him.

"Switch that shit off!" The gun pointed to the TV set this time.

Refentse got to his feet. He had already given himself and his companions up for dead. He walked deliberately, hoping that the slowness of his movements would speed up the visitation of the first bullet into his skull.

He switched the TV off. Guided by the dim lights outside the bar, he went back to his former place.

"Not there, cheeky bastard! Come over here."

He stood up again. As he approached his tormentor, a thought flashed through his mind. What if he kicked his tormentor's stomach! With his boots on, the result could be impressive. But then he thought of the other two men. It was disturbing that he did not know exactly where they were. For the university car had not moved yet. At least there had not been any sound to suggest that it had. The men must still be on the university premises. There was no choice. Refentse went down again, right at the feet of his tormentor this time.

The gunman moved backward until he reached the window. He lifted up the corner of the curtain ever so slightly then moved closer again, toward Jack this time.

"Take off that shit over there!" – pointing with the gun at the public telephone that was in the bar.

Refentse was later to admire the ingenuity of Jack's mind as well as the strength of his muscles. With one attempt Jack successfully pulled off the handset violently so that he had it and its cord in his hand while the boot remained on the counter.

Lerato coughed again. A suppressed cough. Again, Refentse's stomach tightened. He did not doubt that Lerato's unsympathetic cold was more than any robber could bear. His review of his life resumed, with a quicker pace than before. Once more he regretted that Lerato's cold was not being merciful to her. Even in such hard times.

The tormentor said nothing, did not even point his gun at her. Instead, he went back to the window and repeated his exercise. Refentse was glad that the poor soul was left in peace. It would have been doubly painful for him to watch or listen to his sweetheart endure the same drudgery. But shortly afterwards he had a premonition that this was not all.

Exactly what was going on in Lerato's heart and mind in these trying moments was unknown to Refentse. All he knew was that he had not told her that he loved her. This he had meant to tell her before sunset of the following day, but every day had brought with it an increased dread of rejection. And therefore the haunted silence.

Whatever was happening outside did not progress at a speedy pace. The man came back. This time he opened a can of the beer that Refentse had just bought. Refentse would have gladly offered the whole case if he could have persuaded himself that after his gesture of generosity the man would leave them in peace. As it was, he hated the man for opening this one. The man drank quite quickly. One, two gulps and it was gone. He opened another one. The certainty of death did not stop Refentse's bitterness from mounting.

The door opened. Something was thrown into the bar. The man picked it up. Must have been a signal of some sort.

"You remain as you are until I come back. Which could be anytime! Any silly movements, you will serve as an example to the rest that I'm not here to play."

He went out, and just as soon came back. Before Refentse could reach any conclusion regarding the man's voice and accent, which did not sound unfamiliar, his thoughts fell into disarray. Just as well that the man did not take long, for he, Refentse, was about to stand up and leave.

While he switched off the TV, he had heard his friends' voices singing "Amabokoboko aya phumelela ..." chanting their way to his room, only to find that he was not there. He had wondered about the cooking on the stove. But the thought that one of his flatmates would detect the smell when the food overheated and would go to check in the communal kitchen, offered no consolation whatsoever. The friends, if they had left already, would have used the other exit point. He had not heard their voices on their way out.

The man with the gun seemed to be satisfied with their behaviour.

"Good students!" he observed.

Again Refentse started to wonder about the voice and accent. The accent sounded rather forced as it was but he was almost positive that he was familiar with the way this person spoke.

"Do not worry. As long as there are no monkey tricks, you will remain safe. We only came here for the university car. Just be good students. Do not die for things that do not belong to you. We only came for the car that belongs to whites. Or is there any white student here?" he asked rhetorically.

Refentse thought about the exorbitant fees he and all other students were paying. He contemplated the uncertainty of their redemption. Then he visualised his mother's agonised face on receiving news of his death - quick, sharp mental pictures that belittled the efforts of the most advanced of cameras.

As if to accompany his visions, a gunshot exploded from the outside. "Amabokoboko aya phumelela ..." stopped abruptly. A long silence followed. When Refentse's mind quit its blankness and returned to the bar, the silence was still there, in all its impenetrable thickness, as was the heavy presence of the man in the bala-clava.

"Do not worry ..." rattled in Refentse's skull.

OCCASION FOR BROODING

He has already swallowed a few dumpies, as he often does on Fridays. And on other days. The memory of Tshepo competes for his attention with thoughts of what he could say to his mother. And to his friends? Everyone was now surely in a position to say to him: "There's a Jo'burg woman for you!"

Throughout the day, at the University, he has suffered visions of sharp gazes focused on him, and of voices reminding him of what his people had always known would be the inevitable outcome of his stubbornness. The gazes and voices had multiplied in his imagination, becoming sharper and louder by the second. There were moments when he would shrug with fright as he fixed faces, familiar village faces, to the gazes and the voices.

His main wish is to retreat, to withdraw from the pandemonium. The worst torment is the knowledge that what he conjured was what he would see and hear sooner or later. Every moment that elapsed was, and remains, a mighty step toward an ushering of this dreaded moment. Not having chosen to be born, he feels it is regrettable that he should not be left alone to choose how to live.

Entangled in this maze of brooding he forgets for the time being that he himself had done the same to Sammy. That was about a year back. The secret had been well sheltered.

For now Refentse is simply overwhelmed by the painful freshness of his morning findings. He wonders if Tshepo was not truly lucky to have passed away before he got disappointed with life. He lifts the dumpy to his mouth again. But the beer is bereft of the usual refreshing taste. He looks at the setting sun. No warmth there, either. Just the orange at the edge of the clouds that hide it somewhat.

Everything is too quiet for his liking.

He walks slowly into the flat. The music is still playing softly. "See the world through the eyes of a child." His favourite piece. By Stimela.

He presses the volume button. Again. And again ... Until the volume goes full blast.

He unlocks the door that leads out of the flat into the corridor. "See the world through the eyes of a child ..."

He goes back to the balcony. Sits on the balcony wall. Takes another sip of the beer, wondering why it tastes so strange today. Looking onto the street, twenty levels down from where he is sitting, he sees a woman taking a dog for a walk. The sight reminds him of a story Sammy had told him during one of their drinking sessions. It was about the friend's dog, Danger. One day, the story goes, Danger was chasing a mouse. The mouse beat Danger to its hole. While in the hole, it saw Danger blocking the hole with his snout, sniffing angrily as if he would follow suit. Overcome by fear and frustration, the mouse ran out of the hole straight into Danger's mouth.

There was nothing to suggest that the funeral could become one of the most talked about events, not only in Tiragalong and its neighbourhood, but also in such distant places as Nobody and Boyne. Nothing, that is, except that the gruesome death of such a successful youth was in itself enough to make it the talk of the village. Because no one knew the exact cause of the death, creative minds found no difficulty in divining it. His friend Sammy was known to be one of the very few villagers who had a sympathetic view of the calamity.

"For a person of Refentse's calibre," Sammy said, "whose outlook toward life was always positive, the cause must have been very deep indeed."

Refentse's mother could only brood over her son's death. It never occurred to her that she had killed her own son. She had only meant to show him the light. The son was in search of the light, too. He found his own light in the end. This the mother could not comprehend.

"Some things are just too baffling," she said with much sadness.

For those with both imagination and wagging tongues the issue was simple. Here was an educated youth who could not think beyond himself, beer and Jo'burg women. As it was well known in the village, Jo'burg women could frustrate a man. Refentse was often advised to keep away from them. Their words got into his head through one ear and, just as soon, went out the other ear. As it always happens to those who mistake a lion's mouth for a playing field, he got chewed by the lion.

But his mother's strange behaviour forced even Refentse's detractors to change their minds.

"Surely Refentse was bewitched by his own mother," the villagers said.

It was not that the mother had ever been thought of as a witch. But that kind of conduct was associated with witchcraft. The oldest of villagers used to tell stories of witches who fell into the graves of the people they had killed. Only two instances of such bizarre acts, both of which had taken place in the distant past, were known.

None of them had happened in Tiragalong. One took place at Nobody and the other at Nnoko, which shares boundaries with Tiragalong. The two witches, it was said, were new-comers to the art. So their medicines overcame them with their strength, and turned against them. Or, it was said, the deceased's ancestors were too angry and vented their rage on the witches. Nobody knew the truth. But all knew that it was unheard of to fall into a dead person's grave. After consulting doctors in the villages and their neighbourhood the two witches were confirmed as such. They were later thrown out of their respective villages. So when Refentse's mother fell into her son's grave that hot Saturday morning – as she was throwing a handful of soil into it to bid him goodbye – the village was reminded of the two stories. What frustrated the village was that she had killed her own son, using medicines. It was difficult to know what to do with her. In ordinary circumstances she would have trodden the same path as that travelled by Tshepo's murderess.

But the Comrades were not in agreement. Half of them said that, in killing her own son, she had done no one any harm. Killing her own son, who was going to assist her in life, was like committing suicide. It was not something that the society should spend sleepless nights about. Every villager knew that the cry of a person who commits suicide is a drum; when it plays, people dance.

The other half said that Refentse was going to bring advancement to the village. His death was in many ways the death of this advancement. The village had every responsibility to protect itself from the ill will of such night prowlers.

In the end agreement could not be reached. Because the village was going to have to explain their decision to the cruel Mankweng police, it was decided that such accounting would be jeopardised by the split.

Refentse is alone on the balcony of his flat in Hillbrow. Or perhaps he is not alone. Besides beer, Refentse's other companion is the fond memory of Tshepo, of the pain families have to continue to endure because of the sudden deaths of those who should be in some position to relieve them of their poverty.

Refentse and Tshepo attended the same high school. Refentse had been in his first year in the school when Tshepo read for his matric. Tshepo was the first pupil from the school, the only high school in Tiragalong, to study at a university in the South. On receiving his results he was struck by fatal lightning. Grief sent his mother to join him in the world of the ancestors.

What pained Refentse very much was that Tshepo's death was the loss of a role model. Tshepo was not only the first in the village to go to the university in the South. He was also about to be the only teacher, except the principal, with a degree. All the other teachers had teachers' diplomas from the colleges in the homeland of Lebowa – it was going to be a real change having a teacher whose education transcended Verwoerdian food for thought. But to some of these teachers, this was mixed news. They knew that their teaching experience was not necessarily going to secure them a higher position compared to him.

With Refentse the case was different. After all, he had nothing to lose. He was just about to enrol for his first year at the same university when Tshepo died. Tshepo had told him about the advantages of going to study there.

"If you work hard enough," he would say to the younger companion, "you could pass with flying colours. And get a scholarship! The lecturers are also very supportive. One helped me to get my essay published."

Tshepo had something to show for his work. An essay published while he was still in his second year! In his final year he published a short story. He always told Refentse that he was heading for bigger things. Surely Refentse should be equally ambitious! And that was how Refentse came to apply for admission at the institution of higher alienation. But, despite relating the positive, Tshepo had not romanticised the nature of the institution although Refentse did not believe that Tshepo, and other students from impoverished educational backgrounds, could suffer so much at the university. As they say in Tiragalong, to be told is to be deprived; seeing for oneself is like eating. So it was with Refentse.

He first came to Johannesburg in January, 1991. He was an optimistic youth, who had passed his matric subjects. Not quite distinguished, but well enough to be admitted unconditionally to enrol for his degree of Bachelor of Arts. Initially he wanted to study Commerce. But his Mathematics question paper was a bit uncooperative, as his final results showed. Not knowing what else to do, he enrolled for an Arts degree. He had vaguely thought of himself as a journalist, or an editor — although he had no idea what editors did. Now that he could not study Commerce, he thought he could pursue the dreams of his childhood. For he was in the lower primary school when he first encountered the word 'editor'.

After seeking advice — he was always told by his loving mother how important it is for people not to pretend to know — he resolved to study literature. With literature and a course or two in the social sciences, he was told, he should be in a position to be an editor or a journalist. Or even both! So he looked attentively at the year's timetable to see that his subjects did not clash.

English Studies ... Second choice ... It clashed with English Studies. Then he saw something called African Studies on the timetable. He loved Kgadime Matsepe with every drop of passion in his heart. Matsepe was the finest Sepedi novelist he had ever read. Not that he had read much Sepedi literature. African literature written in Sepedi was not readily available in their tiny school library. And, with the raving poverty at home, owning a book was a luxury. Anyway, because of minimal information on what students covered in the African Studies classes, and telling himself that for the first time he would be able to study Sepedi literature without the inhibitions of the secondary school syllabus, he enrolled.

With regard to the other subjects, he had very limited interest in them. They simply completed the empty blocks on his forms. As a result he passed his first year unconvincingly. However, by the second year he picked up a bit. And by the end of the third year, after making his brain sweat a lot, he actually qualified for a post-graduate degree. Now it has to be remembered that not only was he struggling to bridge the gap between his secondary education and university learning, but there were many other problems. Some of his lecturers were an embodiment of rudeness. Dr Lewi, a course supervisor, was one such lecturer. Three moments stand out in his memory of Lewi.

One day in first year a university friend, or fellow sufferer, failed his assignment. Lewi had a way with words. He commented on the poor soul's assignment:

"You have to earn marks. You do not just find them lying in a tray!"

Only the other day he had charged Lerato with looking at him with 'eyes of ignorance'. Lerato was a frail personality, then. She cried silently while a few males enjoyed the joke. Since the other student did not attend the class that day, Refentse was the only other black in the discussion group. He sympathised with Lerato. Particularly because he feared that he was likely to be the next victim of Dr Lewi's linguistic skills. But it had not happened. He had to wait two more months before his turn came.

Refentse received a letter from Lewi. The letter said that he had not attended the required minimum number of discussion groups. As a result, he would not be allowed to sit the June examinations.

Refentse knew it was not true. It could not be. He had attended far more than he was expected to. Fortunately the letter also indicated that it was open to correction.

Appreciating the fairness of the last point, he visited the supervisor. As Lewi's office door was always shut and his hearing was not good, Refentse had to knock hard. Lewi shouted an irritable "Come in!"

Refentse opened the door. He greeted Lewi timidly. The office looked impressive, even when looked at through Refentse's apprehensive eyes. Big books, old and new, packed shelves that almost touched the office roof. Refentse could not help feeling that Lewi must be a very strong and well balanced man, indeed, to have read all these books and still remain sane enough to be able to teach.

"How can I help you, young man?" came Lewi's rather hoarse voice.

Refentse, not having sufficient confidence in his English skills, simply fumbled in his pocket. He produced the condemning document, and handed it over. Lewi gave it a quick glance. He consulted his file briefly. Then followed a sneer.

"Young man!" Lewi's voice came again, as he banged on the table. It was so unexpected that Refentse started. "Young man, according to our records, your attendance at the discussion groups has been less than sparkling. Can you tell us why that is so?"

"That is not so!" stuck in Refentse's throat.

"I ..." he stammered.

But before he could find the right word Lewi intimated that he was not going to argue with first years.

In that moment of frustration, Refentse stood up and walked out of the office. He feared for his life on remembering, while he was already two offices away, that he had not shut the office door behind him.

The alienation caused to first years by the likes of Lewi was difficult to overcome. Even with the support of fellow students and some humane lecturers who did not believe that their work was simply limited to research.

It was worse with the likes of Refentse. Every time he was treated this badly, or worse, he remembered his mother. Their poverty. The two huts in the homestead which promised to collapse at any time. The threat that he might not be able to return to the university due to financial difficulties. No! It was not easy at all.

The following year he had to apply for a study loan. The same happened in his third and fourth years of study. He only received a scholarship when reading for his Master's degree. That was an acknowledgement, finally, of his ability.

He thought of the late Tshepo, and of how his death deprived him of the chance to celebrate with his home-boy. For, like Tshepo, he was busy making a name for himself, and for Tiragalong.

On seeing his progress, Refentse's lecturers constantly told him, in his third year of study, that he could make a brilliant academic. When he was reading for his Honours, one even allowed him to take his tutorial. The experience was so exciting that Refentse witnessed his lecturers' words become a hard fact. Journalism and editing evaporated through his skull into the open air.

But by the time he began to lecture, he could not cope financially. About a quarter of his salary went into repaying the loans. He realised he had agreed to sign contracts that demanded that he now pay more than he could afford. The contracts were not explained to him the way, he now knew, they should have been. His limited English and ignorance of contracts worked against him. It was an unsettling discovery that he had, in fact, authorised his own suffering. Another quarter of his salary was devoured by the tax person . Yet another quarter disappeared in the form of monthly rentals. After paying his furniture instalments, he was left with too little for subsistence, too little even for himself, that is. He had to live on lice, as they say in Tiragalong. And what with family obligations and other forms of pressure, he could think of no way out.

What really depressed him was that his mother failed to understand his problems. And why should she? Had she not spent every cent she could find on her beloved son? The exorbitant tuition fees. The unfriendly transport fares. The new clothes. The everything ...

"Refentse was too inconsiderate," she said. "And too extravagant."

His trusted cousin had told her that Refentse lived for beer. And for Jo'burg girls. In imparting this piece of wisdom to her aunt, the cousin was motivated both by her fear for Refentse's safety with these fast and glamorous girls and a concern for her aunt's peace of mind — both of which could only be achieved through a severing of Refentse's love relationship. ·

As if the two reasons were insufficient, the cousin also had to satisfy her passion for personal revenge. Since Refentse invited the bone of his heart to stay with him at his flat, the cousin had increasingly felt her own influence on Refentse wane. Once there had been the 'good old times' when the cousin just walked into the flat and served herself whatever she liked from the refrigerator, which was often nearly empty, without having to ask for permission. Now Refentse suggested to her that such behaviour undermined the status of the new woman of the house.

The cousin could not allow herself to be trampled down by this newcomer. That the woman was a newcomer was in itself bad enough. That she was also a Johannesburger only smeared her already ugly image with a thick layer of mud. So the cousin wondered how her beloved Refentse could allow himself to be controlled by a girl. She expressed her dismay in sharp words that indicated to Refentse that his mother would know of this love relationship at the earliest possible time. And these strong words expressed her newly found doubt of Refentse's integrity, while simultaneously spiting the newcomer. Since the cousin seldom talked behind people's backs, the three of them were there to swim in the torrents of words as they flowed from her bitter tongue. She observed that her aunt had merely accompanied other women to the clinic; and while they returned with babies wrapped with warmth in their tender arms, she had returned empty-handed. Now, in her old age, she would have no son to take good care of her. So it was that the cousin threatened, when she went home the following weekend, to alert her aunt to the impending fate that awaited her. Refentse knew his cousin well enough to know that there would be difficult times ahead, beginning from the very moment he and his mother's eyes next met.

The danger the cousin envisaged found concrete expression in the fact that Refentse was penniless when he went home — this was only two weeks after payday. He admitted to his mother that he had a lover from the townships of the city and not from Hillbrow, whose reputation for prostitution and crime kept on ascending to the clear skies of Tiragalong as migrants brought fresh wild stories every time they returned to the village. Refentse made his honest admission. And that, really, was what dealt him a blow. Yet, he could not see how he, who loved his mother dearly, could bring himself to lie to her. The truth had to come out. The choice imposed on him by the truth was exacting.

There was a general belief in the village of Tiragalong that Jo'burg women were nothing but parasites. The basis of this popular opinion was not clear to Refentse, if it was to anyone else. Perhaps it was because a number of men who went to work in the South often fell in love with some women there, and subsequently sent too little to their families in the rural site. Perhaps the few who actually married the Johannesburgers were left destitute, without possessions. Refentse knew of one such case in the village. The man lost his property in a divorce case. Whatever the foundations of the belief, Refentse's mother shared it wholeheartedly.

When Refentse suggested to his mother that rural women were no better, all the mother said was: "You break with her, or you are no longer my son!"

He was startled. For the first time in his twenty-four years of life he learnt that his mother could shut her ears to his words. Not only that. She could also shut the doors of her brain to reason. She knew that her son had failed in relationships with young women in Tiragalong.

Refentse recalled the occasion the first would-be lover told him that he was quite a loveable chap. "But," she let honesty take the prize, "you do not own a car!"

He had reflected painfully on all the time spent trying to bring her to a point where she could openly express what she felt. He had interpreted her silence, her apparent unwillingness to tell him once and for all of the state of her heart, as one of those weaknesses he should expect from women. He derived no comfort from learning that, in the long run, silence was simply another way of avoiding stabbing at the hearts of those you loved.

Armed with this fresh piece of wisdom, Refentse was from that day onwards extremely sensitive to the fact of his family's poverty. Wrapped up in a vision of his powerlessness and worthlessness, he had considered suicide. When he told Sammy about his disappointment, deliberately forgetting to mention his gloomy intentions, Sammy had laughed away this woman's honesty as a sign that she did not really love him. He reminded Refentse that his education was sure to soon lift him out of poverty. There were a number of examples in the neighbouring villages — people who rose from the dust of their parents' huts to live in big houses and drive good cars. Sammy, with his patience, dived into the list of these villagers. After which he reminded Refentse, once more, that love and a car were not really an ideal couple for any villager of worth. They were fine if they came your way but you should not make yourself miserable because they did not.

The way Sammy had laughed at the thought that love and a car could go together forced Refentse to reflect that Tiragalong would have a poor opinion of him if the village were to discover why he had decided to commit suicide. He was not one of those people who simply said that death was death and ended there. Refentse's sense of dignity also meant that people should speak well of him while he rested in the grave. These thoughts put him under pressure not to talk to anyone about his contemplated suicide.

Even with the new pressure infused into his life, Sammy's optimism about the future gave Refentse a reason for holding on. And in that way save his self respect from sinking into the muddy pool of suicide. Refentse's new task, since then, was to uproot the poverty at home as soon as he could. With this ambition constantly flooding his mind, he worked hard and with perseverance in the last two years of his student life. And it was this renewed faith in life that led him to another lover.

The second lover, he discovered two months into the relationship, had at least four other lovers. Or rather sexual partners. He learnt this from the New Release, as such partners are sometimes known.

He met the Latest Release when he came from the University. It was during university holidays; he had gone to complete his research essay. On his return the following day, the minibus taxi had problems. Their journey was delayed by no less than three hours. On arriving in Pietersburg, he found there were no taxis to Tiragalong or its neighbourhood. As the village was about forty-five kilometres from the town, he decided to hitch his way home. Walking would have been too much of a bother. Besides, it was too late. Everyone knew that Nobody, through which he would have to go, was full of tsotsis. Who wanted to die just when he was about to complete all the requirements for his BA Honours degree, especially after the terrible alienation and hard work? If there were any such people, Refentse was decidedly not one of them.

He waited on the boundary of the town, on the road to Mankweng. For about an hour he had leaned against the signpost that read 'Lebowa Boundary' on the side facing the town, and 'Pietersburg Grens' on the other side. A car came to a halt.

"Where you going? Want a lift?"

"Tiragalong."

"Throw yourself in, brother."

He lost no time at all. The driver was friendly and talkative. He told Refentse of his sexual exploits. And of other trivialities.

"Yes, I know your village quite well. I used to be famous with the girls there. Not that I am no longer famous. You know Refilwe?"

Refentse nodded.

"She is my cherry. I only won her last week. It is nothing to boast about, really. Everyone knows she is fairly open-thighed. Want a beer?"

Refentse shook his head.

"Just to give you an idea of what I mean, she has got three other boyfriends."

Refentse tried to suppress his emotions. He was often calm and gentle. And generous of spirit. But this frightening piece of news was more than he could cope with. The driver kept his eyes glued onto the rough, stony road while the story continued to flow from his eager tongue with unfailing consistency. The dimness of the light in the car reassured Refentse somewhat that the driver, if he chanced to glance at him, would not see much of his facial expression. It was a little consolation that helped to make him manage his anger for the duration of the journey.

He paid a reasonable fare for his ride. The news was, of course, for free.

When he met his lover the following day, Refentse passed on to her greetings from the Latest Release, who had not really appointed him a messenger. For Refentse's benefit, the lover wondered aloud who this person could be. Refentse did not claim to know him. He only hinted that he knew a lot more than she might guess. He told her, for example, of her partner at Nnoko.

Fearing that Refentse might be irritated by her pretences, she decided to reveal everything about her relationships. She hoped that he would forgive her. Which he did. And, on that note, he left her to herself and the care of the other partners.

His mother knew all this. She might not have known about the once contemplated suicide. Maybe she did not need to know about it, he thought. Maybe parents did not have to know such things before they could listen to their children with two open ears. The thought mingled with the persistent question: What was good about rural women that made them better lovers than those in Johannesburg? After all, he wondered, when people talked about Johannesburgers, were they not referring to people from the rural areas, who were, like himself, in search of green pastures? And when men were generous enough to give their all to their extramarital partners, was that not what provisions of green pastures were partly about? "You leave her, or you are no longer my son ..." The mother's voice, engraved in his mind, disturbed the already confused flow of his thoughts, only to leave him with an even more intense form of brooding.

Things really came to a head when Refentse became the talk of the village. He learnt from Sammy, who had gone home one weekend, of all the bad things said about him. Of how he did not love his mother. Of how his mother was suffering as if her son was not a lecturer. And of many other things.

Refentse was thoroughly humiliated when he went home once more. A number of young women, including those whose morals were poor by the village standards, gave him a piece of their minds. Even the honest woman, whom Refentse had never really stopped loving, talked spiritedly about a country bumpkin who mistook himself for a 'city Awisey'.

When he once more failed to secure an open ear from his mother, Refentse resolved not to return home. But there were people from Tiragalong, working in Johannesburg, who were prepared to come and pester him at his flat. Not only were they prepared. They actually did it. Even his friends, with the exception of Sammy, who knew his problems, said Refentse was wrong not to support his poor mother. He could not go about discussing his domestic affairs with everyone. Their criticism was largely ill-informed. He understood and did not begrudge them.

He found things out for himself. Nothing was blown into his ears by some too loud-mouthed winds.

He had forgotten one of his important documents at the flat. After the first two lectures he went back to fetch the document, for he could not do without it. Not that day, at any rate. Thinking that the bone of his heart might still be asleep, he did not knock. He simply unlocked and marched into the flat.

He found Lerato still asleep. With her eyes and legs open, and Sammy moaning.

FOUNTAINS OF BROODING

A matchstick thrown into the hut from which the shrill screams of Refentse's mother can be heard falls onto a piece of cloth that is wet with petrol. Once more the Comrades of Tiragalong have taken the dress of cowardice off their bodies and are now displaying their bravery, solidarity and co-operation in solving the main problem of the village. Their cause has the support of Comrades from neighbouring villages – Nnoko, which shares the south-east boundary of Tiragalong, Magokobung to the east, Makgwareng to the north, as well as Phuti, which stretches from the northwest to the west of Tiragalong. Were the first village to the south not a bit too far, the Comrades there would probably have also come chanting freedom songs in corrupted Zulu, to assist their fellow sufferers in Tiragalong. For witchcraft is quite a problem in this part of the planet. Especially in the tiniest of the villages, Tiragalong itself.

The problem caused by the incident at Refentse's graveside, which has led to much constipation in the minds of the Comrades, was finally resolved. The split within the Comrade circles was now overcome by sharp intellects, and nearly all young voices in Tiragalong were shouting, as they did a few years ago when they necklaced an old woman to death for having sent lightning to strike Tshepo, "Witchcraft shall be no more!" Refentse's mother is now 'facing the music', as the somewhat educated youth put it.

Clouds of black smoke ascend the skies as petrol catches the tiny flame from the matchstick. The clouds are much blacker than the brooding ones that brought the lightning that summoned Tshepo and, through grief, his mother to the world of the ancestors. They spread themselves to envelop the village. The lush grass, the big mealie plants in the fields, the beautiful fleshiness of the tree leaves, all the greenness in Tiragalong surrenders to the blackness of the smoke. It is as if the Gods have resolved, perhaps once in a lifetime, to bring a miracle to the village and its neighbourhood in the form of black fog.

There is fog everywhere, spreading itself to embrace Nnoko, Magokobung, Makgwareng and Phuti, heading to where nobody knows, travelling much further than the fierce loudness of the Comrades' freedom songs could ever hope to reach.

Mahlodi screams by herself from the heart of the raging flames because her companion, Phaswa, has died just before the burning could begin. When the Comrades went to summon him from his home he had shown signs of protest. In their impatience some of the Comrades had begun to stone him on the spot. By the time they reached Mahlodi's compound his body was already giving signals of bidding the Comrades farewell. None of them noticed the signals. Or perhaps they did, but had little interest in them. The sympathetic few could not display their compassion. A show of sympathy for night prowlers, especially in such trying times, was like whistling to Death which was absent-mindedly passing you by.

In the end Phaswa departed, thus refraining from being turned into braaivleis while still alive. Mahlodi faced the music by herself. Gravesides! Quite dangerous places to be at on a hot Saturday morning.

It began as a rumour. Or maybe not quite what could be called a rumour, for the gossips heard it from a reliable source. The source could not have been anyone but Refentse's youngest cousin, who came to stay with Mahlodi soon after her son's suicide. The news, though so terribly unexpected, gave a powerful justification for the killing of Mahlodi.

Refentse's cousin was sitting in his hut working on his composition. It was not the easiest thing to do. His ability lay more in figures than in creative writing. Besides, the assignment itself was not the most exciting thing, given the topic. 'Our School ...' What could he do with such a dull topic? The school was small, it was poor, with no impressive classrooms or a garden, and was staffed by teachers who were very keen to use a stick on the pupils. They often quoted an English saying about the sparing of rods or something like that. It would surely have been better if the school was Tiragalong High, not Nnoko Secondary School, which the villagers seemed to have little interest in developing. Many parents in Nnoko were sending their children to Tiragalong for their secondary education.

This line of positive thinking about Tiragalong High impressed itself strongly on Leruo's mind. But he could not think of Tiragalong High without remembering Refentse. Although still in Standard Six, Leruo understood enough of life to know that the way Refentse had died was unnatural. It was the kind of knowledge that was bound to distress him. Refentse was not just a cousin; he was also a friend to him.

A gentle knock on the door is followed by an uninterested "Come in!" from Leruo. To his joy, in walk God's blessings! Thabo is much earlier than they had arranged.

"What are you doing so late? You should be asleep by now."

Leruo looks at Thabo. "Asleep by now? Stick on Monday! Our School ..."

"It's that fool giving us homework on a Friday. As if we don't have better things to do. I want to get this done soon so that I have nothing to bother me for the rest of the weekend."

Leruo scratches his head and shakes it slightly. With a hopeful smile he suggests, "Maybe you can help?"

Thabo often had ideas. Also, he was open-handed with them. So together the young pair worked through the assignment. It was about midnight when they completed it.

Thabo, whose parents were fairly rich and gave him some pocket money, had brought with him the glue that he had promised. Now was the moment to have a great time sniffing. It must be good! Leruo had heard Phaswa talk about it during the course of the afternoon. How he used to sniff it as a little boy and how he would see all sorts of things! What he did not hear was that Phaswa was actually criticising it. Not that that would have made much difference, for what he had overheard was enough to tempt him anyway.

When he told Thabo about it, Thabo also became curious to taste what men had experienced in their early days. He offered to sacrifice his pocket money to buy glue. He and Leruo would meet in the course of the night when Mahlodi was asleep.

Just before she went to bed, Mahlodi had gone into Leruo's hut to ask him about something. She was quite impressed to find the two boys doing their homework on a Friday. Especially in the evening, when the less serious children were playing in the bright moonlight in the streets. These two! Theirs was a rare kind of commitment, she repeated to herself numerous times.

Thabo woke up at about four in the morning. Looking out the crack in the wall of the hut to see how dark it was, so that he could dash home before sunrise to ensure that his parents would not find out about his absence, he saw Phaswa coming out of Mahlodi's hut. It looked strange to him that old men should also sleep out. His father used to criticise such men for their boyish conduct. Thabo did not exclude the possibility that Phaswa could have fallen asleep while at his glue, as he himself and Leruo had just done. He was absorbed by this train of thought when Leruo moved in his sleep.

"No, Refentse!" came out of his mouth. The scream gave Thabo a fright. He shook Leruo violently. The latter woke up with a start. He shook his head, rubbed his eyes. Then he gave another piercing scream and dashed for the door, which neither he nor Thabo had bothered to lock. He ran for his life, all the time screaming, "Leave me alone, leave me alone!" But his speedy journey into the unknown was abruptly brought to an end when he bumped into Phaswa.

Phaswa would have been worried that there was something seriously wrong with the boy had his nostrils not caught a whiff of glue as Leruo puffed and panted, held in mid-air by his huge hands. He took the boy back.

Thabo was still in the hut, baffled, but with sufficient presence of mind to snore noisily with the hope that Phaswa would not trouble him.

The Comrades met to take off from where they had failed. When Mahlodi fell into

Refentse's grave not so long ago, the village accused her of being a witch. Especially as practised by those who were not good at it. Many years ago two incidents of this nature took place in other villages. The diviners in the respective villages, when called upon to interpret such strange behaviour, said that one could only fall into a deceased's grave if one had bewitched the deceased.

This time there was no need to consult the doctors. What had happened a long time ago was common knowledge. At that point it seemed that the Comrades could not necklace her because of their fear of Mankweng police. However, the real problem was that they were divided on whether to punish her for practising the evil art. She had killed her own son and that was a family matter, said one section of the Comrades. Others said she had done Tiragalong a great disservice. As matters went, because of the split, they decided to leave her alone. It would have been impossible to justify the retribution they would have suffered at the hands of the police once they were not agreed. As the elders say, lions that do not hunt together get outrun by a limping buffalo, and, as a result, starve.

Now the problem was inadvertently resolved by Leruo.

"I understand your point well," said Comrade Raditaba. "But my point is not that we should punish her because she killed Refentse. He is her own son and we cannot involve ourselves in her family matters. What I am saying is that she killed Tshepo about five years ago. Surely we must bring an end to such behaviour. If we don't, then it will be our turn soon. Unless we all decide not to go and study in the South."

"I support the Comrade over there. Remember, too, that we punished a wrong person for her misdeed. Surely if we can kill the innocent, then we have no reason not to kill the guilty?"

The speaker was Sammy, Refentse's best friend. As he spoke these words, his voice was trembling with anger and his eyes were filled with tears. The most detached of the Comrades could not help being touched. The Comrades were reminded of his oration at Refentse's funeral. As Refentse's friend he was allowed to talk at length about his life. He had emphasised Refentse's sharp vision for the welfare of Tiragalong. He also equally emphasised how generous Refentse always was, so that his education was bound to benefit all in Tiragalong and the neighbourhood. He reminded them of the voluntary library work and teaching Refentse had done for Tiragalong High since he commenced his studies at the University. Everything Sammy had said strongly impressed all present - Refentse's suicide was indeed a loss for the village. And he had rounded his speech off with a befitting praise song for his friend's soul that was now resting in the world of the ancestors.

What Sammy did not hint at in his speech was the possibility that Refentse might have committed suicide because he, Sammy, and Refentse's lover, despite their great affection and respect for him, had nevertheless betrayed him. Refentse had found them in his bedroom on the morning of the Friday when he had returned to his Hillbrow flat to pick up the document he needed for his lectures. His shock deprived him of words. He did not say anything to either of them, he just left for the campus to do his work there. He was to discover that there were times when he could be a most useless teacher who thought more about friendship and sexuality than about books.

When he had returned to the flat in the afternoon his lover was not there. She had feared that he might do something terrible to her. She used to remark to him that quiet people are dangerous because you seldom know what is on their minds. Refentse was the quiet type. But his mind was seldom eaten away by bitterness and ill will.

Sammy, too, did not come, as he often did, to have a drink with Refentse that Friday afternoon. He lacked the courage to apologise to his friend. In the end he was not sure whether, even if he decided to apologise, he would know exactly how to do it. Wrong words might lead him into a deep donga out of which he would not necessarily be able to find his way. He had risked Refentse's wrath. He had no intention of seeing it transformed into action.

Refentse drank by himself that Friday afternoon. But there was very little enjoyment in drinking. It was sunset when he finally found solace by jumping into the street from the balcony of his flat.

Sammy did not give the vaguest hint of these possibilities. As he was sitting down, voices shouted their support. Surely, the voices agreed, the Comrades could not allow Tiragalong to lose people of substance because of the madness of one woman. In the end the Comrades' wrath overcame their fear of the police. And creativity took its toll as Zulu was corrupted in the service of freedom.

It was a fulfilling day for Raditaba.

Raditaba and Phaswa were not friends. It was not just because Phaswa was old and Raditaba was a boy to him. Those who know these things say that Raditaba's father would have married Mahlodi were it not for Phaswa. The two were lovers when Phaswa arrived as a migrant from the South, flashing money in Mahlodi's face as if it were mere sheets of paper. Raditaba's father was poor, as poor as Mahlodi's. Her father was worried that his daughter was getting a little too old and that if she did not take advantage of Phaswa's wealth, marriage would slip through her fingers and it would be humiliating to have a spinster in the family. So it was, that because Raditaba's father did not have money, he was barred from continuing his love affair with Mahlodi.

But that, in itself, would not have been terrible enough to have caused Raditaba to hate Phaswa. As Raditaba and all normal village men, young and old, were aware, marriage was nearly always snatched away by a lucky or daring man. The women of Tiragalong also shared this line of thinking. They did not refrain from trying to woo or seduce a man simply because he had a lover. So Phaswa's rather temporary wealth would not have been a problem were it not for other factors.

Mahlodi, being a woman of remarkable integrity, rejected Phaswa. Even when her father tried to impose his will on her, she remained constant. She remembered well what her father had once told her - that there were times when there was virtue in stubbornness. But when·Raditaba's father could no longer maintain his role in the strained relationship with Mahlodi, he approached the woman who was to become Raditaba's mother.

Phaswa would not leave him in peace. His heart told him that the woman was indeed loveable. Or at least more so than Mahlodi. Phaswa wanted to have a stake in all that was good. He made an effort to follow suit in Raditaba's father's tracks. This time Raditaba's father resolved to declare war on Phaswa. And he was killed in the fight, thus leaving his new love pregnant. Thus what Raditaba resented most was that, when he was born, he had no father to take care of him. As a child, his heart would bleed whenever his playmates talked with fondness of the good things their fathers had done for them. And they talked a lot. His mother was too poor to do what some of these fathers did for their children.

Mahlodi, for her part, had to seek another love. She met Refentse's father, who sadly died shortly after their marriage.

Phaswa came back to her soon after Refentse's funeral, when she was suddenly treated like an outcast. He reminded her that there was always a return to the ruins; it was only to the womb that there could be no return. Since Phaswa seemed to be the only person who showed any interest in her as a full-blooded human being, rather than a scavenging, mysterious, evil spirit, the grudges that she had borne him evaporated like dew in the heat of the morning sun. But, although somewhat of an outcast himself, Phaswa was extremely sensitive to the implications of being associated with her. He suggested that for a start their relationship be secret while they waited for a lull to take root in the village. It would not do to attract further attention to herself, when she was obviously in a grave position. Thus advising her, Phaswa persuaded her that they should only visit each other during the night.

But people also minded their business during the night.

Exactly what Leruo had experienced in his sleep, and shortly thereafter, was unclear. According to Thabo, when he relayed the story to his playmates and friends the following day, Leruo had told him many things. Refentse was still alive, he had said. And so was Tshepo. The two lived in one of Mahlodi's dilapidated huts, the very one that was used by Leruo. They only came out in the middle of the night and went

to work Mahlodi's field. Then they returned before cockcrow in time to avoid meeting people on their way to the busses that daily transported them to their places of work in Pietersburg. Leruo occasionally heard them cry in the night, lamenting their inability to escape the drudgery. When the villagers thought they were burying them, they were merely burying large pieces of wood that magic had caused to resemble them.

It was the kind of frightening news that could not fail to quickly spread throughout Tiragalong and its neighbourhood. When late in the afternoon the blowing horn summoned the villagers to the induna's kraal, neighbours also came to share in the commotion. In the spirit of comradeship, the youth from the neighbouring villages came, too.

The meeting was well attended. One could not even spit onto the ground as it was entirely covered by angry people. As usual, one of the most decisive statements was made by Raditaba. He suggested that the Comrades meet separately, for elders were known to be too disruptive. In their presence no decision to punish the witch would be easily taken. Every time a baboon glanced back over its shoulder, it slowed its pace, he said, so that its pursuer would catch up with it. They were not going to look back like the foolish baboon.

So the Comrades went their own way, leaving the elders greatly puzzled. The Comrades, when angry, could be callous and fierce. The elders were rather afraid of their own children. None of them dared to challenge the Comrades.

Thabo was called to testify as to what he had heard. He said that Leruo had never said such a thing. he added that Leruo also denied ever seeing the late Refentse and Tshepo in Mahlodi's compound.

The Comrades decided to punish Mahlodi all the same. It was obvious that Thabo and Leruo were too frightened to give reliable testimony. It was almost certain that they would not give the kind of testimony that could lead to Leruo's aunt's death. But, of course, even in their madness, people did not just scream in the darkness of a rather cold Autumn morning, running away from the dead, unless the dead were in fact still alive. There must be something of substance to have caused such bizarre behaviour on Leruo's part, the Comrades said. Surely Refentse and Tshepo were still alive. The incident by the graveside had exposed the witch. What Leruo had seen, and in a moment of honesty, when there were no threats of his aunt's impending death, told his friend, Thabo, was confirmation of what was already widely known. As for Phaswa, Raditaba suggested to much applause, his secret night meetings with Mahlodi made it painfully clear that he, too, practised the evil art.

Allan Kolski Horwitz

Graphics by Anna Varney-Horwitz

BLUE

Why do certain images, rather than others, lodge in the mind, resurfacing long after they have imprinted themselves; whether in dreams, snatches of hallucination or reverie, or as fragments of music bursting from the air while trapped in traffic jams, while cooking, washing or making love.

The film is entitled 'Blue'.

Depressed, lonely, melancholy.

But blue is also: peace, freedom, space, tranquillity.

Shirley found the film unconvincing. Why was the main character, Julie, so unrevealing of her feelings? It was to be expected that at first she would be numbed by grief – her husband, Patrice, a famous composer, and their young daughter, had been killed in a car accident – but surely there would be a point when she would react openly and express her anguish and her rage, her sense of impotence. In addition, there was the obvious danger that if she bottled up her grief any one of these emotions could spiral out of control and result in breakdown. However, at the other extreme, if she was wise, there was the possibility of transcendence, in the form of gentleness, leading to an empathy with all people and an understanding of shared pain, a humility built on feeling all losses. Surely the mask would drop? The emotional disfigurement and the vacuum would be unveiled, she would start out again on the torturous road and reconcile with living?

Julie is in a bar, trying to help a neighbour. She finds herself watching television. The program is about Patrice.

Oliver, Patrice's long-standing assistant, displays a photograph. It is of Patrice and another woman, his mistress.

During all the years of their marriage, Julie has had no suspicion of her husband's involvement in another relationship. The revelation is shattering. She is both numbed and enraged.

Was her past happiness real if at the same time he was simultaneously so close to another woman?

Juliet Binoche, the actress who plays the part of Julie, is slightly built, yet conveys a sense of great inner power and control. Shirley greatly admires her poise, her quality of grace softened by woundedness. At times she is so absorbed by Binoche that the dialogue flows past her becoming a stream of sound, dissolving into other auditory components: cars, telephones, the music of orchestras rising ...

Mourning, a woman is thrown into overpowering isolation. While she lives suspended, not knowing if her suffering will end, she hears, in her subconscious, fragments of the music her husband had been composing, his unfinished 'Hymn to Unity', to love and solidarity, to a new age of peace and creativity in a United Europe. But this music is not his composition alone. The key elements have been created by his wife. And with his death, it is finally given to her to complete.

Blue: crystals, a lollipop, a rubbish bag, jeans, a mattress, a pen for correcting music scores. Above all, a pool of blue water in which Julie immerses herself; into which sorrow and tension are released and transformed.

Juliette Binoche has short, black hair that clings round her pale, white face like a helmet. She seems boyish, yet is sensual in a feminine way. Shirley watches her move. There is a coolness that occasionally falters but never visibly alters. The mask remains intact. There is only silence and sadness. Where has she locked up the scream that is surely festering in her, trying to force a way out but being pushed back to writhe in her guts?

Despite Shirley's immediate reaction - that the film isn't entirely credible, that there are sections bordering on melodrama - it has disturbed her, this story of a bereaved woman who discovers her husband was secretly involved with another woman and that it is this woman who is to bear his child into the future. Holding a carton of popcorn in one hand and a large paper cup of cold drink in the other, Shirley watches Julie scrape her fingers against a stone wall till they bleed.

In the dark cell of the movie house, a man in a denim jacket shuffles up the stairs, searching the faces directed towards the screen. He enters a row of seats, brushes against Shirley's legs, and sits down.

The present is always a precipice.

Julie sleeps with Oliver on the night after the accident. Why does this happen?
    On his side the motivation is clear: he has always loved her – but from a distance. Secondly, he wants her help in finishing the 'Hymn to Unity'.

On her side the motivation is more complicated. Is it that she seeks momentary comfort for her pain? Or is it that she feels a violent need to uproot the past?

She leaves him in the morning.

Julie swims, slowly tires and exhilirates the body. Fragments of melody visit her, threads of the hymn. The text of the 'Hymn to Unity' is taken from an ancient Greek poem:

"Without love, one has nothing,
Though one flies with angels' wings.
Without love, one is heavy as a base metal."

The young man slouches, massages his crotch. Shirley ignores him. He continues to play with himself, insisting on her attention. She does not know what to do. The film is very absorbing but he is becoming aggressively exhibitionistic.

"Go away, you stupid man," she calls out. "I'm going to call the manager."

The man stops playing with himself.

It is difficult to believe that Julie can contain her pain without breaking down. It is more difficult to believe that she accepts and befriends her husband's mistress. And instead of being overwhelmed by bitterness and fury, that she congratulates her on being pregnant and offers her the beautiful old house where she and Patrice had shared so much.

It is difficult to believe in such generosity of spirit.

At the end of the film, Shirley and the man both remain seated. The audience files out. The cleaners dawdle in. Shirley refuses to make the first move. She wants the young man to go, wants him to be gone so that she can again visualise and experience the cinema as it was before his arrival and assault on her senses. She wants to purify the atmosphere of his coarseness, his obsession.

She tells one of the cleaners what has happened. The woman laughs. The man is well-known at the complex. He has been thrown out several times. She is surprised that he has managed to sneak back in..

The young man jumps over the seat in front of him and runs out.

Shirley stands up. It is late afternoon. What is she to do? She strolls out into the mall, stops in front of various shop windows and looks at displays of clothes, jewellery, furniture, gardening equipment and medicines. Then she looks at the crowds of people in restaurants and fast food stores — well groomed men and women talking to each other, shopping bags propped up against their chairs.

The hymn is singing itself and she feels hungry.

THE COLOURS OF JOY

TONY'S LETTER

My dearest Shirley,

At first I wanted to write 'Shirlemagne' to show how much I love you and that I can still think of our best times, but my pen has gotten all formal in the spirit of this poisoned situation which doesn't seem to allow any sign of affection.

I'm sitting in Robbie's flat looking at Robben Island and the sailboats in the bay. The sky is throbbing with sunset and, as always, the scene is breathtaking. But I'm feeling really depressed and I'm ready to sleep. I'm only pushing myself to write this letter now because I want to give it to you before tomorrow's meeting. You are still wrapped up in the past and not giving yourself a chance to weigh things up properly. We must find a solution and stop tearing each other up. From my side, I'm still trying to sort everything out, to understand how all this happened and why. I've never known such intensity and so many conflicting emotions. I love you, Shirl but it is a Shirley who has been covered over, who has forgotten herself.

Was this inevitable? We burnt too brightly and I am not used to burning like that? It was only when our passion began to turn into the crucifixion kind that I started to understand how we reap what we sow, and that there are only momentary flashes of grace. But mainly we don't get much of a chance to find our feet. As soon as something comes together, a whole range of dynamics are brought into play and their contradictions start to act out: contradictions of which neither of us were aware before we lived together. There were also contradictions of which we were aware but chose to overlook. Or which seemed minor or secondary at the time and which we decided to ignore, hoping they would go away if we tried hard enough. Or the contradictions which we found positive at first but which later became negative – bits of family history, childhood experiences, past loves, misloves, friendships, other relationships ... and epecially other needs. When you start to live with someone, you begin with a virtual stranger. Then you start to build up a picture, from the inside. You live out nightmares and fantasies. Through the manic and the routine hours; only then can you begin to break the mask.

Shirl, I'm trying to be objective and I don't want to be pedantic so I've decided not to go into detail. It will only antagonise. In any case we've been through the details so many times and they only get in the way and make us shout at each other. What

I do strongly believe is that we don't have to stoop to the level of private detectives and vidoes and all the other humiliating stuff.

If you want a divorce, I will agree to that. If you want to keep everything, I also agree to that. I never married you for money – contrary to what your dear father thinks. My practice is on its feet, I don't need a cent from you. Nor from Bernice. It is the ultimate insult to me. You don't need to go to court so as to block me financially. This really hurts, Shirl, and I beg you to stop it.

I also think back to the months you slept with Jack, without even trying to conceal it. And the night you got drunk at Marlene's and called that American to her bedroom in front of everyone and I had to go out for a drive otherwise I would have killed both of you. And the first time you pushed Bernice against me so that we couldn't move in the corridor because you were holding us together, saying what a wonderful couple we'd make and why don't we try it because everything's so boring.

Since your last exhibition that was the word you kept using about our lives. How flat I'd become, and how predictable and stale all our friends were, and Cape Town and the whole country which you see as a backward pit full of nonentities and philistines. You wanted to live in New York where 'everything's happening', or at least in Paris, or Berlin, where artists have a community and don't live in isolation but help each other and share their visions unlike here where a city of two million people can't even support two or three galleries.

Boring. That's been your feeling the last few years. As if it's my fault. As if it's my obligation to keep you alive, to miraculously transform you and transform myself.

Shirley, is that fair?

Is it my fault you've never gotten the recognition you deserve? No one did more to support you than I did. And as for leaving South Africa, when I finally agreed to explore options, you suddenly got cold feet. I was ready to give up my profession, and you know how difficult it is for an architect to build up a practice, I was ready to give up the rest of my family and a circle of very close friends, all of them, to satisfy you, but your response was to push your sister into my arms so something exciting would happen. And it did happpen. I am not going to deny it.

Bernice and I have been lovers over the past three years. In particular, during the weekends we spent in the cottage at Langebaan. You never wanted to come. You said it blows all the time and the neighbours are idiots. Bernice is a very sweet, kind person who lacks confidence. She waits in the background – where you've always put her even though she's older than you. She was shocked by your proposal but she didn't stop me when I started. And I started because I couldn't believe your vulgarity. You pushed us together and we decided to continue even though, at times, we didn't want to. You played with us and we fell into the game.

When I started this letter, I wanted to write it from start to finish, without a stop, without re-reading, without checking. I wanted it to be completely honest and spontaneous, without censorship, without being strategic. I just wanted to reach you, the best in you that I know and love. But despite these intentions, I've stopped to have a glass of wine and evaluate how far I am. And the amazing thing is that, having read it through three times, I haven't changed a word.

I'm angry at having been manipulated and angry at myself for allowing that to have happened. If only we could exhume ourselves, start again now that the volcano's erupted and overwhelmed us.

I should have insisted we leave. I could have finalised something with Dave Marsh in Bristol. And whether you wanted to or not, I should have just packed everything up. I should have booked us flights and you would have come and very soon you would have enjoyed England and we could have travelled and maybe I would have considered moving to the States despite all my reservations; if only for a while so you could get New York out of your system. You were already in your late-Thirties, Shirl, you wouldn't have danced all night in the East Village with those kids stufffing themselves with drugs. The fact is you've never really known where you want to live so there's an ongoing crisis. You fantasize about leaving, as if that will solve your problems, but you always stay right where you are: right here in Sea Point looking at Signal Hill while you paint out those amazing, inspiring collages of colours.

Yes, you are the strongest artist in the country. That was the thing about you that attracted me from the start. So why, I ask myself, is it so difficult for this extremely gifted, understanding, self-assured, intuitive woman to handle her life?

I repeat: I love you, I want to live with you again. Despite everything, I know we can, in fact, come out stronger. On the other hand, I must emphasize that if you reject what I say, if you truly believe things have gone too far, I will give you an immediate divorce. As I've already said, despite the contract we signed, I'm not asking for a cent of your inheritance. I would only want to take the paintings you have given me over the years. That's all. I don't want anything else.

It's almost midnight. I'd better take this over to you. I phoned you a moment ago. When you answered, I couldn't bring myself to speak. I was overcome by such sadness.

I want you again, Shirl.

Always your's,

Tony

VOICES

Shirley is alone in the studio. The walls are covered with paintings; vibrant blues, greens and browns, swathes of thick paint creating abstractions that breathe with light and depth. But on the easel in front of her is a full-face portrait of a man. The man's features reflect turmoil and growing weariness. She sighs deeply as she studies it. Then she goes out onto the balcony that runs the length of the flat and looks out at the ocean.

As a child she would watch the ships' lights in the bay and the beacon on Robben Island. The beacon was programmed in a rhythm that allowed no variation. It was a constant spark that flashed and died, pulsing, then vanishing, melting into the purple rim of Bloubergstrand. She would watch the lights without blinking for as long as she could. Then she would read her favourite book about a little girl whose mother and father are kidnapped by a sorcerer and locked up in the cellar of a house. And she is the only one who can free them.

Her father's voice is lively, "I'm settling in beautifully. They're treating me like a VIP, Shirl, absolutely five star treatment!"

There is a queue behind him: Louise, her eldest sister, who chatters away with her daughters, and Derek, her only brother, whose son keeps up a constant stream of demands. His whine dominates the background.

"Happy birthday, Dad," Shirley repeats. "Hope they've got enough candles and a decent cake. I know how Derek likes to splurge."

The line is faint, each word echoing, rising up from the cable swaying on the Pacific bed, letting loose a few bubbles, then slipping to the surface to evaporate, pale thuds against the drumskin of heaven.

"He cleaned out the neighbourhood shop. They only had sixty in stock. He had to go specially to town to pick up another twenty-five. It was like the Queen Elizabeth! And you? Are you well, love? Have you seen Tony lately?"

"No."

"And Bernice?"

"No."

"You should go out more. How's that new fellow of yours?"

"Norman sends his love. He's in Durban on business. Really, I'm fine. I've just been out with a friend. We had dinner at the Vineyard, that French restaurant."

Gathered round the telephone, they shout together, "We miss you, Shirl, oh yes, we do, WE MISS YOU."

Her father says, "The weather's wonderful. We're going to the beach tomorrow."

Then Derek takes the phone and tries to say a final, abrupt goodbye on behalf of them all.

"This is costing you a fortune, Shirl. I'll ring off now. We'll call you before they fly back to Melbourne."

But her father speaks again.

"It's a wonderful party. We're only missing you, my darling. You must come soon. Everything's so marvellous here, it's like the old days. I'll make the booking."

The least she can do is phone on his birthday. After all, she is no longer angry with him for what he did to her mother. She has perspective now: they were both oppressors. Each, in turn, used and sacrificed the other. But why did Bessie, who was so strong and resourceful, fail to break the vicious circle that made them both so unhappy? Why did she, despite her intelligence and energy, allow him to dominate? And then, after each crisis and confrontation, allow his sourness and reproaches to provoke her retreat into silence?

Morrie Katz would come back from the furniture shop in Salt River at seven o'clock every evening. They would immediately eat. He would sit at the head of the table and question them about school, checking their class marks, making sure they were always in the top three places.

"Never mind sport. Leave that to the stupid ones. Just get on with your studying. Soon you'll go out into the world and then those marks you sweated for will turn to gold."

"Shirl, is that you? I tried earlier. You were out."

"Yes, of course it's me. Who were you expecting?"

"My God, you're crabby! How's it going? You sound depressed."

"Don't talk nonsense, Norman. I'm just a little tired."

"What are you doing?"

"What are YOU doing?"

"I asked first."

"So what."

"Sew buttons."

"That's an old one."

"It's a good one."

"Don't be silly."

"Don't be stubborn."

"Why shouldn't I be stubborn?"

"It's not your nature to be stubborn."

"You're right. Except about you. I've been missing you. I'm in the hotel. I'm watching TV."

"Missing me?"

"Yes, you and you alone. Don't you believe me?"

"I'm sorry, Norman. I'm tired. I've been working in the studio the whole day."

"Fantastic, darling! You haven't painted for ages."

"Why do you say that? I designed those cards for you."

"Ja, but you said they weren't really art."

"What do you know about art? I did those cards the way you wanted them."

"I know, I know, Shirl! You did a great job! I love them. But you said they weren't really 'Art'."

"What did I say about art?"

"Darling, listen to me, you idiot. I only phoned to say how much I miss your warm little ..."

The intercom suddenly buzzes, drowning out Norman's endearment. She cuts him off and hurriedly says good-bye, then replaces the telephone receiver. The buzzer rings again, even more insistently. She runs to the front door and answers.

It is strange to hear Tony's voice. He sounds calm but firm. She is amazed at her immediate agitation. The wind gusts over the intercom at the ground floor security door.

"Shirley, can I bring up a letter? I'm sorry it's so late but I didn't think you'd be asleep."

"A letter? If it's from your lawyer, give it to Mendel in the morning."

"It's from me, Shirl."

"Whatever you've got, give it to Mendel."

There is a pause. "Please, Shirl." His voice is tremulous. "Please!"

"It's too late."

"Buzz me in."

"No."

"Why not?"

"Give it to Mendel. God, what am I saying? Tear it up! How dare you come here to give me a rehash of all your excuses."

"I'm sliding it under the main door." The wind comes up again as she hears him say, "This is the last time I'll try to communicate with you. I promise."

There is a great banging sound and she wonders if he has smashed the glass door.

"I love you."

She takes the lift down to the foyer. The seagulls cry outside. An envelope is wedged under the main door.

On it Tony has written: TO SHIRLEY KATZ: FROM THE HEART, TO THE HEART.

She slits the envelope open with her nails.

She was the first to say it was unsafe for Morrie to live alone in the flat. Most of his friends were dead, he was sickly himself. And what could she and Bernice offer him? It made sense that he join those of his children who were settled in Australia with families of their own. Besides, Louise had always been more tolerant of him and she had more time.

Before he left, Shirley used to see him every Wednesday afternoon. They would go out for a drive and have tea in the Gardens. Sometimes she would bring him to the flat and show him her paintings. She offered him books about abstract expressionism and pointed out what she'd been trying to achieve but all he did was smile and ask if she was happy, then inquire when she was going to have a child and if Tony's practice was ever going to get off the ground.

Morrie would also visit them on Friday nights. He would sit at the head of the table and mumble the blessing, then quickly gulp the too sweet muscadel as he tried not to spill but always managed to sticky his fingers. Tony told her this praising of the Creator of the Vine made him visualise the sturdy roots thrusting down into their specially fertilised earth, rich grape clusters opening under sunlight, ripening into juicy succulence. Raising his glass, he would propose an ecumenical toast. After coffee they would have a liqueur and watch a video. By ten, when Morrie started to nod off, Tony and the nurse would slip on his overcoat and help him down to the car.

It was also useless for Tony to speak to him about her painting, to try and ignite some pride in him for his daughter's achievements - his youngest child, once the reddest apple in the fruit bowl of his affection; this daughter who never had to earn a living, receiving a monthly stipend from him since the age of eighteen.

The genius of Shirley's work, Tony would say to Morrie, was her ability to invent categories of visual harmony so far advanced that few were currently able to appreciate them.

It has been years since her mother's death.

"Enjoy, my darling," Morrie would say to her. "It's all for you. Enjoy."

She tosses orange peels off the balcony; bright strips spiralling down to the dark blur of the street. She steps back into the studio. All the lights are off. She is unbearably tired but cannot fall asleep again. Despairingly she takes a tranquilliser, collapses into bed and blanks out. But before dawn she is woken by a car alarm. The siren wails out in giant pulses over the palm trees, an adamant howl that forces her to close the windows and the door on the porch. Afterwards she sleeps through till nine o'clock, leaving no time for a bath, only a quick shower and then a frazzled rush to town.

Shirley arrives for the meeting with smudged eye-shadow and an empty stomach. Mendel senses that something is wrong and offers her a schnapps. For the first time in years, she drinks alcohol in the morning and it goes straight to her head.

Tony and Bernice arrive separately. Shirley had demanded that Bernice also come. In addition to seeing Bernice's general reactions for herself, it would be an opportunity to discuss their inheritance.

Mendel meets them at the door to his office. He is businesslike without being nasty. When they are all seated in a small conference room, he quotes the dates and details of the times Tony and Bernice were seen together by the detectives, both at Bernice's flat and at a hotel in Newlands. He lays copies of the videos and the photographs on the polished table. What he does not show is the pit into which Shirley has been thrown during those months. And out of which she is still climbing. And if she is now nearing the rim, too often she still slips down and is swallowed up in the blackness.

They sit in the cream-walled conference room. Shirley watches Tony and Bernice listen in a state of growing shock while Mendel spells out the terms of divorce and the conditions under which she agrees to ever meet with Bernice - the only time she agrees to again be with her in the same room will be at their father's funeral.

Mendel asks when their attorney is arriving.

Tony answers that there is no one representing them, they have come hoping to resolve the matter not to score legal points. More importantly, he wants to hear Shirley's response to his letter.

She hears the wind howling.

Tony insists on her response before allowing the meeting to continue.

Mendel cuts him off.

"I can't see the relevance of that now but let me discuss it with my client. Would you like tea or coffee in the meantime?"

They stand up. Mendel opens the door.

Shirley is aware of the anguish in Tony's eyes. As expected, Bernice has been unable to engage her and has withdrawn, folding herself deep into the leather chair. Now, however, as she leaves the room, Bernice gives her a searching, wounded look as if she is the injured one, the abused. Bernice, the third child, the second girl, waiting for the True Man who will hold her and make her a haven, a world in which none prey upon each other and none speak harshly. Bernice sits in Mendel's office offering the martyred look which has always been imprinted on her face; the lines of which have been progressively deepened by her many disastrous relationships. It was typical of Bernice to allow Tony to talk and express himself while she sat with lowered eyes.

"Why am I so stupid, always trusting? I know Shirley. She wants more and more. And poor dad giving in, always finding ways to look after her, making me out to be an idiot."

Mendel offers Shirley a cigarette. As he raises the lighter to her lips, his thick, hairy fingers touch hers. It is an old-fashioned lighter with a silver case. On it, embellished in flowery strokes, is the outline of a yacht. He holds the flame as his breath sweeps lightly over her. His breath is sweet with the smell of peppermint.

Tony's letter lies folded in her handbag.

She was ten years old. She wanted to be an explorer. They were living in a house with fake turrets and an attic that was empty and unused. She was enraptured by a book that described the great pioneering flights of the earliest aviators, the first aerial crossings of the oceans and continents. The brave aviators were all men. But once she reached the chapter about Amelia Earheart, Shirley knew that she could also take on the challenge of solitude, hardship and danger. More than that, she would glide in the slipstreams of giant birds that appeared out of the sky, invisible to radar, to lead her to the pure, immaculate realm of God. Years later she painted this vision as a Soul floating above a sequence of bodies; the bodies were growing and withering, begetting and dying, while the pristine Soul, emanating silvery blue, pulsated with Eternity.

Yes, she was determined that whatever the pressures, she would make her mark and be applauded. No matter what anyone said, she would present her challenge, she would be a world-class artist. But when the reviews of her first exhibition were dismissive, even denigrating, she was thrown into turmoil. How she hated the critics! They were unimaginative and obtuse, possessors of trivial, one-dimensional minds incapable of being inspired. They said she lacked technique, that her colours were too messy, her sense of composition untuned. They said her style and subject matter were too ethereal, too detached to have relevance in South Africa. The more extreme reviews implied that Abstraction was a CIA plot to take people's minds off the political struggle, and that if her work claimed to be spiritual, it was too esoteric to have popular appeal. For years, despite this negative consensus, despite the public's failure to recognise her art's energy and purity, she was proud to defy such opinions. But that was years ago. Then she had felt heroic and stood her ground. Now she needs to gather her strength and contain the past, in particular, the immediate past, before it drags her down.

She is on the edge of the depression. It needs just a fraction more determination to dig herself out and she will be able to enter a new phase with Norman. But if she is starting to love him, why is she so sharp and irritated when he phones? What has provoked her? She needs him, his comforting, basic appetites, his straightforward, everyday sense that cuts through her morbidity. What has happened is irreversible. Tony's letter is a string of rationalisations. How can she ever forgive him?

Leaning on the balcony railing, she watches the Island lighthouse flick red and green, tantalising the belly of darkness. Further out on the ocean, a ship's arc of lights arrests her eyes.

Shirley stands in front of the kitchen sink washing dishes. The massive, graceful outline of Lion's Head rises above the slopes covered with red roofs and palm trees. Mendel's invitation to dinner has taken her by surprise. She is uncertain whether to accept; there is no doubt in her mind as to the nature of their relationship.

The sink glistens with a gauze of soap bubbles. She enjoys the heat seeping into her fingers. Light slants onto the geranium pot set above the sink and the flowers vibrate with growth. The piano playing of Vladimir Horowitz fills the kitchen. The music swirls over her. She visualises herself at the sink with the sun shining into the kitchen and the shimmering endlessness of the ocean filling the window. She swells with determination to put herself together and recreate the best in herself. And if she is upset with herself for having been short with Norman earlier, what about her father's telephone call just a few hours after her birthday greeting to him? The ringing had broken into her dream. His broken voice continues to sound in her mind.

The painting which stands in the centre of her studio is a portrait of a man in his early forties. He has a high, domed forehead and wide, candid eyes. His lips are full and generous and the nose is straight if a little too broad. The portrait has been there for many months. At first, she worked furiously, hours and hours each day, then abruptly left it. Now all the lines are present, except for the cheeks, half of which are shaded with colour. The portrait challenges her to reach completion but she is disoriented: daylight makes the lips lift in a curve that borders on a sneer. She is bewildered. What more can she do?

The fact is: Tony had served her for almost eight years. And if the buildings he designed were not soaring cathedrals, they were also not the worst commercial and industrial blots on the city. Certainly in regard to her painting, he had been the first to support her attending art school. And once she finished the cycle, 'A Celestial Voyage', he had organised her first exhibition. Afterwards, at the most critical points, it had been his refusal to accept her breakdowns of confidence that had stimulated her return to painting. He was always her champion even when they began living together and she had to fight her family's opposition because he was Catholic. Strangely after Bessie's death, Morrie accepted him. So much so that when Shirley told him about Tony and Bernice, he had refused to believe her and refused to watch the video Mendel's detective had filmed. He had only agreed to look at some of the photographs when she threatened to stop speaking to him if he didn't.

Shirley will never forget the old man trembling as he looked at the photograph of Tony and Bernice kissing in front of her flat. He had sat dumbly in her living room. The next day he phoned to say it was shocking and must stop but that no one could be blamed, it was one of those things that just bursts out. It almost seemed he judged her and Bernice more harshly than Tony; especially Bernice. Tony, he implied, had succumbed to pressures he could not have been expected to resist.

Norman had been present at a Sunday braai to which she'd been invited by one of her casual friends. From the moment Shirley joined the crowd at the swimming pool, he had shown his interest. But, as importantly, despite showering her with attention, despite his transparent desire and constant praising of her beauty, he was slow to make demands, deferring to her every wish and indulging her lack of response.

Slowly, he had saved her. She is not ashamed to admit this. He had saved her by taking her out of herself: entertaining her at restaurants and shows, sending a stream of thoughtful gifts. And for three successive days, at a health farm in the Cedarberg, he had actually made her feel unself-conscious and fulfilled. When they arrived back in Sea Point, she had, at last, welcomed him to her bed.

Mendel is taken aback. Expecting aggression or, at the very least, a defensive sullenness, he has not known how to deal with Tony's composure, his presence that radiated sincerity.

"My client and I must first discuss the letter and, with due respect, I believe we must discuss it in private. This is a very complex and personal matter."

Mendel takes Shirley to his office. There, he is abrupt with her, barely concealing his anger.

"Why didn't you tell me about it? I hope we haven't compromised the case. Besides, we don't have much time. I've got another consultation in half an hour."

Shirley looks aggrieved.

"There's nothing in it. He sets out the same terms. There isn't a single new move on his part."

"Nothing?"

"I told you."

"Give me the letter, please."

"There's nothing new in it. Don't you believe me?"

"I would prefer to read it myself before we jump to conclusions. It may be used as evidence in court and you could be at a disadvantage."

"Mendel, there's nothing in it! In any case, you can't read it now, I've left it at home."

"Then go back and fetch it! We'll adjourn this meeting until I've studied it."

"There's no point to that."

"Let me be the judge of that. We can only stop him getting half of your assets if he's making outrageous demands."

"What can it change? I can never trust either of them again. For over a year he's been trying to win me back but I'm sick of his false repentance."

"What was the offer? Does he agree that you keep both houses and the flat? And your collection?"

Mendel offers her a cigarette. His hand is slightly moist as he raises the lighter.

"I'm saying this for your own good, Shirley. I know all the tricks people use in divorces. I've seen the most unbelievably distorted, unfair settlements. No matter how sharp you are, as your lawyer, I insist on seeing that letter." He pauses. "Otherwise I can't go on with the case."

Tony and Bernice have wounded her raw. Her name is mud, people talk about her in hushed tones, she is pitied but also despised. The divorce talks are unbearably ugly but Tony is giving her no choice, the humiliation is so bad her guts are shrivelled with crying knowing that so many hypocritical, ignorant fools are laughing at her.

Shirley stops herself from responding. She suddenly feels disgusted by Mendel, his short, podgy body, balding and slack.

"He doesn't mention anything about the houses. Christ! Make him lose everything! But I don't have the letter, Mendel. I didn't even open it. I threw it down the rubbish chute."

She knows that she can still alter the portrait, nothing has irrevocably set. She can entirely change that face, make it cramped and mean, inward looking. What prevents her from doing so? Will such changes be true? Will she not be allowing her judgement to be twisted by her private hurt?

This is still the central issue of her life.

They were outside Morrie's flat, standing at the front door waiting for the lift. She'd brought him some poppy seed rolls. The neighbour was there with one of her bridge partners. They were all chatting. When Morrie was introduced to this woman, Shirley noticed how he tried to straighten up and hold in his stomach, smiling in an obviously false way while patting her hand. He was lonely. Of course, he was lonely. But did he have to slobber? Yet she had to admit he had never acted like this while her mother was alive, he had never betrayed her though his friends had affairs and their wives knew what was happening but chose to keep quiet. These women were extensions: mothers and housewives. They had no other means of making their mark. It was a generational thing, this dependence, not a personal reflection on their inadequacy. Though there were a few exceptions like Maisie Levy, who was an estate agent and made as much money as any man. But then, she was a divorcee and had lived alone for twenty years. And sooner or later, everyone slept with her. Except for Morrie. Everyone knew about Solly Lapin and Jack Abrahams. The woman was shameless, befriending the wives so she could get close to their men. But Bessie surprised everyone. She said she couldn't just blame Maisie. "Yes," her mother would say, "with some of us, it's a call of nature we can't resist. And what if you're lonely and there's no other way to attract men?" And as Morrie used to say: "Why God ever made us this way, who knows. It was cruel of Him to make us like this but He did. He gave us Life and for that we have to be grateful. The way He thinks isn't clear to us but it must be clear from His height, and if He wants men and women to make fools of themselves, that isn't Morrie Katz's fault."

"I'm sorry, my darling. I didn't mean to wake you."

"Dad, are you alright? Is everything OK?"

She is befuddled, waking from a dream that was colliding with the thick, half-sobbing voice that she heard rasping into her ear, a telephone call from Sydney jangling into her sleep.

"Shirl, I was never cruel to your mother, not wanting to ... you see, I never wanted to make her unhappy. I promise you, my darling, she meant a lot to me but so often we wanted different things and when we couldn't agree, she would refuse to, to ... you understand? Shirl, she would make me wait and I would get angry. That's what happened and I want you to know. I'm an old man now, I don't want to fight. I've had enough fighting. I want to set things right, I'm ready to go ..."

She experiences a surge of closeness to him, then a gradual cloudiness. How is she to create a single, coherent response?

"I missed you so much after you phoned this evening. I thought, yes, there isn't time. I must say to you what I couldn't ever explain, I must explain why things were like they were. She was a proud woman, Shirl. Your mother was very, very proud. She wanted people to like her and respect her. I gave her everything I could, yes, I did, everything I could, but she wasn't satisfied. So you children saw some terrible things. I don't deny it, you saw some terrible things that I hated, Shirl. I only hit her once and that was because she forced me, she forced me, you know how she could go on and on and on ... I was never cruel to your mother, I never wanted to harm her but she would make me wait and I would get angry ... that's what happened, Shirl, you know what I mean, she wouldn't let me ..."

"She told me about that a long time ago."

"She told you?"

"Yes, dad. And I told her she was wrong. She was wrong to punish you that way. She should have left you long before she got so choked up that she demeaned both of you. It was terribly wrong of her to live with you but refuse to sleep with you."

"She talked to you about this?"

"Come on, dad, that's all she ever spoke about. Her wanting to leave but not having the guts to."

Why had she been so snappy with Norman? It was sweet of him to phone from Durban. But then he is always considerate and patient.

He promises to take her to the Wild Coast Casino, there is a conference coming up. She will love it – the beach and the river mouth, drinks in the evening overlooking the ocean. They will watch dolphins surfing and the fin of a great white shark cut through the waves. And at night there will be gaming tables where she will throw away some of his hard earned insurance commissions.

Mendel has his right hand on the white tablecloth. It is very broad and tanned with well-cropped nails flecked with tiny, white calcium blotches. It grips any other hand firmly when introduced and sifts through documents with authority, pressing buttons, signing contracts. That is its strongest point: it can frame the tightest of contracts for the weakest of cases. Money emboldens, fortifies it. But it is a hand that also excels at stroking and playing with the contours of the female body. In fact, at the level of preference, that is its speciality, though it is also affectionate to children and animals.

Mendel's manicured hand now plays with his silver lighter.

After the appetizers, when he rises and visits the men's room, Shirley takes a pen from her bag and begins drawing on the table cloth but before the sketch can take shape, her cell phone rings.

"It's me again, darling. I'm back at the hotel. What a lousy day, I need cheering up. Are you still my scented sugarloaf?"

"Mm ..."

"My steaming chicken pie?"

"Mm ..."

"My mushroom omelette?"

"With or without chips?"

"With chips."

"Tomato sauce?"

"Of course."

"Lots of sauce?"

"Slinky–slinky sauce."

"Goose and gander, perforce?"

"Who's with you?"

"What do you mean?"

"Who the hell is with you?"

"I don't get you, Shirl ..."

"Answer me, goddamit!"

"No one, I'm alone."

"I don't believe you."

"Why do you say that?"

"I can hear her breathing."

"Don't be ridiculous, Shirl! I'm alone. And I'm feeling shit. I didn't settle that deal and I don't know if we'll make it to the Wild Coast next week ..."

Mendel rests his knee very lightly against hers. Shirley moves back surprised. He continues talking about the meeting, repeating his concern at Tony's offer.

"Don't you want to compromise? He's made out a strong case for at least the paintings. He'll be able to prove that you gave them to him."

"I don't care. Let him struggle to get anything."

"Shirley, don't go overboard. That can prove expensive. The court will consider you unreasonable and award him more than he should get."

"I'll take the chance if it will teach him a lesson."

"What lesson? He's lost you already and that's the biggest loss of all."

Mendel smiles. A waiter arrives, a stocky man with shiny shoes. He brings an ice bucket and a bottle of champagne. Mendel orders oysters. Then he shifts his knee, this time resting it squarely against Shirley's long, brown, bare leg.

She does not react. He presses closer.

"Come on, Shirley, be reasonable. The man needs something to remember you by. The past may be the past but he's a human being, after all, despite what he did ..."

She turns to the window; the harbour lights glow. Mendel begins to slowly move

his knee against her.

She can no longer ignore his action.

"What is it you want now, Shirley? Isn't it time to close the past, to move on, create new ..."

He takes her hand. She faces him, watches him flush, his portly cheeks suddenly rosied, then she kicks him as hard as she can. And when he shouts out, howling with pain and surprise, startling the crowded restaurant, she is in the studio and on her palette is a mixture of yellow and red and green, and on the easel before her the portrait of Tony glows with intelligence and vitality.

She starts to paint.

ASHFORD

A woman has a baby boy. The father of the boy has left her and is living with one of her closest friends. Faced with this double betrayal, she becomes bitter and withdrawn and, some months after the father has moved out, dreams that her son will drown in the river which flows through the grounds of a school called Ashford College. The woman has never heard of such a school but the dream is so vivid that she decides to check if it exists. She finds out that Ashford College is a very expensive private school situated north of Johannesburg and that a river, the Jukskei, runs through its grounds.

At this time she is living far away from the school, in a diametrically opposite direction, so she is not unduly concerned. But gradually, as her baby grows into a healthy and strong young boy, she begins to live in constant fear that somehow, despite her utmost efforts, the dream will come true. Her fear is so great that she considers hanging a sign round his neck:

THIS CHILD MAY NOT ENTER ASHFORD COLLEGE.
HE HAS A RARE DISEASE WHICH CAN BE CONTRACTED
FROM A PLANT GROWING IN THE SCHOOL GROUNDS.
SHOULD YOU FIND HIM WANDERING ON HIS OWN,
IMMEDIATELY RETURN HIM TO HIS MOTHER.

At the age of six, on the night before his first day at school, the boy has this dream: It is a rainy summer morning. His mother drives him to his new school in her old car. They arrive at the ivy covered buildings. She stops in front of a big wooden gate, gives him a kiss, then pushes him out. He stands alone with his brown school case. A tall man in a uniform stands at the entrance. The boy hesitates but the guard motions to him to step forward. The gate swings open. Beyond the well-tended, rolling lawns, he sees the turbulent waters of a flooding river, the bodies of drowned people being swept along. He also sees pots and pans, plastic buckets and underwear in the torrent. He steps back from the gate. As he does so, he wakes up, shivering with fear.

The day after this dream, a distant uncle, with whom they have infrequent contact, arrives unexpectedly. After dinner, the uncle tells them about another of his nephews who is an excellent rugby player. The boy is in the First Team at a prestigious school. He offers to show them a photograph, takes out a copy of his nephew's school magazine. The cover shows the main entrance to a building. The security guard and the gate in the photograph are identical to those in the boy's dream.

Years pass. The mother becomes more relaxed; her son is older and more responsible, more independent. She has told him of her original dream and warned him to keep away from Ashford College. But then, on the night of his sixteenth birthday, they both have the following identical dream:

He is hitch-hiking on a highway. A young, attractive girl of his own age driving a sports car stops to give him a lift. She tells him that she is going to her brother's school; a cross country race is taking place and the prize is very valuable. She asks if he would like to enter, but before he can respond, she removes the purple scarf which holds back her long hair and ties it round his wrist. He blushes and steps into the car. They arrive at the school. He sees spreading lawns that lead down to a trickling stream. Several hundred runners are massed at the starting line. He joins them, and while he stands in the middle of the jostling boys, the girl is swallowed up in the crowd of spectators. Then, as the pistol cracks and the runners shoot off, the dreams diverge.

In the boy's dream, the path along the stream is narrow and the runners are forced to bunch together. They are all fit, psyched up young men, the atmosphere is very competitive and intimidating, but the boy, emboldened by the purple scarf tied round his wrist, is determined to win. Midway through the race, he surges to the front. With a quarter of the course to go, only he and one other runner remain in contention. They enter the final stage. Despite the roar of the crowd, he hears the girl's voice – she calls out, urging him on. As the finishing line comes into view and he prepares for the final sprint, the other runner grabs the scarf at his wrist and pulls him violently to the side. The boy stumbles, falls to the ground. As he lifts his eyes, he sees that the stream's water level has suddenly risen – a flash flood is about to sweep down and overshoot the banks. He scans the crowd. The girl is still shouting support to him, encouraging him to get up and continue the race; she faces away from the oncoming torrent. He tries to call out a warning but before he can open his mouth, the water crashes down.

In the mother's dream, the pistol is fired and the boy sets out on the race. Excited by carrying the girl's scarf, he pushes himself furiously. However, he overexerts himself and twists an ankle. Limping along, he cannot keep up with the other runners. He begins to sweat profusely from the effort and uses the scarf to mop his forehead. Hobbling behind, he frantically wipes the perspiration pouring down his face, but the scarf cannot soak up the flood of sweat. He struggles to breathe. He wrings out the scarf but it remains saturated. He loses sight of the other runners and is far from the girl, the mass of spectators. Sweat gushes down into his nose and mouth. He gasps in panic. As the mother realises that he is about to drown, she wakes.

Years pass. The boy finishes school and goes to university. He begins to spend nights out with young women but his mother constantly warns him against any involvement. She argues that he will be tricked into having a child or that he will contract a fatal sexual disease. The boy, now a self-assured young man, becomes impatient with her negative, doom-laden haranguing and stops confiding in her.

The woman he likes most is tall and has long hair. One day, while visiting her home in one of the wealthy northern suburbs, he passes the triple garage where the family cars are kept and sees a beautifully maintained sports car. He suggests they take it for a drive. The young woman has never before been permitted to drive this car; it is her father's most treasured possession, a very expensive collector's item. But to her surprise, when she asks for permission, her father unhesitatingly agrees. He explains that it is because he likes and trusts the young man.

She covers her long hair with a bright scarf and they set off. They leave the suburbs behind and take a quiet road into the countryside. She drives fast, the car performs well, accelerating and taking sharp corners with ease. Suddenly a rattling sound comes from the engine. Within seconds, a cloud of smoke pours out and she is forced to pull over. Flames rise up. The young man jumps out and throws sand onto the bonnet. Within a few minutes he manages to extinguish the fire. They are overjoyed but after the engine has cooled, the car will not start. It is an isolated area and they have no means of repairing the damage. There is no alternative – he must seek help while she waits. They agree that he should not phone her father unless it is absolutely necessary. So the young man sets off on foot. Before he leaves, he kisses the young woman on the lips. In response, she takes off her scarf and winds it round his neck.

It is the beginning of winter. Already the veld is brown and dry, the air charred and sooty with grass fires. He makes good progress along the winding road. Despite the smokiness, there is also a crisp edge so that when he exhales, his breath turns into little clouds of vapour. The scarf presses against his skin, curls snugly round his neck. It gives off the scent of her perfume, of her body. He inhales deeply, buries himself in her fragrance. Then he begins to whistle. He forgets his anxiety about her father's car and is wholly absorbed in breathing in the young woman's sweetness.

After some time he comes upon a side road which he decides to walk down. Beyond the first bend is a cluster of ivy-covered stone buildings. At the entrance is a big wooden gate with a security boom. Above the gate is a large sign: ASHFORD COLLEGE. Next to the gate stands a guard in a blue uniform. The guard greets him. The young man explains what has happened. The guard replies that he cannot help but that the young man should follow the main path which leads to a reception office where he will find a telephone to call an emergency service. Disappointed but still

appreciative, the young man thanks the guard and enters the school grounds.

In front of him are thick, green lawns stretching down to the Jukskei river. But the Jukskei barely flows; isolated brownish puddles, broken branches and a few ripped tyres litter the riverbed. There is no sign of an office, the buildings near the river bank are all shut up. The school seems deserted. Then, while he is deciding what to do, the guard sneaks up from behind and knocks him on the head with a brick.

The young man falls to the ground and rolls into the river. He lies there, helpless, dazed and bleeding. The guard goes through his pockets. There is only a single ten rand note. Angered by this small amount, the guard grabs the scarf which is still wound round his neck, and pulls it tight. The young man gasps. The guard swears and pulls tighter. The young man kicks out wildly. He catches the guard in the stomach. The guard grunts, squeezes even harder, pushes his face into a muddy pool. The young man cannot breathe, his mouth fills with water. The scarf is now a swathe of fire blotting out the sky. With a last desperate effort he manages to ram a finger into the guard's eye. The guard screams and loosens his grip. The young man knocks him over, picks up a rock and smashes it down repeatedly onto his head.

The guard lies inert. The young man sits quietly in the water, waits for his breathing to steady. In a few minutes he will get up and walk back down the side road to the young woman and the car. But before doing so, he will search the guardhouse and find a spanner. Later he will use the spanner to wedge open the bonnet and repair the damage. And once he has done so, they will drive off without having to phone her father for help. They will hold hands and drive deeper into the mountains.

COURAGEOUS AND STEADFAST

Leaning out of her fifth floor hotel room window, Rose looks up at the rising white moon. The full moon, shining with muted but potent fire, spatters a silvery ribbon onto the amniotic waters of the Indian Ocean. Then she follows the movement of waves across the wide bay. Beyond these regular, seemingly identical waves are the sharp outlines of ships strung with lights, silhouettes of cranes fitted on their decks for hoisting containers. And above them all, at the edges of the moon's radiant circle, is the black thicket of sky merging with the horizon; a swollen mass that descends into the dark welling of the ocean depths.

She has just showered. Wrapped in a soft white towel, she feels refreshed, but earlier in the day she had felt ill. The air-conditioned conference hall made her head throb so the first thing she had done on returning to her room was to open the windows. A layer of humidity immediately covered her. Now, hours later, despite the heat, she still feels a slight chill. In addition, her stomach turns; a sharp churning that makes her wince. This is the third day she has been diarrhoetic. Faced with the abundant and varied hotel buffet, despite her resolution to eat only simple food and to eat as moderately as possible, she has continued to pack her plate. As a result, after breakfast and lunch, as well as after the tea breaks when they served scones with jam and cream, she has been forced to run for the toilet.

The afternoon sessions stuttered, stagnating into a duel between Tshabalala and Ladbrooke: Black Nationalist Capitalist Economist versus White Social Democratic Development Expert. The Civic representatives sat listlessly while the two academics argued past each other. The session facilitator, a mediator from a local NGO, was too weak to intervene, so the subject, 'The Role of the State in Facilitating Small Business as a Tool for Advancing Black Economic Empowerment', was buried under overly technical and abstract arguments.

The afternoon only briefly came alive: the speaker was an older man from one of the small towns in the Northern Cape; a short, strong looking, copper-brown man with a white beard and a large spreading nose. During the tea break after his input, Rose asked who he was. She was told his name was Ivan Legodi and that he had spent twenty-one years in exile.

Rose looks out at the breakwaters jutting into the sea. Along these massive concrete platforms are the distant figures of people fishing for sand sharks. She looks down at the promenade running between the strip of hotels and the beach. The promenade is lit by plastic lamps spaced along the maze of paths weaving between fun fairs and children's wading pools that gleam blue and yellow under the lights. The paths are lined with thick, fleshy shrubs and flamboyant trees under which women are sprawled; shapeless black women clothed in sacks or shabby dresses, some with towels tied round their waists, lying on mats or on the concrete paving. Next to them, arranged in neat rows, are beaded hair-bands, bangles, pouches, belts, earthen and iron pots, grass baskets and cheap leather bags, as well as rows of stone elephants, rhinos, giraffes and buck.

By four o'clock, at the end of the session, Rose had felt tense and exhausted. Now it is eight and she is relaxed though her eyes are still dazzled by the sight of the white bathroom and its gadgets. The shower tap was difficult to adjust. She turned the control dial clumsily and the jet of water that shot out was either too hot or too cold. She had stood in the bath, naked and dry, swearing. Afterwards, once she found the right balance, she lost track of time: eyes closed, skin tingling, steaming under the perfectly modulated jet of water. And while the water poured over her, she heard Legodi's voice, hammering and insistent, "We know that as black people we have suffered much. We know that being poor is the chief reason for our sorrows. But while it is true that we need to create a class of business people, of entrepreneurs who will create jobs and wealth, black people should not view other black people as stepping stones for their individual success. We must not only seek personal gain. We carry the responsibility to look for ways of improving everyone's well-being."

She remembers the rest of the whispered brief history: he had supported a group of MK soldiers jailed at Quatro, the ANC prison in Angola, following the mutiny of 1983. After some of these men were executed, he had resigned as Cultural Representative to one of the East bloc countries. His study grant was cut. Soon afterwards his wife died and he found a job teaching English and politics at a college in Ghana. He remained in Ghana until his return to South Africa in 1994. Since then he had taught history at the local township high school of his home town in the Northern Cape.

The luxurious hotel carpet fills the spaces between her toes. The heavily scented, absorbent white towel clings to her even as she allows it to fall from her shoulders. As it falls, she notices a large, brown smear on the towel. And though this is a three star hotel and there are plenty of clean white towels in each room, she walks back to the bathroom, resolving to scrub out the mark and hang the towel over the balcony.

Rose stares at the dun-coloured streak on the soft, white texture and fills the wash basin with warm water. The stain is a shock. She has not made such a stain since she was five years old. That summer, during the three days a week Ma was away cleaning and washing for Mrs Taylor who lived in Kenilworth, Auntie Geraldine would bring a packet of Marie biscuits and sit with her in the sandy yard and watch her play with the dolls that came from Mrs Taylor's daughters. Auntie would prepare her a bath in the kitchen. She would pour hot water into the big tin basin that was used for laundering clothes. Then she would soap her all over; long, hardened, chapped, brown fingers scrubbing her clean and nice smelling. Rose would feel a stirring, a light warmth mounting from between her legs as the quick fingers played around making her bright. That summer her panties kept sticking in the sweaty crack of her bum. She tried to wipe herself properly but, every night when she undressed for bed, Ma found deep brown ruts imprinted on the cotton. And every night she was reprimanded for being a dirty girl whom God would punish with an infection that would make her privates all rotten. In all the twenty-four years they lived together in that damp, peeling, two-roomed council house with her half paralysed father and her three sisters and two brothers, that had been the only time her mother had slapped her: Rosie, whom Ma loved and spoke to as if she was her sister.

She feels drowsy. Instead of going down for dinner, she thinks of stretching out on the double bed and watching television; she will switch off her mind. On the other hand, she can dress casually and go down for dinner but not eat anything except for a little bowl of soup and a dry roll. The workshop has another day to run. There are important plans of action that need to be finalised. After speaking to those who seem sympathetic, a short walk on the promenade will be restful and sleep will come easily.

Soaping the area of the stain, she scrubs until the water turns yellow, but the brown mark remains visible. She rubs harder. Eventually, after several wrenching minutes, the mark fades. Giving a last rinse, she hangs the towel over the shower rail. Then she walks back into the bedroom and stands naked in front of the enormous rising moon shining on the water. Out of the corner of her eye, she looks at herself in the body-length mirror hanging on the wall and applies a skin cream. Rose watches her hands smoothing and sliding down, moulding over the folds of her body – her black, blue-tinted curls setting off her darting, yellow-brown eyes – and she admits to herself that she is too fat. Her mother is also too fat. But her mother says this is what men want: a soft cushion for warming when the world has denied them.

Aromatic smells rise from the restaurants that line the beach front. There is also the smell of beer soaking into stairways. But these are faint smells, diluted by the sea air. In the township, there is no ocean and there are no ships. There are only garbage strewn streets and streams of water seeping into the dirt roads from burst pipes.

She moves closer to the window; moonlight forms thick droplets of mercury as swathes of celluloid beams wash over the arching belly of water and the beach.

The phone rings.

"Hello! You've been dreaming, comrade!"

It is Modise, the boy from New Brighton: is she coming down to supper? There is something important to discuss, a problem which has long engaged him and for which there is no easy solution. He has also heard about a disco on a boat moored near the docks which is only ten minutes walk from the hotel.

Modise attached himself to her from the start of the workshop but Sithole, whom she likes, has avoided her. His attention has been on a woman named Nomsa, and Nomsa is busy with the German Cottage Industry expert, Schreiner.

Rose tells Modise that she is tired and suggests they talk over breakfast. But as she puts down the phone, the thought of staying in the room and watching television becomes abhorrent. She might as well go down for a drink, just a single gin and tonic to smooth out the roughness. She checks through her clothes: she wants something attractive but not too revealing. It is a pity about Sithole. She chooses a green top, a purple skirt and strap-on sandals. Modise's call has left her no choice. She will have to avoid the dining room. She will skip dinner and have a drink on the terrace.

Legodi is on the landing at the lift doors. Rose looks at him. The green arrow, pointing down, glows. He clears his throat and smiles. She feels shy and does not know what to say. His nose is too big; a curved, sweating nose with deep furrows. When he spoke in the afternoon, it seemed that despite fifty years of political struggle, the successes that are so difficult to consolidate, the innumerable defeats and betrayals that sap ones faith, it seemed as if nothing had broken his commitment to moral progress and solidarity, and nothing had diminished the deep, rich resonance of his compelling voice.

One of the lifts arrives. Nomsa is inside. She greets Legodi in Zulu, then Rose in English. She says how tired she felt during the last session and that she is united with those who want to stop talking theory while outside so many people are jobless, homeless and dispirited.

Rose returns her smile. They have come to know each other a little, having both attended a recent conference in Harare.

The lift reaches the lobby. They drop their keys at reception.

"What are you doing this evening, comrades?"

Rose feels Legodi's eyes on her; they are like foaming, sandy waters swirling round rocks. She remembers his concluding words: "The world is not an easy place, in particular for the poor in either body or spirit. But particularly the body, in that the poor in spirit have always the opportunity to eat the bread of the soul, but those with hungry stomachs are condemned to suffer the blankness, the overriding dullness, fed by their hunger."

The terrace is crowded. Legodi guides them to the only available place, a small side table. He smiles at the nearest waiter. The thick-set man is heavily scarred with tribal markings on his cheeks; his large, squat, glistening head is shaven smooth. He is busy stacking beers onto a tray at the bar but nods back to Legodi.

Nomsa is the first to speak.

"Last night we had the same problem. I came here with Hans. We waited for over half an hour before we got served."

Rose is surprised by her sneering, dismissive tone.

"These waiters crawl around doing nothing. Then once they've finally done you the favour of taking your order, they disappear. But, of course, when it comes to collecting the bill, they're quick to demand a tip. Especially that fat one." She points to the man with the shaven head. "He's the worst."

Rose snaps back, "He looks busy to me. The problem is that there are too few waiters. You know how the bosses are always cutting down on staff. They retrench, then they keep an army of casuals on standby, but it doesn't work, service levels suffer."

"I know all that, sweetie. But why must I suffer? I hate waiting in restaurants. It's boring and I hate being bored."

Rose breathes deeply.

She is shocked by Nomsa's crass attack. But before she can respond to her final banal comment, she is struck by the frangipani tree near the terrace; the night breeze carries the sweet, almost cloying scent to them, and she wants a drink very badly. At the same time she is scared that after the first drink she will want to carry on, with each glass burrowing deeper into a sensation of simultaneous looseness and tightness, of satiety mixed with unease, as if she does not know what she wants when, in fact, she knows precisely what and who she wants, and how the world should conduct itself.

"I'm sorry, I should have introduced myself earlier. Legodi, Ivan Legodi." Legodi rises from his chair. He shakes hands with each of them. "I came late from the airport".

"Yes, comrade, pleased to meet you. I'm Nomsa. I'm from Soweto. And this is Rose Swarts from the Western Cape."

Rose says, "I was very impressed with your speech, comrade. You were honest. The fact is, there is a crisis and it's everywhere, in the cities and in the rural areas."

"We certainly feel it in Huhudi."

"Where?"

"Huhudi, my home town. The Boers call it Vryburg."

Nomsa laughs. "Oh, Vryburg! I had a friend at college who was from there. She said it's a real little dorp. But she said the Civic there has always been strong."

"We are well organised, although I'm told we are not as strong as we used to be, like in the eighties." Rose watches his head move from side to side. "It seems to be the same everywhere."

"Ja, after the unbannings everyone started to relax. We thought our leaders would do everything. That's a good one. We need to work twice as hard now to build something new." Rose waves her hand round the packed terrace. "The bosses are making a fortune again. We're exotic and incredibly cheap for these whites. Nothing's changed. The workers here still get a pittance."

"Would you prefer them not to come?" Legodi asks.

"Who?"

"Would it be better if these tourists, didn't come here and spend their money?"

"That's not a fair question."

"Why not?"

"You know as well as I do – for now we need their money."

"Just for now?"

"But it shouldn't mean we have to bow down."

The waiter with the tribal markings walks up to them. "Sorry to make you wait, people. What can I get you?"

Nomsa barks at him, "You going to be nice now? Why you so slow? Other times you know how to be too quick all right!" then stares across the veranda at the palm trees and the dozing women stretched on mats with their goods.

Rose is dumbfounded by this second outburst.

The waiter has not been rude or disrespectful nor was his expression lewd or in any way untoward; petulance to a man trying to do his job under difficult conditions is unwarranted. Rose's shock is made sharper because, in the past, Nomsa has generally seemed sensitve, progressive. In fact, Rose has hoped to speak to her more openly and find out to what extent they can support each other – by making joint proposals they would have a better chance of influencing the direction and priorities of the Civic movement – and tonight would have been an excellent opportunity to talk about these things, but at this moment Nomsa is being rude and arrogant, acting like a madam.

Rose smiles at the waiter and asks for a rum and Coke.

Looking past him, Nomsa orders a beer, as does Legodi, then she talks about the humidity, the energy-sapping heat that squats on the city.

"Durban's very bad," agrees Legodi.

"It's worse," responds Nomsa. "It's inhuman. My mother's family is from Venda. There it's hot-hot but it's bearable because it's so much drier."

The broad shapes of women sprawled on mats lie in front of Rose. She can see headcloths in the darkness as moonlight splinters along the palm fronds and promenade lamps. Beyond them waves smash down as the tide begins to heave in answer to the huge upward passage of the dead celestial satellite. A hulking woman with a tattered doek on her head staggers under the weight of a bundle of curios.

Rose opens her hands, palms spread to the whitish light.

"It's years since the elections. We've got a wonderful constitution but most of our people have hardly benefited. The only thing that's changed is that some of us now live like the whites." Her palms show several very deep lines. "Everything's collapsed, the whole mobilisation for collective action. Am I being too harsh? We worked so hard for years and then, when we were close, it got taken away."

The waiter arrives with their drinks and hands out menus. This time he smiles and speaks to Rose.

"What would you like to eat, lady? There's two lovely specials tonight. Both are going like hot cakes ..."

"Don't tell me about hot cakes," Nomsa cuts in. "I know what I want. Bring me steak and egg and chips. And I want the steak well done. I can't eat it dripping with blood like the umlungus[40]."

The man lowers his eyes. He looks down at her breasts which almost spill out of the lemon lycra jumpsuit.

"This baboon tried to charm me last night! Made a fool of himself. I think he was drunk. He actually put his sweaty hands on me!"

Nomsa speaks to them as if he is not present, and the waiter turns away, pretending not to listen.

Rose suddenly feels an immeasurable lightness. Why has she been so mistrustful? At last, she understands - does she not know, as much as any woman, how a man can become the lumbering victim of his lust?

"What would you like, madam? We've got prawns on special. Big ones from LM."

"LM? Where's "LM"?"

Rose stares up at him but the waiter looks baffled.

"Why do you still use that name?"

He smiles stupidly.

"Where do you get that name from?

"The boss here, he tells us what to say."

"So you just say what he tells you to?"

The man shrugs. "What would you like to eat, madam?"

Rose taps the table with her spoon. How could he not know that there is no more LM, no more happy hunting ground for whites at Delagoa Bay. On the other hand, she knows the beachfront workers are politically backward; many are traditionalists, semi-literate peasants from the villages in the Kwazulu hinterland - the deep scars on his cheeks should have told her who she was dealing with.

"There's no such place as 'LM'. You've heard about Samora Machel? You know how the Boers killed him? They rigged up a false light. They misguided his plane so as to make it crash into a mountain. He was the president of Mozambique and he lived in M-A-P-U-T-O." Then she hisses, "He fought the Amabulu for you, too, even if your Shenge tells you otherwise. He wasn't their ally drowning us in blood."

The waiter retreats, stands sullenly next to Legodi, his expression telling them what he dares not say: what nonsense coming from a woman, in fact, the second woman this evening to lay into him at the same table. And a bushie[41] on top of it.

He stands stock still and Rose shivers, sensing the massing of his anger. It is so obvious that he is locked into the old chain of killing, of clan fights, endless, sterile wars over cattle and women.

"Alright, baba," Legodi speaks to him in Zulu, "for next time, remember, 'Maputo'. We've had a long day, we're tired."

Rose is infuriated. Why is Legodi giving in to the man's foulness, trying to smooth over the incident? She will challenge both of them. They will realise they cannot fob her off.

"Bring me steak and eggs, too."

She scans the headlines of a newspaper being read by someone at a nearby table.

"The Boers who shot the Ribeiras have been given amnesty. Now there's talk that Hani's killers will also qualify."

The man reading the newspaper is young and smooth with tight Afro curls; a thick gold chain hangs round his neck. He makes her think of the drug smuggler shown on television a few weeks back who was trapped at Johannesburg airport with twenty cocaine-filled condoms stuck up his backside.

"We've forgotten who is who," says Rose. "It's like apartheid never happened. Every single one of those killers is going to walk away. How can admission of guilt be enough? What difference is a one hour public confession going to make to ease the pain of their crimes?"

The waiter returns. "Sorry, madam, there's no more steak. Can I bring you chops?"

"No more steak in this hotel? I don't believe you! You're lying!" Nomsa claps her hands. "Go get the steaks, you donkey!"

Legodi again intervenes. "Please! Bring what you've got. Bring us some chops, baba. Your juiciest chops."

To Rose's surprise, Nomsa laughs. "All right, go bring us good, juicy chops! We're hungry for chops."

The waiter walks off, smouldering.

"That wasn't clever. We'd better cool down if we don't want trouble."

Legodi wipes his beard. Once more Rose stares at him. Is he actually defending this fascist? Then she feels an even greater disquiet: Legodi's face has broken out into a flood of sweat. Looking at his thick, springy beard, she thinks of the pink Christ in the squat church her mother attended on Sundays, the dull brick building that was sterile and clean but still smelt of squalor. The priests were white. They were from England. They were friendly and concerned but distant, explaining how we are all crucified on the crosses we bear. They spoke of patience and doing God's work despite the provocation of the oppressor – and that one should never forget the secret sinner who defiles, the sinner who is each of us.

The moon drifts up over the palm trees. It fills the terrace with a brutal, drowning light. Along the promenade a group of joggers come into view. They pass in a pattern of multicoloured sweat pants and running shoes. But even as she admires their well-toned bodies, Rose feels a sharp contraction in her stomach. It is followed by a second stab of pain. Suddenly she can barely control herself.

"I'm not feeling well ... start eating, please ... don't wait for me ..."

In her haste to rush to a toilet, she knocks a fork on to the floor and, clutching her stomach, runs out between the electronically operated terrace doors into the air-conditioned foyer.

Nomsa is taken aback.

"What's happened? I'd better go and see how she is."

Legodi quickly speaks: "Maybe she wants to be alone. I know when I'm sick I don't like people fussing over me. It puts me under even more pressure."

Nomsa looks at the glass door through which Rose has disappeared and shakes her head, "No, I don't think we should let her suffer in peace. I'll go and check. I'll be back as soon as I can." She rises, then she points a manicured nail towards the waiter." Believe me, tonight he apologises."

Legodi laughs. "You're right, he should, but he won't. So you'll spend the night waiting, and then what will you do?"

"I'll treat him like shit till he does."

"Will that make you feel better?"

"Yes."

Rose bursts into the first floor toilet. There is no one in the perfumed frontal area with its sparkling wash basins and wall-to-wall mirrors. But when she pushes open the door of the first stall, she sees, slumped on the toilet seat, head thrown back against the tiled wall, a young white girl of about sixteen whose face is blank and pale and covered with perspiration, and whose swollen eyes are shut tight; this sweating, tortured head, a strange, tense contrast to the rest of her slender, youthful body.

The girl is dressed in a silver mini-skirt pulled up to her waist; her small, round breasts barely covered by a velvety bikini top and her mane of bleached hair that falls in soft cascades over her knees is partly held back by a plum-coloured head band; her lips are painted black and her extended fingernails glow with a metallic blue.

Despite her own pain, Rose hears the whirring of air conditioning and, very faintly, the laboured breathing of the semi-conscious white girl slumped in the cubicle. She looks at the beads of sweat floating on the pale cheeks and places her hand across the icy forehead that shimmers under the electric light.

The girl opens her eyes.

The sound of waves breaking on the beach as the tide comes up crashes through the chatter on the terrace. Ivan Legodi sips his beer. Earlier in the evening he had sat on his bed in the hotel room and watched a soccer programme on television. The programme showed the highlights of the previous weekend's matches. There was one re-run after another, goal after goal, saves from five different angles. He had sat on his bed following the curve of the ball into the net while the craterous owl-eye filled with dark indentations shone into the room and onto him. And he had inhaled the scents of oil, and curry, and bananas, and sugar cane, and jasmine, and oleander, and tomato bredie, and samoosas, and fried chicken that spread throughout the city, deep into the kloofs and hills that lay beyond the beachfront and its neon strip of hotels, fast-food joints, bars and casinos.

The Indian receptionist does not look at Nomsa as she replaces the telephone receiver.

"I'm sorry. There doesn't seem to be anyone in."

"She may be in the bathroom. She's really very sick."

The receptionist lifts the two razored lines that have become her eyebrows.

"There's definitely no one in."

"Then I'll have to go up."

"I'm afraid our standing rule is that guests meet their visitors in the lobby."

Nomsa stares at her.

"I'm attending the Civic conference So is my friend. She's sick and I need to make sure she's all right. Are you going to phone again or should I call the manager?"

The young Indian woman lowers her eyes. The moon lights up the mirror behind her perfumed, uniformed presence. She looks past Nomsa and dials.

"There's no one in."

Nomsa takes the lift to the fifth floor. Her knocking goes unanswered. Is it likely that Rose has passed out? She waits, knocks again. After a few minutes she wonders if perhaps Legodi was right: respecting Rose's privacy may be the best way to show concern.

Watching the two blue eyes contract, then blur again into vacancy, Rose steps over to the wash basin and cups her hands. Then, as she re-enters the toilet cubicle bearing water for the girl, she feels a sharp prick in the side of her foot.

She shouts out: a syringe is jammed between her instep and a brown leather bag. The tip has penetrated her skin; a glistening stream of blood oozes from the puncture. Next to the syringe, a small black plastic container, dusted with white powder, lies open on the floor.

Rose kicks the syringe aside. Then, looking down at the needle, at the blood on her foot and the frozen girl contorted in the toilet cubicle, she, too, begins shivering. The girl seems so young with her thin white legs, tapering manicured fingernails; her long, silky hair draped like a princess's while a tide of sweat floods across her drawn face.

"Shit, I"m cold! Cover me!" The girl shakes her head wildly, then abruptly stops. "Close the door! What are you doing here? Leave me alone! Get out! Do you hear me? Fucking get out of here!"

Nomsa grunts as the waiter brings a tray with three plates of chops, eggs and chips. On one side is a heap of plastic packets containing vinegar, Worcestershire sauce, chutney and tomato sauce. The waiter sets down a plate. As he does so, several chips slide off and fall onto the table cloth. Nomsa looks up sharply. The waiter ignores her and, turning to Legodi, sweeps the chips into his hand.

"Sorry, chief." He sets down Legodi's plate.

Legodi shuffles his cutlery.

"Go ahead, comrade," says Nomsa. "The food's getting cold."

Legodi begins cutting the meat, soaking strips of tender chop in the yolk of the fried eggs that sit next to the chips.

"It can be hard work having to listen. Hau! That last session ... They were really

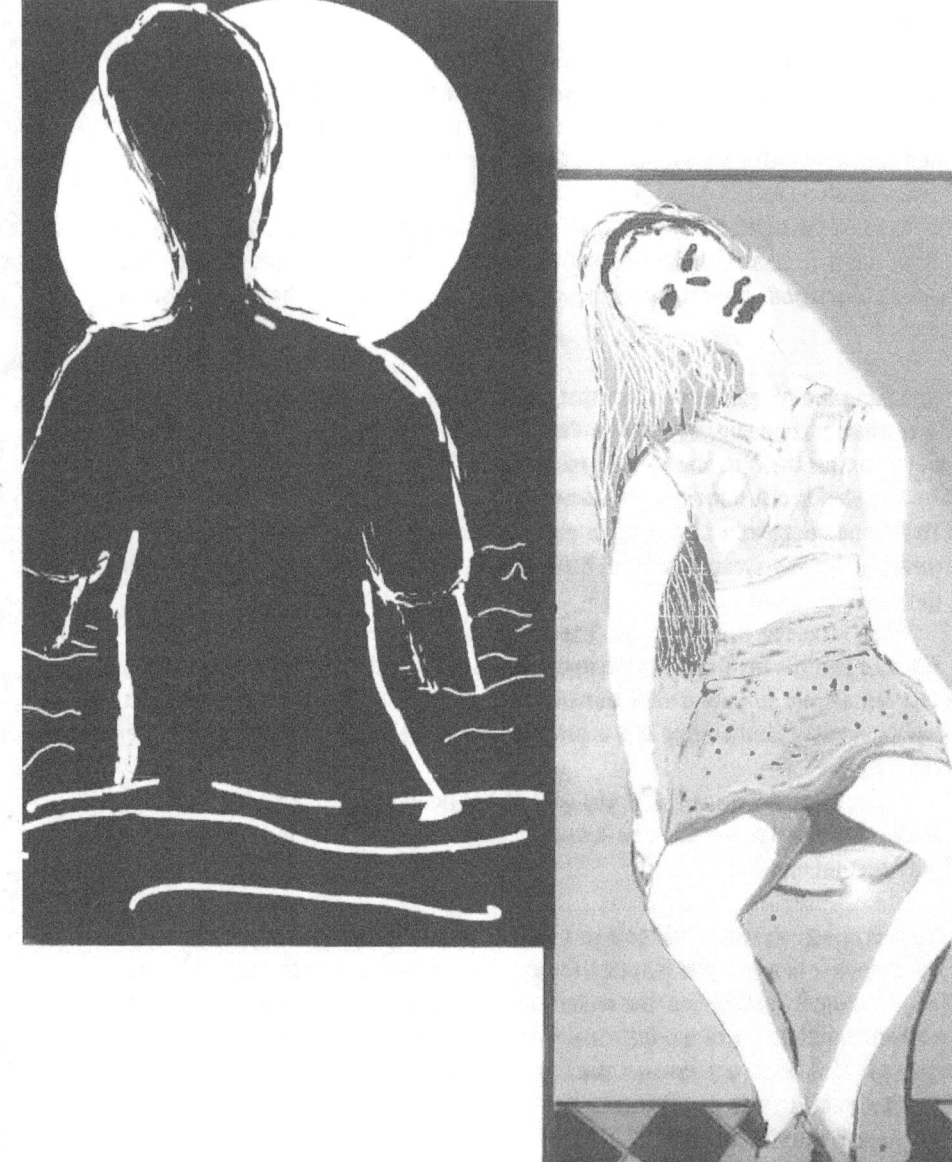

going at each other!"

A country and western singer in a rhinestone cowboy suit sets up a microphone stand. The terrace vibrates with his voice and the buzzing conversations of the groups of white people, locals from Gauteng and the Free State goldfields as well as foreigners, Germans and English, perspiring in cotton seaside clothes.

Legodi seizes a chip with his fork and rams it into his mouth.

"They flash all the things they have and we go for it. We don't think about their real impact. We just swallow what they produce. We don't analyse where it's leading us."

He stops chewing. Nomsa laughs and says, "The minute you opened your mouth, I knew you were another one of those disillusioned but still loyal Nkrumah types."

Legodi pauses, swallows his mouthful and sighs, points again to the surrounding tables.

"How long will it take for us to have an equal relationship with these people?"

The moon rises up to his hand and Nomsa sees a gold wedding ring flash and spring over the heads of the palm trees, and then spiral down to light up the sleeping eyes of the worn out women who lie on their grass mats under the trees and the gashed canyons of the moon.

The white girl's eyes are dilated and wet. Still slumped in the hotel toilet, she tosses about in foaming waves off a breakwater. Swimming towards her is an enormous mouth filled with razor-sharp teeth. But she is powerless to shout out or move. The brown-ringed mouth is almost upon her — she is sucked in towards it.

Moonlight reflects from the toilet window as Rose steps onto the beach. The tide has risen, white-topped swells crash onto the sand. Her toes dig in and she rubs them, relishing the sharp, wet grinding against her skin. Then she walks into the water. There is a momentary searing as the salt laps over the wound where the syringe had pierced her. She closes her eyes. The waves wash her as she sings the song Auntie Geraldine sang while soaping her clean.

GLOSSARY

1   Nou ja, kerels, wat – Yes, gentlemen, what
2   Nee, jong – No, youngster
3   Wat makeer? – What's wrong?
4   Ek is ou Crime, ek – I'm old Crime, I am
5   Toyi toyi – South African protest dance based on military movements
6   Asseblief, my baas, hy is my kind – Please master, he is my child
7   Mosadi – Woman
8   My baas – My master
9   Viva – Long live
10 Buya – Come
11 Vuka – Wake up
12 Izwe Lethu – The land is ours
13 Sizobabamba nezingane zabo – We will catch them together with their children
14 Sizobabamba – We will catch them
15 Sizobadubula ngombayembaye – We will shoot them with guns
16 Nang' uSobukwe – Here is Sobukwe
17 Ha bashwe bana ba baloi – Let the children of witches die
18 My gat, mos man – My arse, man
19 Uyibhubhezi – You are a lion
20 Moer – Cunt
21 Volk – Afrikaner nation
22 Donga – Gorge
23 Ousie – Sister
24 O s'ka nhlanyetsa wena – Buzz off/beat it
25 Ka mma ruri – I swear by my mother
26 Mhlambe unga thola e ou encha – (Who knows) you might meet a nice guy
27 Ngwanenyana ke wena? Can't kuku eo ya gago – Young woman, you better curb your disgraceful sexual appetite
28 Ngaka-ya-ditaola – Bone throwing diviner/medicine man
29 Mosadi ke tshwene, o lewa mabogo – A woman's worth is her hands
30 Tampus – Alcoholics
31 Mjeremane – The Germans
32 Brakkies – Small dogs
33 Lekker krap – A good itch
34 Boemelaar – Hobo
35 Homola wena – You shut up
36 Kgosi, re botse – Hey, chief, tell us
37 Ba-gaetsho! tlang le bone se-tsoga bahung– Oh people, come see the one who woke up from the dead
38 E'sbotho leso – That worthless bum
39 Seazi abanqono thina – We know worthier people
40 Umlungus – White people (Pejorative)
41 Bushie – Coloured person (Pejorative)

www.ingramcontent.com/pod-product-compliance
Lightning Source LLC
Chambersburg PA
CBHW050127030726
47505CB00007B/2077